By Edward P. Hamilton

,,

A HISTORY OF MILTON, MASSACHUSETTS

THE FRENCH AND INDIAN WARS

ADVENTURE IN THE WILDERNESS
*The American Journals of
Louis Antoine de Bougainville
1756-1760*

FORT TICONDEROGA
Key to a Continent

Fort Ticonderoga

KEY TO A CONTINENT

Fort Ticonderoga

KEY TO A CONTINENT

by Edward P. Hamilton

WITH AN INTRODUCTION BY
Nicholas Westbrook

FORT TICONDEROGA • TICONDEROGA • NEW YORK

ISBN: 1-56715-053-5

FIRST EDITION PUBLISHED IN 1964 BY
LITTLE, BROWN AND COMPANY, BOSTON.

SECOND EDITION PUBLISHED IN 1995 BY FORT TICONDEROGA
WITH THE PERMISSON OF THE MASSACHUSETTS HISTORICAL SOCIETY.

PRINTED IN THE UNITED STATES OF AMERICA

THE COVER: Detail reproduced from an original printed and water-colored map in the collections of the Fort Ticonderoga Museum. *A PLAN of the TOWN and FORT of CARILLON at TICONDEROGA; with the ATTACK made by the British Army Commanded by Genl. Abercrombie, 8 July 1758* was published by Thomas Jefferys, "Geographer to . . . the Prince of Wales," as sheet 36 in his 1768 atlas, *A General Topography of North America and the West Indies.* Jefferys based his cartography in good measure on manuscript maps of North America in General Jeffery Amherst's headquarters collection. Jefferys' published map is derived from a British copy made for Amherst from "the original . . . taken amongst the Papers of M^r de L'aubiniere Engineer 1759 at Quebec." Canadian-born Lotbinière had been engineer for the French construction of Fort Carillon (Ticonderoga). Amherst's copy is now in the collection of the William L. Clements Library, Ann Arbor, Michigan.

In Memory of Stephen Pell

Contents

	Prologue	3
1.	They Followed the Waterways	5
2.	Gunfire Wakes the Echoes at Ticonderoga	19
3.	Martyrdom on the Mohawk	25
4.	A Fort Rises in the Wilderness	33
5.	Montcalm Takes Fort William Henry	54
6.	Defeat at the Log Wall	72
7.	Amherst Planned Well	87
8.	"In the Name of the Great Jehovah . . ."	101
9.	Britain Loses the Waterway	115
10.	Ticonderoga Becomes the Northern Bastion	129
11.	Britain Wins the Lake, Too Late	145
12.	The Fort Awaits Assault	163
13.	A New Year Opens	172
14.	The Last Surrender	188
15.	Surrender at Saratoga	200
16.	The Fort Holds Fast	215
17.	Two Centuries of Peace	225
	Bibliography	231
	Index	235

Fort Ticonderoga

KEY TO A CONTINENT

Edward Pierce Hamilton (1897–1972) on the occasion of his appointment in 1957 as Director of the Fort Ticonderoga Museum.

Introduction

||||||||||||||||||||||||||||||||||||||||||||||||||||||||||

FIRST PUBLISHED more than 30 years ago, Colonel
Edward P. Hamilton's *Fort Ticonderoga: Key to a Continent* remains the best concise history of this National Historic
Landmark. Unfortunately for the thousands who remain
curious about the history of Fort Ticonderoga, the 1964 commercial hardcover edition quickly went out of print. For years,
copies have been available only on the rare-book market for
upwards of $40 and $50. To make this important book available
once again, Fort Ticonderoga proudly publishes this reprint
edition so that a new generation can appreciate the work
of one of the century's leading American military historians.

I never met Edward Pierce Hamilton (who is still known
here only and respectfully as "the Colonel" or "Colonel
Hamilton" by staff and Trustees who worked with him from
the 1950s until his death in 1972). His presence remains palpable
at what he lovingly called "the great stone fortress," Fort
Ticonderoga. He shaped the museum's collections and interpretive themes, giving still-evident emphasis to the Seven
Years' War and to matters of 18th-century technology. Part
of a generation of gentleman-amateur museum directors,
he confidently moved museum practices forward at time when
the field was rapidly becoming more professional. He asserted
a standard of scholarship for the museum, in his own work
and in the museum's publications, which we still strive to meet.

The stern, no-nonsense face of 60-year-old Colonel Edward P. Hamilton stares out of the formal portrait published in ***The Bulletin of the Fort Ticonderoga Museum*** announcing his appointment as Director of Fort Ticonderoga early in 1957. The slight frown, the direct, penetrating look, the set lips, the three-piece Harris-tweed suit all bespeak a stern old soldier whom even his good friends considered "gruff and stand-offish," a man of "very definite ideas and instructions." Behind a stiff shell of reticence bolstered by partial deafness was a proper Bostonian, courteous and proud, methodical and disciplined, a man remembered as "always thinking, always innovative," highly regarded for his firmness, his rigorous standards for himself and others, his own meticulous craftsmanship, his unquenchable curiosity, and his authoritative knowledge of colonial sources. Yet his surprisingly personal writing style suggests something of the inner man: "very warm and human under the veneer," and "interesting to be with." "He was not one for pomposity; he was such a gentleman, he didn't need it."

Hamilton's book stands in a long New England literary tradition that includes Nathaniel Hawthorne and Francis Parkman, telling again the story of one of the best-documented and well-visited historic sites in North America. Here, during a bloody and dramatic quarter-century, the superpowers of the 18th century contested for empire. In those few years, in the course of a generation, first one empire was lost by the French — and then another by the British, scarcely more than a decade later. "A new nation under heaven" was born in the shadow of the Fort and its outworks on the Vermont shore defiantly named *"Mount Independence."*

After the Revolution, the twin allies of history and landscape drew travellers, artists, and historians, beginning with future presidents Jefferson and Madison in 1791. During the

19th century, authors and antiquarians including Reverend Timothy Dwight, James Fenimore Cooper, Nathaniel Hawthorne, Flavius Josephus Cook, Francis Parkman, and Seneca Ray Stoddard gathered and retold the stories and folk tales about the role of this Fort in the birth of the new republic. Their work amplified the patriotic resonance of the site and vividly evoked telling features in the landscape, keeping alive the memory of heroism and sacrifice at this hallowed place.

Early in the present century, Stephen and Sarah Pell undertook the reconstruction of the ruined Fort which had been in Pell family stewardship since 1816. With the steady progress of their pioneering restoration work and the corresponding growth of museum collections on exhibit, the audience increased spectacularly, spurred by the advent of inexpensive automobiles and paved roads after World War I. To meet the needs of those visitors, Pell commissioned a modest guidebook, *Fort Ticonderoga in History* by Helen Ives Gilchrist, in the early 1920s. By the early 1930s, Pell's own work in restoring the Fort and assembling the collections had reached a plateau. He turned to retelling the story himself, and in 1935, published *Fort Ticonderoga: A Short History*, drawing almost exclusively upon the extraordinary manuscripts that he had collected for the museum archives. Kept in print by the museum for almost sixty years, his brief book offered the vividness of first-hand experience but lacked a broader narrative context.

Colonel Hamilton's 1964 *Fort Ticonderoga: Key to a Continent*, first published half a century after the restored Fort opened to the public as a museum, was a milestone in the interpretation of the Fort's role in the colonial and Revolutionary Wars. The stories springing from "the warpath of nations" and the larger-than-life heroes who passed through the portals of the Fort fired the romantic imagination of

Hamilton, as they had done for earlier generations. Placing the Fort consistently at center stage of this great drama, Hamilton set the Fort's story within the broad context of that century of warfare. Hamilton blended primary sources from the Fort's own rich collections with those at the Massachusetts Historical Society, and other collections. His essay draws precision and authenticity from his own military service in this century's two world wars, his vivid sense of engagement in conversation with his predecessor historians, and his intimate knowledge of the landscape of these strategic waterways, in the valleys of Lake Champlain, Lake George, and the Hudson River. From these threads came the enduring power of this book: Colonel Hamilton loved to explain, in very clear and plain words, how things work. "He would spend as much time with a child as with an adult. He enjoyed educating."

When *Fort Ticonderoga: **Key to a Continent*** appeared in 1964, Colonel Hamilton had been Director of Fort Ticonderoga for seven years, extending a relationship which had begun with his generous donations to the museum thirty years earlier. He continued as Director almost until his death at age 75 in 1972. His leadership of the Fort Ticonderoga Museum was in fact what he often called his **third** career. He trained and worked, he said, as "an [hydraulic] engineer for a number of years, then [pursued] investment work for many more, interrupted by war service, and finally . . . operating a military museum and writing history." His biographer reports that his third career "gave him his greatest happiness."

Hamilton was born in 1897 on the outskirts of Boston and spent his life focused on Boston and Boston institutions. He graduated from Harvard, having studied American history with the great Frederick Jackson Turner, who preached the decisive impact of the frontier on American culture. During

World War I, Hamilton served in the field artillery of the U.S. Army. After the war, he returned to Harvard for advanced work in engineering, and then practiced and published for a decade as a hydraulic engineer. But already he was combining his historical and engineering interests in a pioneering study of windmills on Cape Cod, published in the mid-1920s. Then, as economic conditions began to change, he launched a second, twenty-five-year career in investment management.

During this period, Hamilton continued his mechanical and engineering interests, repairing and building clocks (the supreme test of an amateur machinist's skill); fashioning one-off hood ornaments for his sports cars; developing and restoring an outstanding collection of historical firearms; and researching and building meticulous scale models. In 1936, Hamilton began making a series of donations of 18th-century firearms and scale models to Fort Ticonderoga (see the list below). In World War II, he again responded to the nation's call, serving finally as a highly-decorated colonel of field artillery in the Italian campaigns.

After the war, Hamilton's historical interests increasingly engaged him. During the middle years of the 1950s, he became active in the affairs of the Boston circle of exclusive, elective historical organizations: the Club of Odd Volumes, the Massachusetts Historical Society, the Colonial Society of Massachusetts, the American Antiquarian Society, the Society for the Preservation of New England Antiquities. Colonial Williamsburg called upon his expertise on colonial windmills, dating back to his Newcomen Society essay on Cape Cod mills written just out of graduate school. "My only excuse," recalled Colonel Hamilton modestly, "is that Williamsburg could not find anyone else in the country who knew anything about them at all, and they learned I knew a little, so I got tagged." To confirm that his historical and engineering research really **worked**, Colonel Hamilton characteristically built an exact large-scale model, equipped with sails made from "an 18th-century linen handkerchief belonging to a royal lady." Just as characteristically, the final test was in the taste: "I have eaten excellent corn bread made from meal ground" by the full-size recreated 1710 windmill. The mill he designed for Colonial Williamsburg still runs, mesmerizing visitors today.

The sudden death of his wife in 1955 provoked another career change, this time settling Hamilton into new challenges as historian and museum administrator, divided between Boston and Ticonderoga. In 1956, he was elected "Cabinet-Keeper" (or chairman of the collections committee) of the Massachusetts Historical Society, a position he held until his death. That same year, he retired from the investment business and accepted appointment as Director of Fort Ticonderoga.

Hamilton, Fort Ticonderoga, and the Pell family were already well acquainted in 1957. For the previous twenty years, Hamilton had been a frequent donor of artifacts and active contributor to the not-for-profit organization Stephen H.P. Pell had created to carry on the preservation of Fort Ticonderoga. During those years, Hamilton had come to know well both the museum's founder, Stephen H.P. Pell, who passed away in 1950, and his son, John H.G. Pell, who succeeded his father as Managing Director. (In 1965 Hamilton would write a biographical essay about Stephen Pell for Clifford Lord's anthology about seminal antiquarians and museum founders, **Keepers of the Past**.)

Hamilton worked intimately with John H.G. Pell during his entire tenure at Fort Ticonderoga. John H.G. Pell had been both President and Managing Director for seven years when he appointed Hamilton to succeed him as Director. Pell's own increasingly active academic and business responsibilities precluded the same daily, hands-on attention to Fort affairs his father had managed. Hamilton's scholarship, business acumen, and on-site presence during the Fort's full season created a symbiotic relationship with Mr. Pell and the Fort Ticonderoga Association from which the historic site benefited.

In the 1950s, attendance at Fort Ticonderoga and other Adirondack attractions was rocketing as baby-boom families sought to discover their American heritage through direct experience of landmark sites. The demographic boom coincided with an accelerating economy. People flocked to the cool mountains and lakes of the North Country in the years before air-conditioning and home swimming pools were generally available. At Fort Ticonderoga, a series of bicentennials of major events of the French and Indian War offered additional incentive for visits. Many a young boy (including this one) raised on Kenneth Roberts' novels, stimulated by the series of historical prints commissioned by the Glens Falls Insurance Company, and watching "Hawkeye and the Last of the Mohicans" on television, found Fort Ticonderoga a compelling family destination.

Hamilton's first formal role at Fort Ticonderoga was his appointment in 1954 as a member of the Bicentennial Committee charged with planning an appropriate commemoration of the 200th anniversary of the beginning of construction of the Fort by the French in 1755. The relationship fit well, and in 1957 Hamilton was appointed the first non-family Director of the museum. Hamilton began his new assignment at Ticonderoga planning another bicentennial celebration, this one celebrating Montcalm's great 1758 victory over the British who out-numbered the French forces by five-to-one. The next year, he played a leading role in orchestrating the basin-wide 350th anniversary celebration of Champlain's "discovery" of the lake which bears his name.

At the same time, Hamilton commissioned expert assessments of the museum's renowned manuscript and firearms collections, and undertook their cataloguing and improved care. He hired the museum's first full-time professionally trained curator of collections. He hiked the landscape around the Fort, armed with his surveyor's transit, and prepared detailed engineering drawings to document the structure and condition of the surviving 18th-century fortifications at Ticonderoga and Mount Independence, including the Fort itself. He laid the groundwork for a fresh interpretation of the Fort's role in history, giving particular emphasis to its role during the Seven Years' War. He helped inaugurate what we know today as "living history," beginning an interpretive program of daily tours by guides in period clothing, accompanied by live-firing demonstrations of 18th-century artillery. He revived a program of 18th-century military music, encouraging Scottish piping in particular. He developed imposing museum dioramas of several of the most dramatic scenes in the Fort's history: the Black Watch attacking the French lines in 1758; the capture of the Fort by Ethan Allen and the Green Mountain Boys in 1775; the American fleet and the Great Bridge to Mount Independence under construction in 1776. He resumed the program of restoration, correcting the problematically reconstructed northeast "watchtower" and substantially completing the shell of the East Barracks. He oversaw the engineering and installation of extensive water and sewerage systems that would make a small town proud. He placed the museum's journal, *The Bulletin of the Fort Ticonderoga Museum*, on a more scholarly basis and inaugurated a panel of distinguished advisory editors. He made the Fort active in community historical affairs, resurrecting the Ticonderoga Historical Society in the 1950s, rejuvenating the Forest Theater Indian Pageant after its founders were unable to continue in 1961, and collaborating closely with the New York State Historical Association, then still partially headquartered here in Ticonderoga in the Hancock House.

When Hamilton's "third career" at Fort Ticonderoga ended with his death in 1972, he had already begun planning for the American Revolutionary Bicentennial. The museum had also just received news that Fort Ticonderoga was among the first twenty-six museums in the country to be accredited by the American Association of Museums, in good measure a tribute to his leadership.

Hamilton's first research and writing project at Fort Ticonderoga was a brief history of the Champlain Valley, *Lake Champlain and the Upper Hudson Valley*, prepared for the 350th Champlain anniversary in 1959. With an appropriate historical symmetry, Hamilton's *last* work for Fort Ticonderoga was a similar pamphlet prepared for the Revolutionary Bicentennial, *The Champlain Valley in the American Revolution*, published posthumously in 1973.

"I spend spring to fall operating Fort Ticonderoga, and when the Fort closes return to Boston and devote the winter to research and writing," said Colonel Hamilton, summarizing the rhythms of his third career. During those fifteen prolific winters, Hamilton managed to produce four major books, five pamphlet-length monographs, and numerous articles for the journals of the American Antiquarian Society, the Massachusetts Historical Society (MHS), and his own museum. Throughout, his scholarly attention remained largely focused on the French and Indian War and was rooted in the collections he lived with summers at Fort Ticonderoga and in winter quarters at "the Mass. Historical" where his former corner office is now the Hamilton Memorial Room. Hamilton's deep familiarity with the MHS collections and warm relationships with staff there enriched the collections of Fort Ticonderoga and brought numerous MHS manuscript treasures to publication in **The Bulletin of the Fort Ticonderoga Museum.**

At the Massachusetts Historical Society, Hamilton immersed himself particularly in the papers of Francis Parkman, the great 19th-century historian of the conflict between France and Britain for control of North America. Parkman's work inspired and shaped Hamilton's. Like Parkman, Hamilton read widely in the primary sources, believed in the importance of examining the landscapes of conflict first-hand, and wrote for a broad, general audience. But Hamilton also absorbed some of the perspectives of his exemplar. Like Parkman, Hamilton saw the French and Indian War as a moral drama between France and England: the French regime as despotic, and the British as virtuous. (His anti-French cultural bias sometimes seemed visceral to his friends: Offered *escargot* as part of a proper French dinner at the Fort, Colonel Hamilton responded, "This is strictly against my New England conscience!")

Parkman's influence took a more indirect form as well. In the Parkman Papers at MHS, Hamilton encountered a transcription of the journal of Louis Antoine de Bougainville, aide-de-camp to the French general, the Marquis de Montcalm. Parkman had acquired an incomplete transcription but had not been allowed by descendants to use Bougainville's forthright journal in preparing **Montcalm and Wolfe** (1884). Hamilton recognized the significance of Bougainville's candid account, calling it "by far the best single piece of source material we have concerning the French and Indian War." Hamilton prepared an annotated translation of Bougainville's journal which he began publishing in *The Bulletin of the Fort Ticonderoga Museum* in 1962. A hardcover edition was published by the University of Oklahoma Press in 1964; this essential journal of the period remains in print today. Hamilton absorbed Bougainville's point-of-view, and his biases. With Bougainville, Hamilton honored Montcalm but considered the French-Canadian gentry fatally corrupt. With Bougainville, Hamilton disliked and distrusted Montcalm's Indian allies. Hamilton depersonalized "the Indian," treating many nations as a single faceless people, an undifferentiated culture of "Stone Age savages," helpless in the face of liquor.

The twin perspectives and congruent biases of Parkman and Bougainville pervade Hamilton's *The French and Indian Wars*, published in 1962. Hamilton intentionally used the plural, "wars," in the title to indicate that his scope was more than just the final war of the 1750s, but embraced as well the earlier conflicts the English called the wars of King William, Queen Anne, and King George. Reviewers praised the work as the best single-volume study of the century-long warfare between Britain and France. Hamilton had absorbed Parkman's multi-volume study of the French regime in North America. Hamilton had also closely studied Lawrence Henry Gipson's 15-volume study of imperial Britain in *The Great War for Empire* (1936–1970), emphatically annotating the museum's copies!

Undaunted by following such magisterial efforts, Hamilton brought special emphases of his own. Applying the precepts of his mentor, Frederick Jackson Turner, he stressed the importance of frontier geography, but noted especially the pattern of strategic waterways in shaping the contrasting character of French and British activity in North America. Still the engineer, he also paid particular attention to matters of technology: the size and shape of boats, the function of muskets and the knapping of flint, the logistics and rate of fire of 18th-century artillery. Repeatedly, he was able to bring the authority of personal experience to the topic. Curious about the efficient operation of a 17th-century matchlock gun, Hamilton machined a replica based on one in the museum collection and experimented. He wrote with certainty about what it **felt** like to fire a 12-pounder from the walls of a fort (nearly killing a skunk in the King's Garden in the process), and the **taste** of spruce beer ("Surprisingly enough it has a distinct beer taste and is comfortably warming. We made some here at the Fort according to the old formula [which he had found in the journals of General Jeffery Amherst], and so we know.").

Hamilton recognized from the beginning of his tenure here that Fort Ticonderoga needed a strong, comprehensive one-volume history. For the 1959 Champlain anniversary, he persuaded his Harvard classmate and by then a highly regarded Revolutionary War historian, Bruce Lancaster, to prepare a brief history of the Fort for teenagers, ***Fort Ticonderoga: The Story of a Fort***. The on-going editorial conversations between the two old friends helped frame up the broad story of the site in Hamilton's own mind. Then building first upon his own personal expertise, Hamilton researched and wrote on the century of Anglo-French wars and the Fort's role in those conflicts. At the same time, to flesh out his intended comprehensive history of the Fort for the adult reader, Hamilton began exploring the Revolutionary and War of 1812 history of the Fort and Champlain Valley. He prepared for publication in ***The Bulletin of the Fort Ticonderoga Museum*** key documents concerning the American Revolution (e.g. the orderly books of Anthony Wayne, commander here during the awful winter of 1776–1777, and the letters of Wayne's comrade in arms, Persifer Frazer) as well as several trial essays ("Was Washington to Blame for the Loss of Ticonderoga in 1777?"). Culminating his enormously productive first seven years at Fort Ticonderoga, he published *Fort Ticonderoga: Key to a Continent* in 1964. Sadly the book was perceived to be parochial in focus, and thus did not receive the critical review in scholarly journals which *The French and Indian Wars* had enjoyed two years earlier.

One can fault Colonel Hamilton for paying scant attention to Indians, blacks, and women, people whose experiences admittedly received scant attention in the contemporary diaries and journals of white participants in these campaigns. Today, historians require a more sensitive and complete understanding of the Native American presence and culture at Ty through the last 400 years and beyond. They see a more nuanced appreciation of the relationships between governors and officers from the mother country and their provincial comrades in arms on both the French and British sides. We recognize now that, in fact, "history was [**not!**] silent in the Champlain Valley" during the pre- and post-war eras in the 18th century. Born in the 19th century, Hamilton virtually ignored "modern times" and the 19th- and 20th-century history of the Fort and the Ticonderoga peninsula. But in the early 1960s Hamilton was writing within the context of his own era and in the context of his own training in history half-a-century earlier. These issues are the challenge of our generation and the next. We can pursue such questions and sources only because he blazed a trail for us thirty years ago.

Edward P. Hamilton's *Fort Ticonderoga: Key to a Continent* remains an important book today. Here you will find the dramatic story of the Fort told in lively, concise prose. You will meet first-hand, and hear in their own words, everyone from officers to private soldiers, telling both of broad strategy and the daily slog and tedium of army food and fatigue duty. You never forget the geographical significance of this narrow chokepoint on the great water highway linking New York and Montréal. You taste the spruce beer, smell the musket's black powder, and heft countless bateaux over the portages.

Millennia ago, enduring stories of arms and men around the ancient Mediterranean were sung by Virgil, Homer, and Herodotus. Edward Hamilton spins equally stirring tales of valor two centuries ago on these lake shores.

— NICHOLAS WESTBROOK
Director
Fort Ticonderoga

Fort Ticonderoga
July 1995

* * *

I am grateful for the reminiscences of Fort Ticonderoga Association Trustees (including Stephanie Pell Dechame, William P.C. Hudson, J. Robert Maguire, John Bigelow Pell, Stuyvesant B. Pell, and Louis Leonard Tucker), and the staffs of Fort Ticonderoga (especially Ruth Fitzgerald and Linda J. Edson) and the Massachusetts Historical Society (Stephen T. Riley, his successor as Director, Louis Leonard Tucker, and Librarian Peter Drummey). Their reflections appear throughout in quotation marks.

A Bibliography of the Historical Writings of Edward Pierce Hamilton

"Some Windmills of Cape Cod," *Transactions of the Newcomen Society*, vol. V (1924-25).

"Early Industries of the Neponset and the Charles," *Proceedings of the Massachusetts Historical Society*, vol. 71, (1953-1957), pp. 108-123.

"The Diary of a Colonial Clergyman, Peter Thacher of Milton," *Proceedings of the Massachusetts Historical Society*, vol. 71, (1953-1957), pp. 50-63.

"Milton Firsts," in *A Brief History of Milton, Massachusetts*, Milton Historical Society, 1956, pp. 42-44.

A History of Milton, Massachusetts, Milton Historical Society, 1957, 275 p.

"Robert Hewes and the Frenchmen: A Case of Treason," *Proceedings of the American Antiquarian Society*, vol. 68 part 2 (1959), pp. 195-210.

Lake Champlain and the Upper Hudson Valley, Fort Ticonderoga, 1959, 47 p.

Guide Book to Fort Ticonderoga, Fort Ticonderoga, 1959, 16 p.

editor, "Nathaniel Wheelwright's Canadian Journey, 1753-1754," *The Bulletin of the Fort Ticonderoga Museum*, vol. X no. 4 (February 1960), pp. 259-296.

"An Historic Mortar," *The Bulletin of the Fort Ticonderoga Museum*, vol. X no. 4 (February 1960), pp. 299-303.

editor, "Letters from Ticonderoga, 1776, [from Persifer Fraser]," *The Bulletin of the Fort Ticonderoga Museum*, vol. X no. 5 (February 1961), pp. 386-396; vol. X no. 6 (January 1962), pp. 450-459.

"Parkman, Abbé Casgrain, and Bougainville's Journal," *Proceedings of the American Antiquarian Society*, vol. 71 part 2 (1962), pp. 261-270.

editor, "Bougainville's Journal: An Introduction," *The Bulletin of the Fort Ticonderoga Museum*, vol. X no. 6 (January 1962), pp. 419-449; vol. XI no. 1 (December 1962), pp. 5-34.

editor, "A New Description of Fort Ticonderoga," *The Bulletin of the Fort Ticonderoga Museum*, vol. XI no. 1 (December 1962), pp. 35-48.

The French and Indian Wars: The Story of Battles and Forts in the Wilderness, Garden City, New York, Doubleday and Co., 1962, 318 p. *Mainstream of America Series* edited by Lewis Gannett.

"Was Washington to Blame for the Loss of Ticonderoga in 1777?" *The Bulletin of the Fort Ticonderoga Museum*, vol. XI no. 2 (September 1963), pp. 65-74.

editor, "The Wayne Orderly Book [10 July 1776 to 15 October 1776]" *The Bulletin of the Fort Ticonderoga Museum*, vol. XI nos. 2-4 (1963-64), pp. 93-154, 177-205.

editor, "The Diary of Henry Sewell," *The Bulletin of the Fort Ticonderoga Museum*, vol. XI no. 2 (September 1963), pp. 75-92.

"The Battle of Plattsburgh," *Vermont History*, vol. 31 no. 2 (April 1963), pp. 94-105.

"Unrest at Caughnawauga, or the Lady Fur Traders of Sault St. Louis," *The Bulletin of the Fort Ticonderoga Museum*, vol. XI no. 3 (December 1963), pp. 155-160.

Adventure in the Wilderness: The American Journals of Louis Antoine de Bougainville, 1756-1760, translator and editor, Norman, University of Oklahoma Press, 1964, 334 p.

Fort Ticonderoga: Key to a Continent, Boston, Little, Brown & Co., 1964, 241 p.

The Village Mill in Early New England, Sturbridge, Massachusetts, Old Sturbridge Village, 1964, 24 p. OSV Booklet Series #18.

"John Henry Lydius, Fur Trader at Fort Edward," *The Bulletin of the Fort Ticonderoga Museum*, vol. XI no. 5 (December 1964), pp. 270-280.

"Stephen Hyatt Pelham Pell," in Clifford Lord, ed., *Keepers of the Past*, Chapel Hill, University of North Carolina Press, 1965, pp. 223-231.

Chocolate Village: The History of the Walter Baker Chocolate Factory, January 1966, 14 p.

The French Army in America, Ottawa, Museum Restoration Service, 1967, 108 p. Historical Arms Series #7.

"Colonial Warfare in North America," *Proceedings of the Massachusetts Historical Society*, vol. 80 (1969), pp. 3-15.

"Colonial and Revolutionary Artillery," *The Bulletin of the Fort Ticonderoga Museum*, vol. XII no. 5 (December 1969), pp. 313-327.

"The French Colonial Forts at Crown Point Strait," *The Bulletin of the Fort Ticonderoga Museum*, vol. XII no. 6 (October 1970), pp. 393-399.

"Maurice Cary Blake [memoir]," *Proceedings of the Massachusetts Historical Society*, vol. 81 (1970), p. 212.

editor, "The Journal of Archelaus Fuller, May-November 1758," *The Bulletin of the Fort Ticonderoga Museum*, vol. XIII no. 1 (December 1970), pp. 5-17.

"John Bradstreet," *The Bulletin of the Fort Ticonderoga Museum*, vol. XIII no. 2 (June 1971), pp. 137-150.

editor, "Memoir on the Defense of the Fort of Carillon," *The Bulletin of the Fort Ticonderoga Museum*, vol. XIII no. 3 (1972), pp. 197-226.

"General John Thomas," *Proceedings of the Massachusetts Historical Society*, vol. 84 (1972), pp. 44-52.

The Champlain Valley in the American Revolution, Albany, New York State American Revolution Bicentennial Commission and the Champlain Valley Committee for the Observance of the Bicentennial, 1973, 20 p.

A small collection of the personal papers of **Edward Pierce Hamilton** is held by the Massachusetts Historical Society. His administrative papers as Director of the Fort Ticonderoga Museum are preserved in the Thompson-Pell Research Center at Fort Ticonderoga.

Memoirs

Stephen T. Riley, in *Proceedings of the Massachusetts Historical Society*, vol. 84 (1972), pp. 113-117.

[unsigned] in *The Bulletin of the Fort Ticonderoga Museum*, vol. XIII no. 3 (1972), p. 241.

Donations by Edward P. Hamilton
to the Collections
of the Fort Ticonderoga Museum

Four-barrel, over-and-under pistol, 1936.

Wheel-lock pistol, 1937.

1773-74 silver watch, 1940.

Two British gorgets, 1940.

Pocket pistol with folding trigger, 1946.

Dragoon pistol, 1947.

American holsters, 1947.

Pair of dueling pistols "Presented by the Duke of Hamilton to G.W.," 1955.

Scale model of the gunboat "Philadelphia," 1956.

Scale model of the row galley "Washington," 1957.

Silver-mounted Queen Anne pistol, 1967.

Tooth-puller, 1969.

Pocket scales, 1970.

Prologue

IT WAS ONLY a puny little fortress far out in the wilderness of North America, yet six times within less than a generation great armies marched to assail it.

No fort anywhere in the world has a history such as that possessed by Fort Ticonderoga, yet its active life was but a score of years. Indians, incited, equipped and often led by Frenchmen, slipped silently southward from its gray stone walls to raid the unguarded settlements of New England and the York colony. Sometimes they brought back an unfortunate Englishman or two, whom they knocked on the head and boiled in their brass kettles on the flats below the forts. Occasionally an expedition of Frenchmen stopped there before moving on south against the British. Here it was that Montcalm's army of French regulars, Canadians and Indians assembled in 1757 for the march against Fort William Henry and the siege that led to massacre. Scarce had another year fled before Abercromby, sitting in his tent far from the battlefront, repeatedly flung his great army against the high log wall built by Montcalm's little host. Hour after hour the battle was joined until nightfall at last brought surcease and saw some sixteen hundred British dead and wounded.

Another year rolled by, and Amherst at last seized the fortress, held this year by only a petty garrison of Frenchmen. Long years of peace were to follow, years during which the great stone walls fell into decay, until in the spring of 1775 Ethan Allen thunders demand for surrender in the name of the Great Jehovah. Once more a year passes, and the pitiful, smallpox-ridden American army recoils from its vain attempt at the conquest of Canada, and pauses at Ticonderoga to catch its breath, heal its sick and to hold the frontier against British invasion. It succeeds, but in the following summer, that of 1777, Burgoyne takes the place, shamefully evacuated without fight by its defenders, and marches on to meet his fate at Saratoga. But before the invaders are finally checked at Bemis Heights, gallant John Brown leads an attack on the garrison left at Ticonderoga by the advancing British, succeeds in part, but fails to capture the old stone fortress. Six times armies had marched against the little fort in the course of twenty years; thrice it held, and thrice it fell. No other fort in history can boast of such a record. Such was Ticonderoga, the key to the vital Champlain Valley.

ONE

They Followed the Waterways

THROUGH THE narrows at Ticonderoga pressed the great highway of colonial North America, the only practical route between New France and the British colonies, the path that must be followed by all who traveled between the two regions, be they fur traders, stealthy smugglers or great armies. Quite rightly has Ticonderoga been called "The Key to a Continent." He who held the narrows determined who might pass and when.

Today we take roads, highways and great turnpikes for granted, and we have no appreciation of the difficulties of travel in colonial times. In the middle 1700's there were almost no roads in North America, save along the seacoast. A trip over the shore road from Boston to New York normally required at least a week on horseback, ferrying over several rivers. From Boston a road ran west to Worcester and on to Springfield, crossed the Connecticut on a ferry, and then, more trail than road, struggled up the Berkshires, "over mountains that rise like going upstairs," then down to lower levels and on to Claverack on the Hudson, where it met the New York–Albany post road. Yet a keg of rum or a bale of imported sailcloth could move more cheaply and usually more speedily by water, around Cape Cod, along Long Island Sound, and up the Hudson to Albany, than it could had it gone by wagon or pack horse across the Berkshires.

By about 1750 there was a second road to Albany which passed north of Worcester, crossed the Connecticut near Deerfield, and then, probably more pack trail than road, followed up the valley of the Deerfield River, across rugged Hoosuck Mountain, and then over more gentle terrain passed through Williamstown and on to Albany. Robert Treat Paine, who went west in 1755 by this route to serve as chaplain with one of General William Johnson's regiments, has left us a journal and a quaint road map. He recorded that the road west of Williamstown was smooth and level.

The New York–Albany road must have had its attractions and been well served by its inns, for in 1759 General Amherst walked all of its one hundred and sixty miles on foot on his return to New York after the conclusion of the year's campaign. There was a second road to Albany on the west side of the Hudson. The Boston–New York shore road extended to the north at least as far as Portsmouth and south to Annapolis.

Roads west into the foothills of the Appalachians were few in 1750. One ran from Philadelphia to Harrisburg on the Susquehanna, and then, probably only a narrow trail, swung southward through Chambersburg to cross the Potomac near today's Hagerstown, Maryland, and then, now again a wagon road, led down the great Valley of Virginia, the Shenandoah, at least as far as Staunton. Nearly a century later it would be the Valley Pike of Stonewall Jackson's day. Near where the Chambersburg trail crossed the Potomac, it was joined by a road from Alexandria through Frederick, which continued on up the Potomac Valley toward the mountains to Fort Cumberland, the most advanced British post in all this region. Braddock's men would march westward over this miserable road, taking just under a month to cover about 125 miles. South of this Frederick road another ran direct from Alexandria to Winchester in the Valley.

From Chambersburg the pack trail of the fur traders extended west to the Forks of the Ohio, where Pittsburgh stands today. A few years later General Forbes would make it into a wagon road, when he advanced slowly but surely to the capture of Fort Duquesne. From Fort Cumberland another such trail headed toward the Ohio, and it outlined the route Braddock's road soon would follow. But these in 1750 were only trails, narrow and fit only for man or horse; much widening, blasting and corduroying would be needed before they were fit for heavy wagons.

One must not think a colonial road to have been anything like those of today, when almost all have been given a bituminous or concrete top. Look for the crudest, roughest country road that you can find, and you will have an idea of about what they were like — muddy or dusty, rutted and at times almost impassable in places. The day of the stagecoach was still half a century in the future.

Man went by water in colonial North America. The rivers of the country were the highways for both trade and war. Coastal commerce was carried by thousands of little vessels, and the few coastal roads could not compete with waterborne carriers of provisions and merchandise. Tidal rivers and deep estuaries in many places allowed the coastal trade to proceed well inland. The Connecticut was navigable to Hartford, the Hudson to Albany, Chesapeake Bay to Havre de Grace and Head of Elk, the Potomac to Alexandria, and the James to the falls where Richmond was settled in the late 1730's. Further advance westward beyond these points required other forms of transport, travel by foot, by horse and pack train or by small river craft, dugout, barge, canoe or bateau.

A host of little sailing craft plied all along the coastline from Georgia to Nova Scotia, while scows, barges and gondolas were rowed, poled or sailed up and across the bays and estuaries. Goods moved between seacoast towns by water, not by land. And moreover they moved faster that way. The week-long (and often longer) trip by road and ferry from Boston to New York could usually be accomplished in not much over half of that time by going overland to Providence and then by water for the rest of the journey.

Any real penetration of the interior had, practically speaking, to be made by water. The great Appalachian mountain chain determined that. Extending from almost the banks of the St. Lawrence all the way south to the new colony of Georgia, these mountains presented a great barrier to any land movement westward. True, you could penetrate them on foot, but at most you could carry only perhaps seventy-five pounds—which must include food and your personal equipment before you could add traps, trade goods or merchandise. Or you could take a string of pack horses, each carrying a load of some two hundred pounds; but this must include at least some forage, for grass was always scanty in the great forests. A boat, on the other hand, would take any load you wanted, provided the craft did not become too large to handle on the inland waters, and it could be paddled, rowed or poled with much less effort than was required to force one's way through the primeval forests and over the rugged mountains.

Water transport, of course, had its drawbacks — waterways did not always go where one wished, and often they were interrupted by falls and rapids, or became too small or shallow. Recourse then was made to overland carry of boat and cargo — portaging, it was called — until another waterway was reached. Certain portages were of great strategic value and in many cases forts were built to control them. Examples are Fort Niagara, which covered the vital passage to the Far West; Fort Edward, where commenced the two portages to Lake George and Lake Champlain; and

Fort Stanwix on the Mohawk waterway. At important and often used portages improvements sometimes were made to facilitate passage. Road work of course was important, and at Niagara the French at one time kept ox teams permanently stationed, while at the short but busy carry by the falls of the Oswego River some genius devised a series of rollers so that bateaux could be rolled across without necessity of unloading them.

Fortunately the rivers of North America so interlaced their tributaries that portaging was usually necessary only for a few miles at most, a minor inconvenience in view of the relative ease of the rest of the journey. By far the longest water route of North America was that up the St. Lawrence over a number of short portages to Lake Ontario, then a fairly arduous carry by Niagara, followed by travel on the open lakes all the way to the site of the future Chicago, where at times of high water a bateau could often be floated over the divide into the headwaters of the Illinois River, then on to the Mississippi and New Orleans.

The other great disadvantage of water transport was that for at least three months the rivers and lakes in northern parts were frozen solid. But this was not too serious, for military campaigns were usually undertaken in summer. In winter a man could haul his furs or trade goods behind him on a sled over the frozen water surface almost as easily as he could have paddled or poled. Here the British had a real advantage over the French, for their waterways were open longer. Spring came late in New France.

Unfortunately for the British colonists, practically all of their rivers led only into the mountains and furnished no thoroughfare to the west, but there were two most important exceptions; the Mohawk corridor, and that of the Hudson-Champlain Valley. The Mohawk River, interrupted by two or three waterfalls which required only short carries, ran from the Hudson due west to today's Rome, New York, in those days called "The Great Carrying Place." A relatively short land carry then led overland to the waters of a tortuous and swampy creek which, by twisting through humid, mosquito-ridden woods, at last entered Lake Oneida, whence the Oswego River flowed, with but a single waterfall, into Lake Ontario. This was Britain's only water route to the west, and it was of vast importance. Indians had long brought furs eastward along the Mohawk to Albany, and by 1721 the fur trading post of Oswego on Lake Ontario had been established. This post at once became a thorn in the flank of New France, for not only did it represent a British penetration into lands claimed by the French King, but it also very largely diverted furs from the French West to the Dutch merchants of Albany. Moreover, this westward corridor gave the British direct access to the waters of the Far West and an opportunity through intelligent use of naval power to control all that vast land. Today it is hard to understand why Britain, thoroughly imbued with the vital importance of her navy on salt water, failed to extend similar thinking to the great inland lakes of North America. Had she done so, the last French and Indian war would have been concluded much sooner and with greater ease.

Farther to the south conditions were quite different, for all the rivers had their headwaters in the lofty Appalachians and their river valleys faded out into the mountain slopes. Water transport speedily came to an end, and only man's two feet or the pack horse could penetrate the great mountain ranges, which, forming a massive barrier all the way from the Mohawk to the plains of Georgia, cut off the seaboard colonies from the great West.

Geography was kinder to the French, for nature had given them waterways which offered easy access to the Great Lakes, the waters of the Ohio and even the Mississippi itself. Thus the French could establish posts beyond the mountain barrier and attempt to hold the heartland against an advance of British settlers. This they were able to do with considerable success, largely through the use of raiding Indians who were based on French forts in the Ohio country. These posts, although relatively easy of access by water from Montreal, were nevertheless at a great distance from their base of supply, and it was not expedient to attempt formal military action eastward through the mountains, here just as much a barrier to the French as to the English. Offensive Indian raids backed by forts capable of defensive action were sufficient to hold the colonists in check south of the Mohawk. Major military expeditions by the British would be another matter, but such expeditions were still in the future in 1754. To the north two opposing civilizations, the tight despotism of New France and the separate little independent democracies that were the British colonies, faced each other at relatively close range in the Hudson-Champlain Valley, where the great north-south waterway of colonial days made passage simple and easy. The British pushed up the Hudson and the French up the Richelieu into Lake Champlain. It was on this great waterway of North America that the two would first meet in battle.

Most of the watercraft used on these inland rivers were a product of the country, new to European eyes. The earliest of all was probably the log dugout, a form of boat common to primeval man, but abandoned by the Indian in later centuries. During the colonial period and later white men on the Hudson made highly refined dugouts, well shaped and thinned down to fairly light weight. In the mid-1700's, at least, these dugouts were usually propelled by a man standing and paddling with a short oar. Dugouts were quite narrow and must have required a nice sense of balance. The really important boats of fresh-water North America throughout many years were the canoe of the Indian, the bateau of the white man and, to a lesser extent, the whaleboat.

The northern Indian made his canoe of birch. It was surprisingly like our modern version except that birchbark instead of painted canvas formed the waterproof envelope. The bark, however, did not furnish the structural strength, for under this outer envelope long thin wooden strips gave lengthwise strength just as they do in our modern canvas canoes, and there also were many light ribs. Had an Indian canoe of two hundred years ago been covered with canvas instead of birchbark it would have been little different from its modern counterpart. One perhaps wonders how an Indian, working only with tools of stone and bone, could have fashioned these long slender strips of thin wood. If the proper kind of wood is thoroughly soaked and then sufficiently pounded with a smooth stone it can be peeled off in thin layers, each growth ring in sequence. These then will split easily along their length, giving the wooden strips necessary both for canoe-building and basket-making. When dried out again the wood regains most of its strength. A birchbark canoe was an excellent and long-lived watercraft and needed only occasional patching of the bark as holes or cracks made their appearance. These canoes varied in size from those intended to carry two men and their baggage up to the master canoes of the Great Lakes region, thirty-five feet long or more and carrying a crew of eight or ten in addition to some three tons of trade goods, provisions or furs.

Farther to the south, not far south of Ticonderoga, there were fewer and fewer birch trees suitable for canoes, and the Mohawks were forced to make theirs of elm bark, a much less suitable material. When wet it becomes soft and flabby, when dry it shrinks badly and often develops splits. The elm canoes were usually made each year and then discarded, although sometimes attempts were apparently made to preserve them by burying them in damp sand. All in all they were considered to be a most inferior form of boat. They differed basically from the birch canoe in that the heavy thick bark alone was depended on for lengthwise strength, and only a few ribs were used.

The white man's workhorse was the bateau, a double-ended, flat-bottomed, lapstreaked boat of shallow draft. It was much like the modern Gloucester dory except for the small stern transom characteristic of the latter. The bateau was the common watercraft of inland North America, and it was built in thousands, yet no complete specimen is known to exist today. The bottom plankings of a number have been found in Lake George in recent years, but most of their ribs and side plankings have rotted away. There is, however, still hope that a complete specimen may yet be found, or at least reassembled from separate parts. The Maritime Museum at Greenwich, England, has a contemporary drawing giving lines and dimensions of two colonial bateaux, while the Swedish naturalist Peter Kalm, a great traveler, has left us a clear description of bateaux that he had seen in 1749. Those in use around Albany were usually from eighteen to twenty-four feet long with a greatest width of about three and a half feet. The sides, particularly amidships, were nearly vertical, making it easier to pole the craft in shallow water. Such a shape made a poor boat indeed for the rough water of an open lake, and bateaux for such employment had more flaring sides than those intended for river work. Kalm, an observant man with an inquiring mind, wrote that he had seen nothing like these bateaux anywhere in Europe. The design may have developed in America to suit the local needs, or it may well be that the resulting form is the simplest and quickest one suitable for shallow water that can be nailed together. The type appears in America in clearly defined form at least by the early 1700's, and, save for the considerably

modified lumberman's bateau of later years, it completely
disappears in the early 1800's. Oddly enough, the Roman
pleasure galleys recovered from Lake Nemi shortly before
World War II, and later burned by the Germans, had tend-
ers which from photographs appear to be practically identi-
cal in form with the bateaux of our colonial days.

These boats varied in size from the smaller ones in use
around Albany to great craft up to forty-five feet long, capable of carrying as much as twelve tons. These larger examples, usually rigged with sail, were for use on the Great
Lakes or the Mississippi and were too large for many of the
smaller rivers. French bateaux normally were considerably
larger than those of the British, a fact which worked much
to the former's advantage in the last French war when bateaux of the two nations met on Lake Ontario. It was then
found that the British could not stand up to fire their muskets for fear of capsizing their craft, while their enemies could.
British bateaux used on the Mohawk averaged about twenty-
five feet long overall. Lewis Evans, mapmaker and geographer, wrote that the usual Mohawk bateau was manned by
two men and would carry freight of about three-quarters of
a ton, just about what was considered a wagonload. The
examples that carried Abercromby's army over Lake George
to its 1758 attack on Fort Carillon at Ticonderoga each carried
twenty-two soldiers and their provisions for a month. These
typically consisted of two barrels of salt pork, four of hard
bread or flour, and a few sacks of dried peas, rice or cornmeal,
giving a total load, both men and provisions, of about three
tons.

Charles Carroll of Carrollton, who went north to Canada in 1776 as a commissioner of the Continental Congress,
kept an interesting journal. It tells us that the bateaux then
being used to move troops down Lake George were thirty-
six feet long by eight wide and could hold thirty to forty

men. They had a mast to which a small squaresail or a blanket could be fixed, but this was useless unless the wind came from almost directly astern. Some of these boats even had awnings. Carroll was interested to see that General Schuyler had devised a machine at the foot of Lake George which picked each bateau out of the water and loaded it on a special four-wheeled carriage for transport over the portage down to Lake Champlain.

Bateaux could be hurriedly and roughly built. Sometimes, as in examples found in Lake George, part of the bark was left on the ribs, so crudely were they finished. The planks for the sides and bottom, of course, had to be sawed out from logs, either with two men and a sawpit, or, if one were in luck, by a little water-powered sawmill. It is on record that six men could put an average bateau together in two days, including sawing the planks. This is only a little longer than Peter Kalm found necessary to build an elm-bark canoe.

The gondola appeared on Lake Champlain in the Revolution, but the name, if not the precise form, is found as early as the closing years of the seventeenth century in New Hampshire. Those built on Lake Champlain in 1776 were flat-bottomed craft of about forty-five feet in length, carrying a fairly heavy cannon in their rounded bows and a smaller piece amidships on either side. They had a single mast with square mainsail and topsail. The stern was pointed with a little rake and carried a rudder, and the craft was built with quite heavy timbers. Gondolas were intended to be rowed quite as much as sailed. They were poor sailers except before the wind, but could stand surprisingly rough water. I had often wondered about their ancestry and searched for an indication without success until I realized that the gondola was merely a great bateau, its bow rounded and enlarged to support the weight of its forward gun, and its timbers strengthened throughout to carry the weight of its cannon.

On the larger rivers and lakes barges were sometimes used. They were merely great scows. Lewis Evans wrote that those on the Delaware River were made like troughs, forty or fifty feet long, six or seven wide and perhaps three deep, their ends sloped on the underside to decrease water resistance. They drew little over a foot and a half when loaded. On the lakes both nations launched little sailing vessels during the Seven Years War — some for cargo-carrying, others armed for battle, and none probably much over fifty feet long; but during the Revolution both the Americans and the British had rather sizable warships on Lake Champlain. In 1756 the British were well on their way to possessing quite an imposing little navy on Lake Ontario, but they dawdled too long and Montcalm's spirited raid on Oswego caught most of the vessels either on the stocks or still without armament. During the colonial period neither side appeared to appreciate the decisive effect that a naval supremacy on the Great Lakes would have on the contest for Canada. The French after the fall of Oswego had acquired, through construction as well as capture, an important little fleet, yet they failed to utilize it. Bradstreet's dash against Fort Frontenac was made only in bateaux, and it caught the French fleet tied up in harbor, crews understrength on some vessels, while others were both unmanned and unrigged. There were of course serious problems in maintaining a fleet on western waters, particularly that of safeguarding the vessels when winter had locked them fast in the thick ice, easy prey for the torch of a raiding party. One certain but somewhat drastic solution was to unrig and empty the hull and then sink it safely below the surface until spring allowed the process to be reversed. These problems, difficult as they may have seemed, could have been resolved, and had the effort and money of Braddock's vain attempt on Fort Duquesne been devoted to putting the British Navy on Lake

Ontario, the war would have been materially shortened.

Finally, the whaleboat deserves a brief mention. They were used for scouting on Lakes George and Champlain by Robert Rogers and his Rangers. These boats were collected on Cape Cod, Martha's Vineyard and Nantucket and taken up the Hudson to Albany and then over the portage to the lakes. We do not know just what they were like, but it seems probable that they were little different from the later New Bedford whaleboat except that they would have no centerboard, and probably no sail. Their light weight and the ease with which they could be rowed made them ideal for scouting expeditions. In the course of one raid Rogers carried his whaleboats from Lake George to Lake Champlain about six miles overland and across a mountain chain as well.

Mention was made earlier of the Hudson-Champlain waterway, the great thoroughfare along which nations, first Indians, then French and British, and finally British and Americans, were to meet in battle for centuries. From a point some two score miles north of Albany the Hudson River runs, straight almost as a tightened string, due south to the city of New York. The little oceangoing vessels of colonial days could ply their way north to Albany, and there discharge their cargoes, which then would be carried either by wagon over the sandy plains to Schenectady and on up the Mohawk by water, or, if intended for the north, a combination of water transport and land carriage by the little falls and rifts of the upper Hudson would bring the goods to Fort Edward, built in 1755 on the site of Lydius's trading post of earlier times. Here there was a choice of overland routes before the Champlain waterway could be attained. One could proceed over the almost water-level carry to Fort Anne, or, as an alternative, climb the steep carry up to the head of Lake George. Both were about the same length, some dozen miles or so, but once Fort Anne was reached there remained another similar distance along the twisting, muddy Wood Creek, where muskrat houses were seen by the hundreds, and there were great marshes where the wild duck lay in vast flocks. The Lake George carry gave access to some thirty-five miles of travel over the waters of one of the most beautiful lakes of North America, and then, down-hill over a mile-long carry, one reembarked his bateau or canoe into Lake Champlain, some twenty miles north of the mouth of Wood Creek. There remained a hundred miles of travel before the northern end of Champlain was reached, and one entered the Richelieu River, tributary to the mighty St. Lawrence. There were two or three short rapids in the Richelieu, some or all of which could be run if the water was not too low. At worst they were but minor portages.

And so the Hudson-Champlain Valley with only minor annoyances allowed free travel from New York all the way north to Montreal. This was the route of the smugglers and of trade, and when war came, it was only by water transport over this great thoroughfare that the tools and supplies of combat could be carried. The Hudson-Champlain waterway connected two very different civilizations, doomed to mutual attempts at conquest, and it is obvious that military effort would necessarily be canalized along this great artery of North America.

The place where the Lake George carry enters the narrow southern arm of Lake Champlain was called Ticonderoga by the Indians, and, controlling as it did both routes between the lake and the Hudson, it was the critical point on the entire waterway which extended from the Atlantic to the St. Lawrence. From Champlain's 1609 fight until Burgoyne was at last overcome at Saratoga in 1777 men were to fight for this critical point on the narrows of Lake Champlain. He who held Ticonderoga did indeed hold the "key to a continent" in his hands.

Gunfire Wakes the Echoes at Ticonderoga

CHAMPLAIN, the great French explorer, was the first white man to visit Ticonderoga. In the summer of 1609, wishing to adventure southward up the valley of the Richelieu into the great lake of which he had heard the Indians speak, he joined forces with a war party of Hurons and Montagnais. These Indians, itching for a profitable skirmish with their bitter enemies, the mighty Iroquois of the Mohawk Valley, heartily welcomed the addition of the white men and their death-dealing firearms, something as yet unknown to the Iroquois. The expedition worked its way south upstream against the current of the Richelieu River until the rapids at Chambly were encountered. It soon was evident that the Frenchmen's shallop could never be gotten upstream past this obstruction. Champlain accordingly selected two companions from the crew and sent the craft back to the tiny outpost of Quebec, where his fortified garrison house had been built the year before. Sixty Indians and the three Frenchmen carried overland around the rapids their equipment and twenty-four birchbark canoes, smallish ones really, each intended to hold only two Indians and their baggage. All climbed aboard, and there could not have been much room to spare. They paddled upstream and soon met more rapids at the place later to be called Ste. Thérèse. Then something over a score of miles up the now placid river brought them to the waters of the great lake we now call Champlain.

Each night the party landed, threw up birchbark shelters, and then built a barricade of tree trunks around them. A canoe or two scouted ahead for a few miles looking for signs of an enemy, but soon returned. No further guard was maintained, and all the Indians went to sleep, trusting their "manitou" to keep them safe until morning. Each evening the medicine man made magic to prophesy, to keep away evil spirits and to put a "hex" on the Iroquois. The expedition paddled southward, keeping a weather eye out for the enemy, and soon it was decided to travel only by night, hiding in the woods during the daylight hours. No Indians lived in these regions, but they were the hunting grounds of the warring nations. Split Rock, near today's Essex, New York, was said to mark the boundary line between the Canadian and the more southern Indians. He who passed beyond this point in those early days was certain to have warlike intentions. In later years it would no longer be so, but in Champlain's day battle was the only objective of passage beyond Split Rock.

South of this point the lake becomes more narrow, and once Crown Point — Pointe à la Chevelure (Scalp Point), the French called it — is reached the width is only that of a great river. It was at about ten in the evening of nearly the last day of July that the party arrived in the vicinity of the narrows at Ticonderoga, and there they encountered a flotilla of Iroquois elm-bark canoes, headed northward and bent on mischief.

The two parties, that of the Iroquois much the larger, closed their canoes tightly together and lay to just out of arrow range. Insults, threats and badinage were exchanged, and the Indians from the Mohawk then landed on the little peninsula of Ticonderoga, where they hurriedly built a barricade of tree trunks and bushes. The Canadian Indians lashed their canoes together with long poles and held a position of safety offshore. Soon two Iroquois canoes paddled out with envoys who asked if the northerners would fight. The reply was that they would like nothing better and that that was what they had come for. How confident must the Iroquois have felt, seeing their enemy only a third of their own number, and how certain of victory. The Canadian Indians knew no fear, for they trusted in the magic of the white men's firearms, whose power they had already seen demonstrated in their northern villages. All agreed that it was foolish to attempt to fight in the dark, and that the battle must wait for daylight. The remainder of the night, according to Champlain, was passed in songs, insults and dances, although how one could do a war dance in an overloaded canoe, and at night at that, is not easy to comprehend.

At daybreak Champlain's party landed in a crowd, the Indians forming a screen in front of the explorer and his two companions. The Iroquois, some two hundred in number, rushed out from their rough barricade, expecting to overawe the invaders by their numbers alone. Three chiefs wearing great feathers on their heads led the van. The Canadian Indians rolled aside their center ranks, revealing Champlain with his arquebus, loaded this day with four leaden balls. The two companions slipped into the cover of a patch of woods on the flank. Champlain now started forward toward the Iroquois, who had halted in their mad rush at their first sight of a white man. He does not tell us whether or not he wore any armor that day, but his appearance even without a shining breastplate would have been wildly unlike anything the Iroquois had ever seen. Despite their astonishment they set arrows to their bows and prepared to let fly. But before they could the Frenchman delivered his fire from a range of only thirty yards, aiming at one of the chieftains. Two of the Iroquois leaders fell, while a third Indian was wounded, so lucky was the shot. Undaunted by the noise and smoke of this new and undreamed-of weapon, the southern Indians let fly their cloud of arrows, but no one was seriously hurt. If Champlain wore no half-armor he certainly must have had on a padded jerkin, and the Indians had wooden shields, proof against any arrow.

Then one of the Frenchmen on the flank let go with his weapon. This second clap of thunder was too much for the Iroquois, and they took to flight, pursued for a short distance by Champlain, who got off one more shot, dropping another two or three redskins. Pursuit was continued for a distance into the heavy woods, while the whooping and wildly exulting Hurons and Montagnais killed a few more of their enemies and seized about a dozen prisoners. Soon all returned to the scene of the battle, and it was found that only about fifteen or sixteen of the victors had been wounded, and that all injuries moreover were slight. It was a mighty victory, but most unfortunately for Canada it would long be remembered by the Iroquois and would lead to bitter reprisals over many years to come.

The victors feasted, sang, danced and made merry for about three hours, during which time Champlain apparently visited the little river which connects the lake of his name with Lake George, although he did not spare the time to go as far as the latter. The Iroquois were still in the vicinity in considerable numbers, and the risk of ambush existed. It is probable that he went only as far as a canoe could take him, that is, to the lowest falls on the river, where later the French would build a sawmill.

By this time it must have been about midday, and the expedition took to its canoes, now greatly overloaded with prisoners and plunder. Very likely they added a few of the elm-bark canoes of the enemy to their flotilla. After about three hours of paddling northward they went ashore, probably a bit north of the present Crown Point bridge. A fire was lit and a prisoner selected for torture. Champlain gives some of the bloody details. After listening for a while to the shrieks of the unhappy victim he begged the tormentors to put the wretch out of his misery. They objected to discontinuing their sport. At last the Frenchman could stand it no longer and his arquebus put an end to the suffering of the Iroquois. Then the Indians cut out his heart and tried to make the other prisoners eat it, but in this they had no success.

Various thoughts have been advanced over the years as to the exact location of Champlain's fight, and of course it can never be precisely determined. It obviously was somewhere on the peninsula upon which Fort Ticonderoga stands today, although claims have been made for Crown Point, largely because the latitude recorded by Champlain's crude astrolabe more nearly approaches that of this place than that of Ticonderoga. Two specific points disprove Crown Point's claim. Champlain stated that he saw the river through which Lake George discharges into Lake Champlain, and he also reported that his party returned north three hours after the battle. Thus there would not have been sufficient time to paddle on from Crown Point to Ticonderoga and to return. The other point, and a very definite one, is that on Champlain's map of 1632 he clearly marks Lake George and its outlet, and shows by a number keyed to the legend that it was on the peninsula, on the north side of this river, that the fight took place.

Champlain returned to Canada and no white man would see Ticonderoga for years to come. Not many miles to the south, however, Henry Hudson that same summer was exploring the river which was later to bear his name, and scarcely a month after Champlain's skirmish the Englishman was in the vicinity of Albany, less than ninety miles from Ticonderoga. The first tentacles of the two civilizations which were to clash for nearly a century over the control of the Champlain Valley had almost met in that year of 1609. When at last France and Britain joined in decisive battle in that vital valley, it was at the site of Champlain's encounter that the issue was to be most bitterly contested. And again in the American Revolution this same spot would be the enemy's objective for two successive campaigns.

For years to come, however, Ticonderoga would, after Champlain's departure, be merely a name in the wilderness, and over a century was to pass before the white man attempted settlement in the region. Until nearly the end of the seventeenth century the French would restrict their habitations to the banks of the St. Lawrence and the northern parts of the valley of the Richelieu. Albany was established by the Dutch as a trading post by 1614, soon to be followed by Fort Amsterdam at today's New York, but the Dutch-British occupancy of the Hudson Valley would not advance north of the Mohawk until well into the following century. And so Ticonderoga would remain merely the name of an almost unknown place in the forests of North America while New France was slowly consolidating her tenuous hold on the St. Lawrence and English immigrants were pouring into New England to populate a new land and to establish a way of life quite different from that existing elsewhere on the continent.

THREE

Martyrdom on the Mohawk

FOR A GENERATION after Champlain's battle at Ticonderoga the Iroquois refrained from attack on the French, but they remembered and nourished revenge deep in their savage hearts. The Dutch at Fort Orange (now Albany) traded muskets for their furs, and by 1640 the Iroquois possessed at least thirty of these weapons with which Champlain had first confounded them in 1609. As their acquisition of firearms increased, so grew the enmity, still largely concealed, of the Iroquois against the French. With their new muskets they carried war to the Hurons of Georgian Bay and the Algonkins, but, save for a minor incident or two, they left the French alone. Then at last in the summer of 1641 the brittle peace snapped and open war broke out as Iroquois raiding parties appeared along the St. Lawrence. It was not a continuous war at all, but a sporadic one in which little parties of bloodthirsty savages suddenly burst from the woods, did what damage they could and promptly disappeared again into the wilderness.

In the early summer of 1642 Father Isaac Jogues of the Society of Jesus, a gentle and unassuming priest, timid but of an indomitable will, was sent from the Huron Mission of Ste. Marie on the shores of Georgian Bay to Quebec to secure much-needed supplies. He was returning westward with a party of two score Hurons and three lay missionaries and had passed by Trois Rivières and then Montreal Island, where only a month or two before Maisonneuve and his devoted little band had established the mission colony of Villemarie, still but a few tents and huts enclosed in a rough palisade. A little west of Montreal the Ottawa River enters the St. Lawrence through the Lake of the Two Mountains, really only a widening of the former river's shores. At the upper end of this lake there are a number of little islands, and here on the northern riverbank, Jogues's Indians noticed the tracks of some raiding Iroquois. These appeared to be relatively few in number, and the Hurons felt safe in continuing on their way.

The waters of the river here ran swiftly, and the canoes accordingly closely skirted the shore where the current was less. Suddenly some thirty Iroquois rose up from among the tall reeds and grasses along the river's margin, and poured upon the dumfounded Hurons a fusillade from their newly acquired weapons. Thirty muskets sent their bullets at forty men sitting in canoes at a distance of probably not over twenty or thirty yards. One Huron was wounded in the hand — such was Indian marksmanship on this occasion at least.

Another band of the invaders appeared on the opposite shore and the surprised and terrified Hurons splashed ashore and took to the woods in flight. Many of them escaped, and one of the four Frenchmen also was successful. Several friendly Indians, however, were killed or disabled. Father Jogues, from concealment in some bushes, watched the conclusion of the affair and could probably have remained safely in hiding until the Iroquois withdrew. But when he saw the two Frenchmen in the hands of the enemy, his conscience told him that he must share their fate, and he emerged from hiding and gave himself up to the howling savages. He immediately received a beating, and most of his fingernails were torn out by the roots, ripped off by Indian teeth. Then the Iroquois chewed one of the priest's fore-fingers until the bone was crushed and splinters of it pro-truded. The other Frenchmen received similar treatment, but the Hurons for the moment suffered no tortures.

The torment of the missionaries did not long continue, and soon the Iroquois with their twenty-two captives headed eastward down the St. Lawrence. They stopped at the mouth of the Richelieu, where the heads of the slain Hurons were set up on the top of stakes and crude pictures of Jogues and the other prisoners were sketched on the trunks of trees. Then the party ascended the Richelieu and went on up Lake Champlain, while the Frenchmen suffered agonies from their untended wounds and the fierce heat of summer. Eight days after the capture they met, probably a little north of Ticonderoga, a war party of two hundred Mohawks bound on a raid on the Canadian settlements. The newcomers, with shouts of excitement and a joyful volley of musketry, at once cut clubs and formed a long double line. The prisoners were forced to run the gauntlet, but the priest could make it only halfway and fell to the ground beneath the blows. Then he was further mishandled, a fingertip burned, another crunched by Indian teeth, and threatening gestures made of cutting off his nose. But soon the sport lost interest and the northward-bound party proceeded on its way. They were to meet surprise, for only eleven days after Jogues and his captors had left the Richelieu's mouth a French expedi-tion arrived there to build a fort, the first of the many that were later to follow in the Champlain Valley. The new stockade was not quite finished when the war party got there, but it was complete except for a single gap, where the French made a successful stand, and the savages were beaten off.

Father Jogues's captors continued on to Ticonderoga and

then along Lake George, at last quitting their canoes at today's village of Lake George and continuing overland. The
priest, suffering greatly from his wounds and bruises, was
forced to carry a part of the Indian booty, the goods originally destined for the Huron Mission. They crossed the Hudson, at this time of year flowing sluggishly in its rocky bed,
and almost certainly followed the valley of the Sacandaga,
today flooded by a great reservoir, and on to where Amsterdam now stands. The lowest of the three Mohawk towns
was but a mile or two upstream. Today the great Martyr's
Shrine of Auriesville covers the site of this vanished town.
The trip from the Lake of the Two Mountains had taken
thirteen days. The prisoners were at once greeted with clubs
and stones, while the priest had his two remaining fingernails
torn off. Then all the youth of the town lined up for the
gauntlet; but now a new proceedure was introduced, as Mohawks inserted themselves at intervals in the file of prisoners
and forced them to slow their progress through the ranks of
their tormentors to a walk.

At last the center of the village was reached, and here
further torture awaited. Jogues's left thumb was hacked off
at its base, a customary Indian mayhem before the day of
firearms, since it prevented use of a bow. The next day the
captives were taken to the second village, a couple of miles
upstream, and subjected to further torments, such as being
staked out naked on the ground while Indian children tossed
hot coals at them. Two days later they were moved on to
the third town, a few miles east of today's Canajoharie. Here
Jogues, stark naked, suffered greatly from cold and wet, but
otherwise he received only minor mishandling. One of his
companions, however, was less fortunate. This man hitherto
had lost no fingers, but one of the Mohawks, noting the
fact, at once sawed off a forefinger with a clamshell.

This was the end of the priest's worst physical suffering,

but he still led a miserable existence, scantily clothed in fragments of cast-off Indian garments and eating little but unripe squashes and cornmeal mush occasionally enriched with bits of fish or sun-dried meat. The Dutch at Fort Orange soon learned of the prisoner and tried without success to ransom him from his captors. Jogues still lived in fear and received many threats, but fortunately they were only threats. One of his two companions was adopted by a Mohawk, while the other was murdered in the presence of the Jesuit, who also bowed his head for the tomahawk but was left unharmed.

Father Jogues by now had largely recovered from his injuries, although his hands would always be fearfully maimed. He was treated as a slave and taken on a fall hunting trip. The Indians had a custom of dedicating their slain deer to one of their divinities, which Jogues believed devils, and accordingly he refused to eat any of the meat, which was to his mind accursed. And so he nearly starved in the midst of plenty. His food at times was, he recorded, deer entrails, boiled fungus, frogs eaten whole and cornmeal mush. It is most probable, however, that at times his captors fared no better. By the new year of 1643 his position became somewhat less miserable; a Frenchman at Fort Orange gave him a suit of clothes, and he commenced to study the Mohawk tongue, at last feeling that he probably would be allowed to live. He even managed to secure some paper from the Dutch and wrote several letters, one of which, directed to the governor of Trois Rivières, was actually delivered by an Indian to the fort at the mouth of the Richelieu.

By some extraordinary chance Father Jogues was able to retain possession of at least two books of religion, and with these and his increasing knowledge of the Indian tongue he started missionary work, probably largely among the Huron slaves. He was now left relatively free to go where he would among the Mohawk villages, and, being an unusually swift runner, he could probably have escaped had he wished. But he felt that he now was doing some good for his faith and so decided, for the present at least, to remain. The good Dutch dominie Megapolensis of Fort Orange befriended him, and the priest even visited the Dutch settlement upon occasion.

Father Jogues at one time had accompanied a fishing party of Mohawks to the Hudson at a point some twenty miles below Fort Orange, and on returning to his village by way of this post he learned that an Iroquois raiding party had suffered disaster through, they firmly believed, the letter he had dispatched. Accordingly they were out for his blood. And so at last he decided to escape and sought safety with the Dutch.

The little outpost which was to become Albany was the northernmost settlement in the Hudson Valley in 1643. It was a puny little place, "a wretched little fort called Fort Orenge, built of logs with four or five pieces of cannon . . . and as many swivels." The entire population was but a hundred living in something over a score of houses. There was an active trade with the Indians, who for their furs received guns, kettles, knives, axes and cloth as well as many other items of trade goods.

The Dutchmen were kindly and sheltered the priest in secrecy from his searching Indian hosts, until he could safely be put on shipboard. Eventually the Indians were placated by a sizable ransom and ceased their search for the priest. At the Hudson's mouth was the Dutch settlement of New Amsterdam, and to Father Jogues, after years in the wilderness, it must have seemed a real metropolis with its fort and garrison of sixty soldiers, its large stone church, the governor's house of brick and the storehouses and barracks. The population, some scattered over the island of Manhattan, totaled four or five hundred. Jogues was told by the governor that eighteen different languages were spoken there, while half as many sects worshiped as they pleased.

After further adventures, minor in nature compared to those he had survived, Father Jogues reached France on Christmas Day of 1643, a year and a half after his capture. A few days later he knocked on the door of the Jesuit college at Rennes, where he was at first taken for a beggar. Word soon reached Paris of his extraordinary misfortunes, and the queen sent for him to tell her the story. The modest priest shrank from the homage of the Court and longed to return to Canada. Under Church law, the fearful mutilation of his hands prevented his saying mass, but a sympathetic pope granted him a special dispensation. He sailed westward again in the spring of 1644, and for the next two years was retained at various duties in the little town of Quebec.

In the early summer of 1645 Mohawk peace emissaries appeared at Trois Rivières, bringing with them that companion of Father Jogues whom the Indians had adopted. In dress and appearance he now was a Mohawk, but it was largely due to his efforts that this embassy of peace had been undertaken. Council followed council and wampum belt followed wampum belt until at last, after days and weeks of councils and feasting, peace was declared. But it was a tenuous one that would not last.

The Canadian governor in the spring of 1646 decided to send an ambassador to the Mohawks in an attempt further to cement the peace. Father Jogues, in view of his knowledge of both the language and the region, was the logical candidate. With one white companion and a few Indians he started south, wearing on the advice of the Indians a civilian doublet instead of his cassock. They reached the northern end of Lake George on the eve of Corpus Christi, and the priest, in honor of the day, named the lake St. Sacrement, a name that would endure for more than a century. From the southern end of this lake the party followed the Sacandaga trail until they reached the Hudson, where, borrowing canoes from an Indian fishing party, they started paddling down the river to Fort Orange. Here the priest received a hearty welcome from the Dutch and a few days of rest were taken. The embassy then moved up the Mohawk to the scene of the priest's former captivity. What thoughts he must have had upon seeing again the place of his torment! The reception given him by the Mohawks was such as was due an emissary of a power with which it was desired, for the moment at least, to remain at peace. His Huron converts were certainly glad to see him, and some of the Mohawks appear to have been reasonably cordial. Father Jogues delivered his belts and speeches and shortly returned to Canada without incident.

A month or two later in that same year it was decided to attempt to found a mission on the Mohawk and Father Jogues was designated as its head. He started south in the late summer. Meanwhile, there had been a change of feeling among the Mohawks and one of the clans, the Bears, believing that Jogues had put a curse on their nation, were all for war and demanded the priest's death. The Turtles and Wolves, however, defended him and wished to maintain the peace. A war party of young Bears met Father Jogues and his companions somewhere south of Lake George, seized and stripped him, and took him back prisoner to the lower Mohawk town, where he promptly met martyrdom from an Iroquois tomahawk. Such was the sad end of this gentle, timid and yet iron-willed priest, who later would be canonized by his Church.

FOUR

A Fort Rises in the Wilderness

FOR A SCORE of years after the death of Father Jogues the Champlain Valley saw no white man, and the region remained the hunting grounds of the Indian. Over the northern half of the region the Algonkin held sway, while to the south the Iroquois hunted without fear of ambush. Raids northward on the puny Canadian settlements by warriors of the Five Nations had, by 1665, become so troublesome that the French King at last took notice and sent a regiment, the hard-bitten Carignan-Salières, across the ocean to curb the raiding savage. The governor of Canada believed in carrying the war to the enemy and in 1666 he led his forces south in a raid on the Indian castles of the Mohawk Valley. The expedition went astray, met a party of Dutchmen from Albany, then two years a British possession. The Dutchmen saved the Frenchmen from near starvation, and the disgruntled raiders struggled north again to Canada, the first military expedition of white men ever to pass through the narrows of Ticonderoga. Later in that same year the Frenchmen tried again with better luck, found and burned five of the Mohawk towns and thoroughly cowed that tribe of the Five Nations. The Mohawks never forgot their humiliation, and, despite treaties of peace and friendship, they waited their opportunity for vengeance. Albany and the New Netherlands meanwhile passed back into Dutch hands for a brief period before becoming, in 1674, the British province of New York.

In 1689, fifteen hundred bloodthirsty Iroquois, mindful still of their villages burned a generation before, hit La Chine, a Canadian settlement a little distance upstream from Montreal, in a bloody raid. The French governor, the fiery and short-tempered Frontenac, convinced that the English had incited the raid, in revenge turned his Canadians and Indians against the little hamlet of Schenectady. This was Canada's first attack on the British colonies, forerunner of a half-century of bloody warfare. Britain at once retaliated with an attempted thrust northward, which never got beyond the southern end of Lake Champlain, and by two minor raids on the Canadian settlements on the St. Lawrence. It was in the course of the last of these, Peter Schuyler's raid of 1691, that Ticonderoga is again mentioned in our history, for the raiders rested there at the narrows for a day or two on their journey and built an additional canoe. There was a little further, but minor, action back and forth along the great waterway, while Canadian raids shifted eastward to fall on the settlements in Maine. Then peace was made, a peace which soon was broken when Queen Anne's War erupted. Although this new struggle commenced in Europe in 1701, no action took place in America until two years later. A truce existed in effect along the Hudson-Champlain Valley, for neither the French nor the Dutch of Albany wished to interrupt the profitable smuggling trade which was carried on between the two colonies. So for many a year the narrows of Ticonderoga enjoyed a quiet peace, broken only by the splash of the smuggler's paddle, and history had no tale to tell.

Gradually the French pushed southward up the valley of the lake until in 1731 they built a stone fort at Crown Point, a fort which was fated to exist for a generation and yet never see a hostile action. The British meanwhile had advanced their settlements northward up the Hudson to the region of old Saratoga, now called Schuylerville. Only some sixty miles separated the two opposing civilizations. King George's War broke out in America in 1744 and lasted for four years, but they were relatively peaceful years save for minor strife on the borders. The great event of this war was the New Englanders' capture of Louisbourg, but in the Champlain Valley little of note took place.

Peace between France and Britain endured for a few years after the Treaty of Aix-la-Chapelle in 1748, but it was a peace that could not last. Two great empires were in conflict and this was but a breathing spell. The first real clash was to come in America and beyond the Alleghenies, where the French were advancing their frontier posts and stockaded forts into the great valley of the Ohio River. In 1749 a number of Virginian and London capitalists had formed the Ohio Company in order to speculate in lands in that desirable region. Its emissaries were now pushing westward, while at the same time independent English fur traders, a rough and undisciplined crew, were encroaching more and more into lands each nation believed to be its own, and bringing out many of the furs so essential to the economy of New France. King Louis considered the Appalachian Mountains the westward boundary of the colonies of Britain, a view King George and particularly his American subjects were far from accepting.

By 1753 the French had established Fort Le Boeuf on the headwaters of the Allegheny, only a relatively short portage from Lake Erie — up to now, and for a few years yet to come, uncontested French waters. The stockaded fort was about a dozen miles south and slightly east of today's Erie, Pennsylvania. From Le Boeuf one could easily descend by water all the way to French New Orleans on the Gulf of

Mexico. The governor of Virginia in 1753 sent young George Washington to the Ohio to order the French garrison of Le Boeuf to cease their encroachment and depart. The commander at the little fort of course spurned the demand, and Washington journeyed back through peril to Williamsburg to report the rebuff to Governor Dinwiddie.

In the spring of the next year, 1754, a party of Virginians was despatched westward over the mountains with orders to build a fortified post at the Forks of the Ohio, the junction of the Allegheny and Monongahela Rivers, the Pittsburgh of today. Scarcely had they started their work before a large body of Frenchmen suddenly appeared, descending the Allegheny from Fort Le Boeuf. The Englishmen were quietly and firmly ejected and told to go home across the mountains. Meanwhile the Virginia governor had raised additional troops and sent them west under the youthful Lieutenant Colonel George Washington to reinforce the new British post on the Ohio. They were too late to save the post, whose builders had already started their long trek homeward. Washington's little army met them, learned the news, and then soon encountered a party of reconnoitering Frenchmen. The first armed clash of the new war took place, a war which at last was to end with France stripped of Canada. Reinforcements quickly arrived from Le Boeuf and Washington was penned up in the hurriedly built Fort Necessity at the Great Meadows, near Uniontown, Pennsylvania, besieged and forced into surrender. This petty engagement, far away on the frontiers of North America, opened the great "Seven Years War," which, however, would not formally be declared in Europe until two more years had passed. In America it really was the "Nine Years War."

Although peace officially continued between the two nations in this summer of 1754, each knew that open war was inevitable and each made preparations to initiate it in America. The British King sent General Braddock and two regiments of regulars overseas. An expedition was to penetrate to the Ohio and throw out those Frenchmen who had dared to encroach on His Majesty's domains. Braddock was also to chase the French away from their post near Niagara Falls and from Crown Point on Lake Champlain. None of these missions could be considered acts of war in British eyes. They were merely police actions to eject unlawful intruders. The French, of course, would believe otherwise and feel, perhaps quite rightly, that Britain had started a war.

Paris meanwhile had been far from asleep, and an army of nearly four thousand regular troops crossed the Atlantic under command of General Baron von Dieskau, an officer of considerable experience. Some five hundred of the soldiers had the misfortune to fall prey to the ever-watchful British navy, but the remainder reached the St. Lawrence in safety. They would be the backbone of the army that Montcalm would often lead to victory over the next few years. A few reinforcements would trickle in from France, but only a few. New France had its own regular army, the regiment of La Marine, but it was small, of dubious quality and had officers of little experience in formal warfare, although often most effective in the wilderness campaign. There also was Canadian militia, but like all militia it was a most dubious tool, poorly armed and undisciplined. The little force of hard-bitten French regulars was the weapon Montcalm would wield so effectively over the next four years.

Braddock's unfortunate attempt on the new Fort Duquesne at the Forks of the Ohio is beyond the scope of this book, but he accomplished logistic wonders in moving his force over the mountains and nearly succeeded in his mission. He deserves better of history than he has received.

The northern drive against Crown Point was to start from Albany. The army, composed entirely of colonial regiments, assembled there on the flats under command of General William Johnson, fur trader, Indian commissioner, politician and one of the great men of colonial North America. Word of this impending attack soon reached the ears of Canada's Governor Vaudreuil.

In the spring of 1755 the southern bastion of New France in the Champlain Valley was the fort at Crown Point, an unusual fort in that its principal structure was a high tower-like redoubt. It was a dozen or so miles north of the narrows at Ticonderoga. The British had no real defense north of Albany, for stockaded Fort Lydius, where the portages for Lakes Champlain and George left the Hudson, had been burned during the last war. Such had also been the fate of the post at old Saratoga. Johnson's mission was to seize Fort St. Frédéric at Crown Point, but he appreciated the threat to New York offered by the undefended Hudson corridor to the south. Accordingly he moved up the river and commenced building a new fort on the site of Lydius's stockaded post. He called it Fort Edward, and for years it was to be a main defense of the Hudson Valley.

By late summer von Dieskau had his army at Crown Point —seven hundred French regulars, sixteen hundred Canadians and seven hundred Indians. The fort, quite a small one at best, and at this time only twenty-four years old, had fallen into poor condition. Masons feared to work on its walls lest they collapse. Yet this was Canada's southern outpost on the vital Hudson-Champlain waterway. In the first week of September von Dieskau started south, hoping to surprise the workmen at the new Fort Edward. In planning his expedition the general, new to America, made a grievous mistake, for he put his trust in Canadian militia and Indians, and left all but two hundred of his regulars behind. There is no need here to go into the resulting battle at any length. Johnson had left troops to continue work on the new fort, but he took most of his men on to the southern end of Lake George. In colonial days it was a rare occasion indeed when Indians could be persuaded to attack a fort — they preferred easier game. Von Dieskau's Indians refused to have anything to do with the camp where Fort Edward was just starting to arise, even though as yet it was quite indefensible. Accordingly he moved on against Johnson's main body at Lake George, and, after successfully ambushing a large force unwisely sent forward by the colonial general, he attacked the main body of troops barricaded behind breastworks hurriedly contrived out of tree trunks, wagon bodies and bateaux on a ridge bordering the shore of the lake. The regular French troops fought valiantly and suffered terrible losses, while the Canadians and Indians earned but little glory that day. Von Dieskau's attack was foiled, and he himself was wounded and captured.

The defeated French fell back to their boats on the western arm of Lake Champlain, receiving another mauling on the way from a party of British reinforcements. They retreated north to Ticonderoga and encamped. Johnson, wounded in the battle, failed to pursue and held his army at Lake George, his mission unaccomplished. Yet his victory, the only one gained by the British in America this year, made Johnson a baronet.

Canadian Governor Vaudreuil may or may not have heard of Von Dieskau's defeat when, on 20 September, he directed his wife's nephew, de Lotbinière, a young Canadian engineer officer, to build a fort at Ticonderoga. De Lotbinière had studied military engineering in France, but he had never seen active service in the field or garrison duty in a fortress. Nevertheless the young engineer had no doubt of his ability to design and build a fort in the wilderness, and his family connections gave him a much freer hand than any other officer could have enjoyed.

The peninsula which extends southeastward into Lake Champlain at the outlet of Lake George is composed largely of rugged rock, but when de Lotbinière first saw the place it apparently was so covered with trees and bushes that one could not see more than thirty paces in any direction. Nevertheless he staked out the outline of the fort on the ground and set to work. Later, when the outer end of the peninsula was stripped bare, it became apparent that the fort could have been better located, but it was then too late.

Work on the fort began in mid-October of 1755. De Lotbinière's first care was to provide some sort of winter quarters for the workmen, and relatively little was accomplished on the actual fort that fall and winter. He had two regiments from which to draw his labor force, La Reine and Languedoc, about six hundred and fifty men in all, and there certainly must have been some civilian artisans, such as foremen and carpenters. Soldiers were paid for their labor, in addition to their regular pay. The next year at Fort Frontenac on Lake Ontario this additional pay was at first a franc, then it was lowered to fifteen sous, three-fourths of a franc, but even this latter sum was a most welcome addition to the soldiers' meager pay.

The British were not ignorant of the new fort that was building, and scouting parties kept the peninsula under observation at frequent intervals. Robert Rogers, most famous of the colonial rangers, viewed the place at the end of September and reported that there were about three thousand men camped on the point, engaged in laying the foundations for a fort. A week later he rowed up Lake George with a party of fifty but failed to get any view of Ticonderoga, although his scouts managed to observe the force camped at the head of the portage. In mid-October Rogers returned to Lake Champlain, scouted around Crown Point, scalped a soldier there in full view of the fort, and examined Ticonderoga on his return trip. He reported about two thousand men in camp there but no further details.

And so it went, frequent reports from scouts but few specific details beyond the fact that the French were obviously building a fort, until in December Thomas Poor brought back word of four barracks within the outline of the walls, and twenty-one small huts, covered with boards or shakes, outside. He saw about four hundred men, he thought, felling trees and sawing planks.

It seems highly probable that there was little further progress on the fort now that cold weather had really set in — cutting and hauling firewood would take much of the time of the troops. De Lotbinière reported that the walls were seven feet high before freezing weather put a stop to the work, but I am inclined to believe that he stretched matters considerably in view of what Montcalm found the following spring.

French documents tell us that by February of 1756 there were twelve cannon in place as well as some smaller pieces, while eight more were at hand but not yet in position. An outpost with defensive works had been established at the head of the portage coming from Lake George, and the garrison now numbered some two thousand in all. More workmen and some Indians had evidently arrived since the previous fall. The fort itself apparently as yet amounted to very little and probably consisted of scarcely more than the base upon which the walls were to be erected. It had been necessary to level off an even footing, cutting rock away here and building up masonry there to form a foundation for the wooden facings of the walls. These main walls, the major defense of the place, were composed of heavy oak timbers, fourteen or fifteen inches square, laid horizontally one on top of the other. There were two such wooden walls, ten feet apart and tied to each other with cross timbers dovetailed in place. The space between was then filled with dirt and rubble. This form of construction was cheaper and quicker than one using masonry, and from the immediate military point of view better, since cannonballs would become harmlessly imbedded in the wood instead of shattering the stone facing. The drawback, of course, was the rotting of the timbers. In the end, for a permanent fort, stone was cheaper. Initially timber was used at Ticonderoga, later to be replaced, in part at least, by stone.

The campaign of 1756 was to bring no important action to the Champlain Valley. Neither the French nor the British was yet ready for a major clash in that region. Each was busily engaged in building its major outpost, and until that was accomplished there could be no thought of aggressive action. The new French fort at Ticonderoga, first called Fort Vaudreuil, soon acquired the delightful name of Carillon, presumably, tradition tells us, because the music of the waterfall in the little river falling down from Lake George sounded like a chime of bells. Johnson's men had started their fort in 1755 at the scene of von Dieskau's defeat, and they called it Fort William Henry.

Louis Joseph, Marquis de Montcalm, reached New France in the spring of 1756 to replace von Dieskau as commander of the field army. He was subordinate to the vain and jealous Governor Vaudreuil, and the two men were to clash constantly until Montcalm died from the wounds received on the Plains of Abraham three years later. The newly arrived general was sent west this first summer to attack the important British post of Oswego on Lake Ontario, the outpost that guarded Britain's access to the Great Lakes and the fur harvest of that vast region. The mission was brilliantly achieved, the first of the memorable deeds which Montcalm accomplished before his death.

This spring another regiment of regulars, the Royal Roussillon, was sent to Fort Carillon, and by July there were some five thousand men there in all. The regulars amounted to about two thousand, and much of the remainder must have been Canadian militia and workmen, with only a relatively few soldiers of La Marine, a regiment which numbered under nine hundred in all and furnished garrisons for the three cities of Canada as well as many of the western posts.

The fort advanced slowly. On the other hand, progress had been made, for by mid-July, 1756, all four bastions had been raised to a height of at least seven feet, and some thirty or more cannon were in place along the walls. Montcalm, a volatile Provençal, naturally was impatient and not at all pleased with the youthful and inexperienced engineer who, trusting to his most influential connections, went his own way and did largely as he pleased.

Graft was rampant in Canada, and it had become increasingly so in the 1750's. The notorious Bigot, who had learned his trade as commissary at Louisbourg before the 1745 siege, became the *intendant,* the economic czar, of Canada after the peace of 1748, and he proceeded to exploit the possibilities open to him and his associates in a grand manner. The Canadian governor was charged by the King with all military matters and all dealings with the Indians, but, practically speaking, all executive, economic and police measures were under the intendant, whose powers, in effect, were really greater than those of the governor. When this most important officer was dishonest, or even only unobservant, the opportunities for peculation were vast. Bigot gathered around himself a coterie of grafters whose operations were immense, in scope relatively greater even than those of Tammany under Boss Tweed. Opportunities were endless in the new land, and even well-intentioned men were forced to sanction illicit operations to a greater or lesser extent, even if they themselves received no direct benefit. New France was considered a Utopia for ambitious and impecunious young Frenchmen in the first half of the eighteenth century, and many a bankrupt courtier sought a Canadian appointment so that he might make or recoup a fortune. This perhaps could be done honestly, but it was soon learned that dishonest methods were quickest and were not questioned. All was excused in a land of easy morals.

While Governor Vaudreuil must have been cognizant of what was taking place, he apparently never secured any direct benefit from these operations of his friends and associates. He was, however, much to blame for not at least attempting to curb these excesses. The real answer, however, may have been that Bigot's powers actually were so much greater than those of the governor that the latter was powerless to act.

Living costs were much higher in Canada than in France, yet the pay of the regular officers, in theory the same as in Europe, was soon being disbursed in inflated paper money, and no allowance was made in any way for the greatly increased cost of mere existence. The Canadian officers also suffered, of course, but many of them engaged in extracurricular activities, usually more or less illicit. Such operations, even if desired by the more strait-laced French professional officers, were seldom if ever open to them. Thus many an officer was forced into debt.

One simple source of profit, open in practice only to officers of the Canadian regiment assigned to western posts, was to trade to the Indians for furs those goods which the French King sent as gifts. Another practice commonly available, since companies were almost always understrength, was to draw rations and equipment for the full theoretical company strength and to sell the excess. Neither of these methods would have been open to regular officers who came overseas with Montcalm. There is little doubt that some of the regulars succumbed to the opportunities they found existing and the spirit in which even the highest Canadian officials viewed illicit gain. The great majority, however, and all the senior commanders appear to have held themselves rigidly aloof from these activities.

Probably the greatest chance to make a fortune open to one not of the topmost echelon was given to the officer charged with building a fort in Canada. Several avenues were open to him, some accepted by Canadian practice as proper and correct, others less so and therefore conducted more or less under cover. The ultimate result, after all had taken their share of the spoils, was that it cost just about twice as much to build a fort in New France as it did in the home country. While some of this undoubtedly resulted from distance and the difficulty of operating in the wilderness, a very large part of the excess cost was represented by graft.

One plum considered the rightful perquisite of the officer building a fort was the canteen concession. It was particularly true in a place like Ticonderoga that a soldier had nothing upon which to spend his pay, both his regular pittance and those extra francs received for work on the fortifications, except on wine and brandy at the canteen. At Ticonderoga, Le Roux, keeper of the canteen, sold wine for just twice what it cost at Montreal and brandy three times. In the same way the farther one went away from Montreal the greater the cost of the soldier's ration. In 1756 the value of the soldier's daily portion of food was ten and one-half sous at Montreal, while at La Chine, only twelve miles upstream, it was twenty-seven sous. A small bit of this fearful increase of course was chargeable to transport costs, but most of it was due to graft. The King gave daily to each soldier about a pound each of bread and salt pork, perhaps half as much of dried peas, and an allowance of wine. Save for salt and other condiments, that was all. At times fresh beef was issued, but salt pork was usual. Sometimes when a barrel of salt pork was broached, it was found to contain only the heads and feet of pigs. In times of scarcity, and they often reigned in New France during this last war, salt cod was substituted for some of the pork and the amount of meat and bread reduced. At permanent posts vegetables were grown and there always was the chance of securing fish and game, but food at Ticonderoga in these years was neither plentiful nor very attractive. Montcalm at one time, in order to set an example, even tried eating bread made partly from *"grouillée"* (squirming) flour — flour constantly in motion from the activity of the vermin within it.

The profit of the canteen was great and continuing. The longer it took to build the fort, the greater the engineer's profit. Thus de Lotbinière had no real incentive to expedite the construction at Ticonderoga, but instead had every reason to make the work drag out. A French regular engineer officer who served at the fort estimated that the annual profits of the canteen at Carillon amounted to 100,000 francs, certainly equivalent to $150,000 today. Another moneymaking opportunity was open to anyone who had a little capital. De Lotbinière paid his workers in paper chits, rather than the usual Canadian "card" money which was bad enough in itself. If one had hard money at Carillon he could buy "card" money at a material discount, and then with this latter currency he could acquire de Lotbinière notes at anywhere from one-half to three-quarters of their face value. Then, if he sent these chits to the treasurer at Montreal, they would be exchanged for their face value in "card" money less a small discount. The process could then be repeated. It was even said that de Lotbinière kept a clerk at the fort who would expedite these various exchanges.

A third operation, illicit and open only to the engineer himself, was quite out of the ordinary. The sand used in the mortar — much of the later work at Carillon was in masonry — had to be hauled a hundred or two hundred yards from the sandpit, so horses were provided by the engineer, although presumed to be hired from various fictitious owners. De Lotbinière had to pay for the oats the horses ate, but hay and shoeing were provided by the King, as well as the supply and repair of the wagons used. Twenty-five francs, say thirty-five dollars or so in today's values, was paid for each trip, but it was considered too much trouble to bother to count the number of trips actually made, so it was assumed that each horse made sixteen or seventeen trips a day. There were at least fifteen horses in 1756 and each horse must have grossed about ten thousand francs a month. This seems almost astronomical and would be hard to believe were the figures not reported by an honest professional officer recently arrived from France. Another officer has left a record confirming this operation, but he put the proceeds at a considerably smaller figure, believing that the seven horses working in 1758 earned de Lotbinière 120,000 francs in all, a sum certainly not to be despised.

De Lotbinière, as constructing engineer, certified for all work done, and no one appears to have audited his figures. It is most probable that a material part of the engineer's immense receipts were distributed to associates and subordinates — he offered a third share in the canteen and horse concessions to a regular French officer who worked with him at Carillon, and who refused the offer in scorn — but he must have made a very sizable fortune through his operations. Today we would consider this an illegal and ill-gotten gain, but it appears that de Lotbinière stayed within the letter of the law of that day, just as did Governor Vaudreuil.

The former was not arraigned nor the latter found guilty in the wholesale trial of Bigot's crew after the fall of New France.

Montcalm returned to Carillon after his capture of Oswego, and was discouraged by the lack of progress in the fortifications. As late as the end of September he noted that it would be at least another month before the fort could be considered fit to defend itself against an attack. The general found that he had to ride herd on de Lotbinière to keep him engaged in essential work, otherwise he would be distracted into unproductive channels. The slower the progress, the greater the profit. It is quite possible that the criticism of the young engineer which has survived is unfair to him, but it comes from several sources, biased perhaps, but each of them has a reputation for accuracy. De Lotbinière was not dishonest according to the standards of New France; he was merely working a good thing for all that he could. And whatever one may say he did get Fort Carillon built.

In 1756 a lime kiln and a brick works were in operation by summer, and work was started on a sawmill at the lowest falls on the river flowing out of Lake George, Rivière la Chute, the French called it. There evidently was no experienced millwright available and the mill could not be gotten to operate this season. Water-powered sawmills were still rather a novelty in Canada; the first ones had been built by captive New Englanders or Yorkers, history does not say which.

Once the Ticonderoga peninsula had been cleared throughout its lower end in order to secure an open field of fire, it was found that the fort did not effectively command the passage through the narrows. The range was too great for accurate fire. Accordingly a redoubt, actually a small separate fort, was built this summer on the extreme tip of the neck of land. When the British at last secured Ticonderoga in 1759 this redoubt, then built of stone, was still incomplete. Hence it seems probable that in 1756 this structure, then called the Grenadier Battery, was only of log and dirt, a temporary defense, later to be replaced by a more permanent work.

By the fall of 1756 the outlines of the uncompleted fort were much as they are today with one major exception. As one enters the fort, one crosses a flat stretch, bounded on the south by a high wall lined with great bronze cannon and on the north by the southern bastions and curtain wall of the fort itself. This little plateau and the great retaining wall which holds it in place are later additions, perhaps built by the British in 1759, perhaps Revolutionary in origin. In 1756 a large storehouse stood on the original hillside just in front of the present arched entrance into the interior of the fort. It was built, like the fort walls, of squared horizontal timbers and carried cannon on its roof. Actually this storehouse was a ravelin, square rather than triangular in shape, covering the southern curtain wall and the main entrance to the fort. Its cellar, hewn out of solid rock, was used to store a great number of the casks of wine upon which the garrison depended.

As the winter of 1756-1757 approached, the fortress, still only partly completed and built of earth and logs, was at last in condition to put up a reasonable defense against an attack. There were now thirty-six cannon mounted on its walls, a third of them 18-pounders carrying a five-and-a-half-inch iron ball. The storehouse covered the southern curtain by cannon on its embrasured roof. There was now a small fort, perhaps merely a blockhouse, at the head of the falls on the east shore of Lake George. Fort Carillon no longer need fear a sudden raid. But this the British had no thought of attempting, so shocked and handicapped were they by the loss of Oswego. Their activities in the Champlain Valley this year would be limited to pushing on the construction of Fort William Henry near the scene of von Dieskau's defeat at the head of Lake George.

Montcalm returned to Carillon after his victory at Oswego, and with him came his excellent aide-de-camp Bougainville, whose voluminous journal tells us of conditions at Ticonderoga during that late summer and fall of 1756. Bougainville was a brilliant young Frenchman, trained as a lawyer but also skilled in mathematics, who had served the French ambassador in London. He knew the English and their language, was interested in everything and recorded it all in his journal. Moreover he and Montcalm were deep in each other's confidence. (The young officer transferred to the French navy after the end of the war, explored the South Seas, introduced the Bougainvillea flower to Europe, and died an admiral and a count of Napoleon's empire.)

The general and his aide reached Fort Carillon on 10 September. Progress since his earlier visit seemed to the general to be very slight. Although about five hundred men were working daily on the defenses, little appeared to have been accomplished since late spring. Montcalm, moreover, thought that the fort should be about twice its actual size, capable of holding a garrison of five hundred instead of the three hundred that the present structure could shelter. Three of the four bastions, those spurs which projected out from each corner of the square fort and provided flanking fire along the face of the curtain walls, were in a practical state. There was a camp at the foot of Lake George, where an enemy coming from the south must land, with an advance camp a mile farther south along the lake shore, whence two bateaux daily reconnoitered the waters of Lake George. Over eleven hundred men were deployed at these outposts out of a total force of less than three thousand, but this still left an ample force to work on the fort itself. Each nation's army harassed that of the other with petty raids in the Lake George region, but fort-building was the only real order of the day.

Bougainville recorded early in October that the work went very slowly:

The soldier, corrupted by the amount of money he here receives, and by the example set by the Indians and the Canadians, breathes an air impregnated with independence, works with languor. The engineer is almost never at the works, it is to his interest that the fort should not be completed promptly. He has the exclusive privilege of selling wine (it sells at 55 [sous] a bottle [almost three francs]) and all the money of the workmen, even the soldier's pay, go to his canteen. Besides he has built this fort of horizontal wooden timbers, in a region where stone, limestone, and sand are found abundantly, where, in obtaining stone with which to build, the ditch is created at the same time, where there doubtless is timber, but where men are lacking to cut it, square it up, haul it, where there are neither wagons nor horses. [The sand-hauling horses evidently appeared later.] Odd business! This engineer gives the workmen certificates which have the value of money without anyone assigned to control them, and all these certificates come back to him.

A few days later he complained that there was no wine for the regular issue, not even for the hospital; only the canteen had it for sale. Indians and British rangers prowled around, and Bougainville noted a scalping of a soldier and a maidservant at this time, between the fort and the advance posts.

Since the defenses of Carillon were not yet sufficiently strong, and winter was unpleasantly near, Montcalm decided to erect palisades of vertical logs along the weaker portions, and the soldiers, told this must be done before they could go north to their winter quarters, worked with vigor.

Bougainville recorded that a French regular officer, probably Captain de la Pauze, had succeeded in fixing the sawmill that "the Vauban of Canada could not make work. Unfortunately it is to the interest of this Vauban that the work drag out. The canteen must have its business." All the French regular officers who left us journals seem to have made bitter remarks about de Lotbinière, perhaps because of the contempt of the regular for the colonial, perhaps on account of the character and actions of the young engineer. My own belief is that de Lotbinière was an ambitious young man with little experience but most powerful connections who saw a chance to make a fortune and did, while always keeping within the law as it was then interpreted in New France. His intentions, unlike those of Bigot, were not evil.

In mid-October Montcalm's aide-de-camp had another complaint: "Now we are without candles. For the last fortnight the officers grope their way to bed in the dark, an inconvenience, but a far greater one for the bakery and the hospital. . . . They melt salt pork into tin lamps and use it instead of oil. I admire with what consistency and industry they here take every means of squandering away the King's money. Candles which come from France with much difficulty are fearfully expensive, oil made in [this] country from fish and very little in demand because of the war goes for almost nothing; and so in all the posts they burn candles and send no oil although [Montcalm] often has asked for it."

Bleury at last arrived with his flotilla of bateaux loaded with wine, and all were again happy, released from having to drink spruce beer or even, horrid thought, just water. Spruce beer was made by boiling the tips and small branches of the spruce tree, adding molasses and yeast to the resulting liquid, and letting nature take its course for a very few days. The result is mildly alcoholic and surprisingly enough tastes like beer. (I know, for I have made it.) Bleury had the concession for ferrying supplies to Carillon, and he was paid slightly under a franc a pound for carriage. Each of his great bateaux — he brought fifty-four in this convoy — carried some three tons. Bleury also brought wine, brandy and poultry on his own account for sale to the garrison. It is most evident that here was another Canadian well on his way to making a fortune.

At last, late in October, Montcalm, convinced that there was nothing more that he could accomplish before winter closed in on Fort Carillon, started north to Montreal. The garrison he left in the fort was composed of a hundred and fifty regular troops, one hundred soldiers of La Marine and about fifty workmen. There would be plenty to keep them occupied, for they would have to cut and haul at least three thousand cords of firewood in order to make life endurable in the fort as winter seized the Champlain Valley in its frigid clutches. One hundred skilled woodchoppers would need at least a month to cut this amount of wood, and much more to haul it into the fort. There could be little complaint of lack of exercise at Carillon this winter of 1756-1757.

FIVE

Montcalm Takes Fort William Henry

FORT WILLIAM HENRY was the most advanced post of the British in the Champlain Valley. Sir William Johnson had commenced its construction in the summer of 1755 after his defeat of von Dieskau at the Battle of Lake George. It lay at the southern end of that lake, a fort with four bastions, built of stout wooden cribwork filled with earth. The fort was a fairly formidable structure, but not very large, capable of holding a garrison of only some four hundred men. A competent officer, Major William Eyre, had built it, but its defenses on the west needed further improvement.

In March of 1757 the Marquis de Vaudreuil, governor of Canada, sent his brother, de Rigaud, to assail the fort in a winter raid. Sixteen hundred French regulars, Canadians and Indians plodded their way southward on snowshoes, dragging their supplies on sleds over the ice and snow of Lake Champlain and then on up Lake George. Their hope was to surprise the garrison or at least to scare it into surrender by the size of the expedition, but Major Eyre still was in command, and he was on the alert for trouble. The French took no artillery along and they at once found themselves powerless against the grapeshot and musket fire of the British garrison.

Any stockaded fort, if sufficiently manned and provisioned, and commanded by a wide-awake and capable officer, was safe against attack by musket fire alone — artillery was needed to breach the walls. A stout earth-and-timber fort, such as William Henry, required for its reduction the heaviest of artillery, particularly one or more of the 13-inch mortars which could toss 200-pound explosive bombs deep into the heart of the defenses. Without such artillery the French were helpless. Rigaud's attack was not pushed home and the adventure failed. The assailants succeeded, however, in burning many bateaux and some larger vessels, as well as various out-buildings, a decided embarrassment to the British.

The Marquis de Montcalm had made a victorious start to his American campaigns when, shortly after his arrival here in the early summer of 1756, he had captured and destroyed Oswego, the important British post on Lake Ontario. Now, as the campaign of the following year got under way, he prepared to move against the next British encroachment in the pathway of New France, Fort William Henry.

Montcalm's task was to be made easier, although he probably did not yet know it, by the fact that Lord Loudoun had taken a great army off on an abortive attempt against Louisbourg, the mighty French fortress on Cape Breton Island. The depleted forces guarding the New York frontier were left under the command of General Daniel Webb, a sick and not overly competent officer. The French assembled at Ticonderoga and there completed the final preparations for the advance up Lake George. Battalions of regulars, La Reine, La Sarre, Languedoc, Béarn, Guyenne and Royal Roussillon, covered the flats below the fortress. Along with them there was a horde of painted Indians, howling, dancing, stealing and, when occasion offered, boiling captured Englishmen in their pots. Then there were the Canadians, some men of La Marine Regiment, but mostly militiamen, along with a few volunteers, some three and a half thousand in all, not trained troops, but excellent for the hauling, rowing and digging which was to be endured. Ticonderoga hummed with activity.

While Montcalm held long and solemn council with staid old Indian chiefs, Ottawas, Chippewas, Menominees and Potawatomis, the young braves, tired of salt pork and eager for fresh meat, ran riot, butchering the draft oxen needed to haul the supplies up the mile-long portage to Lake George. Not even Montcalm's own poultry was safe from pillaging Indians, and there was little the French dared do, lest their touchy Indian allies should quit in a huff. Already a few, satiated with a handful of prisoners, had left for home, warning of what could happen in a much greater way.

Bougainville wrote home about these savage allies, ". . . Indians, naked, black red, howling, bellowing, dancing, singing the war song, getting drunk, yelling for 'broth,' that is to say blood, drawn from 500 leagues away by the smell of fresh human blood and the chance to teach their young men how one carves up a human being destined for the pot. Behold our comrades who, night and day, are our shadows. I shiver at the frightful spectacles which they are preparing for us." Such were the allies that the French were leading against the British defenders of William Henry.

Montcalm brought eighteen hundred Indians on the expedition, some eight hundred Christian redskins from the missions, accompanied by Abbé Piquet and two other priests, and almost a thousand wild Indians from the region of the Great Lakes, with one priest and several partisan leaders and half-breed interpreters in their train. Father Roubaud, the Jesuit missionary at St. Francis, went along with this Indian contingent, and left a graphic account of his experience. "Imagine a great congregation of savages decorated with all those ornaments most capable, to the European eye, of disfiguring one's appearance, vermilion, white, green, yellow, black made with soot or the scrapings of cooking pots; the face of a single

Indian unites all these colors methodically applied, with aid of a little grease which serves as pomade. Behold the paint which goes to work on these dress occasions to embellish not only the face but even the head, almost all close-shaven except for a little tuft of hair saved on the very top as a point of attachment for bird feathers or some bits of wampum or some other such trinket. Each part of the head has a special ornament, the nose has a pendant, there are others for the ears, which are hung there from childhood and have by their weight so elongated the earlobes that they reach to the shoulders . . . a shirt smeared with vermilion, a wampum collar, silver bracelets, a great knife hung on the chest, a belt of varied colors, but always burlesquely assorted, shoes of moose hide, that is the dress of the savage."

A scouting party of French and Indians had paddled up Lake George and had succeeded in destroying a considerable body of reconnoitering Englishmen, volunteers from New Jersey, commanded by Colonel Parker. Many were killed, but a number of prisoners were brought back to the Indian camp at Carillon. Father Roubaud wrote home about what happened to some of these unfortunates. "My tent had been placed in the middle of the Ottawas. The first object I saw on arriving there was a great fire, and wooden spits stuck in the ground, denoting a feast. There was one indeed. But, heavens, what a feast! The remains of the corpse of an Englishman, skinned and the meat half cut off! A moment later I saw these inhuman beings eating, with famished greed, this human flesh. . . . What was most sad was that they had forced a half score of English to be spectators of their infamous meal." Father Roubaud protested without avail, and a young warrior replied in bad French, "Thou hast a French taste, I an Indian one, this meat is good for me," and he offered a choice bit of broiled Englishman to the priest.

Councils with Indians continued as Montcalm outlined to

his savage listeners his plans for taking Fort William Henry. Most of the redskins enthused, but the crafty Iroquois contingent held back, saying that they would have to consult their elders, who were not then present. Suddenly nearby in the forest a great tree fell with a mighty crash, an augury to the savages, but of what, of success or of disaster? The quick-witted Montcalm at once and without hesitation announced that thus would William Henry fall before their victorious advance, and the Indians howled their approval.

The expedition was to advance in two divisions, one by land along the western shore of Lake George, where rugged mountains, thick forests and slimy marshes made progress a constant struggle. The larger party, which Montcalm would lead, was to move by water, a much easier trip, even with the artillery and supplies. The movement was to start on 29 July, but the Indians protested that they were not yet ready, and Montcalm was forced to postpone the advance. Another great powwow was held, and all the Indians, the Christianized of the eastern missions and the heathen of the Far West, promised obedience and unity of action. Now the Iroquois, scenting blood and loot, decided to come along, and immediately claimed the honor of leading the advance, a request it was unwise to deny them. Then each tribe presented Montcalm with bundles of little sticks, each stick representing a warrior in the roster of their contingent. In all there were 1799 of them, 820 mission Indians, the rest untamed savages of the great west.

Somewhat over a third of the army started overland on 30 July, while the remainder in the early morning two days later clambered into their bateaux and canoes, after having spent much of the previous night hauling their cannon and supplies up the steep portage between the lakes. The Indians had left behind in their camp, hanging on a tree, a cloak, a breechclout and leggings as an offering to their manitou.

Three French priests, who had intended to say mass at this very spot, asked Montcalm if it was right to say mass at a place where sacrifice had been made to the devil. Montcalm promptly replied that undoubtedly it was better to say it there than not say it at all.

The vast regatta spread out over Lake Champlain, a majestic sight indeed, but what most impressed young Bougainville, accustomed as he was to the sight of great European armies, were the hundred and fifty birch canoes laden with naked, painted savages. Father Roubaud recorded that when they passed the scene of Colonel Parker's defeat they found many signs of the disaster, stranded whaleboats and a great number of corpses, mutilated and in some cases hacked into pieces. Twenty-four hours later at the appointed place the two parts of the expedition met, the land contingent having arrived the day before, exhausted by endless struggle with steep mountains, pathless forest and fallen tree trunks, and all this through heat as great as armies ever met in Italy. Advance continued both by land and water, and by midday of 2 August the French halted at a point some five miles from the British fort. Reconnaissance was at once pushed forward, while the army went into bivouac and rested. Shortly before daybreak the next morning the troops advanced the remaining distance by land and Fort William Henry was soon surrounded.

There followed the normal routine of besieging a fortress. A trench would be pushed forward from some hillock relatively near the fort, and in a diagonal direction to give cover from enemy fire. At a convenient place a cross-trench would be dug and here the first battery of siege guns and mortars would be placed. Their fire would cover the further advance of the trench as it zigzagged ahead to the next battery position. Batteries might be and often were carried to within two hundred yards of the walls of a fort, because only from such a short range could the cannon of that day develop sufficient accuracy to concentrate their fire on the section of wall it was desired to breach. Such was Montcalm's procedure, and the first battery opened fire early on the morning of 6 August from a range of about four hundred and fifty yards against the west side of the fort.

There actually were two positions defended by the British, for only about four hundred men of the entire army of over two thousand could be accommodated within Fort William Henry itself. The remainder took up a position on a large and rocky knoll nearly half a mile from the fort and separated from it by a marsh and a brook. This place was hurriedly stockaded and barricaded against attack, but it lacked any appreciable artillery and was too far from the fort to be of any real assistance. In effect the body of nearly two thousand men stationed here sat out the entire siege almost solely as spectators, except for one futile sortie. Lieutenant Colonel Monro, a competent officer of British regulars, had now replaced Eyre as commander of William Henry.

Montcalm did not have a force large enough to invest the whole area completely, but this was hardly necessary since relief could come only from one direction, the south, by the road from Fort Edward on the Hudson. The camp of the Indians was placed across this road, thus completely cutting off all British communication to the rear.

The siege proceeded in the usual fashion, the British attempting with their artillery and small arms to delay the digging of the trenches and the emplacement of the enemy guns, the French trying to get their cannon and mortars into sheltered positions from which they could start battering down a wall of the fort. Their fire was concentrated on the weak point about which warning had been given the previous year. All this was normal and conventional in the eyes of a European-trained soldier, even though carried out in the

MONTCALM'S MAIN CAMP

FRENCH BATTERIES

LAKE GEORGE

THE WHARF

RAVINE

TRENCHES

FORT GARDEN

THE FORT

ROAD TO FT. EDWARD

ENTRENCHED CAMP

FORT WILLIAM HENRY
1757

Adapted from Ann Rocque's map of 1765 in the Collection of the Mass. Hist. Society

LEVIS' CAMP

YARDS

0   100   200   300   400   500

DE LA CORNE'S INDIAN CAMP

Fort William Henry, 1757

wilderness against a fort with walls of wood rather than of stone. The Indians, of course, furnished the discordant note. Instead of sending out scouting parties as they had been told, they all trooped into the vicinity of the fort, excitedly watching the French fire their cannon and hiding in the gardens to take potshots at the British. This did little good except to waste powder. Their scouting did, however, produce one prisoner and a dead man, whose waistcoat concealed in its lining a letter from General Webb at Fort Edward to Colonel Monro telling him that he could expect no aid, and that he had better make the best surrender terms he could. This put the game right into Montcalm's hands, but he held the letter for a day or two before sending it to Monro under a red flag of truce, red since the French colors were white.

General Webb had reinforced the fort before the attack, leaving himself only sixteen hundred soldiers at Fort Edward. He has been accused of being a craven for not coming to the rescue. He originally had intended to, then becoming more cautious, felt that he must assemble more militia for the defense of the Hudson corridor before he dared move forward. He had some justification. An advance through that wooded country had grave dangers and there is some question what he could have done once he got near the fort. The final surrender was occasioned to a considerable extent by the bursting of most of the fort's heavy guns and mortars, and only a new supply of artillery or a powerful sortie could have saved the day. The former, Webb could not have gotten to the fort, the latter would have been almost impossible to carry out, so well did the terrain protect the attacking French. Moreover it would seem from reports of the battle that the active defense was left almost entirely to the small garrison in the fort itself, while the very much larger body in the barricaded camp on the high ground did little but watch. Would the presence of another thousand or two English have saved the fort? There seem to be grave doubts. Nevertheless Webb probably should have tried to do something, but he was the man on the ground, and the decision was his. He believed that Montcalm had an army of eleven thousand men, and knew that his own little force at Fort Edward was, save for some scattered regulars and untrained militia levies, the last defense of the Hudson, of Albany, and perhaps even of New York City itself. Had he been able to visualize some of Montcalm's problems, lack of food and supplies, a jealous and carping governor, and militia and Indians both frantic to go home, he might not have been so cautious. One is always prone to think of his own troubles and seldom of those of the other side.

At one time there was a short truce and an Abnaki told a

member of the British party in bad but understandable French: "Ah, no surrender, well! Open fire then, and my Father will then shoot his great cannon, then defend yourself well, for if I capture you, there will be no quarter." Dire warning of what was to come, but Montcalm failed to heed.

The French poured their artillery fire against the cribwork walls of the fort, gradually reducing them to mere piles of dirt, and little by little overpowering the answering fire of the defenders. One by one the British guns burst; and smallpox ran riot through the garrison. Once it was learned that no relief would come morale broke down, and it became obvious that the case was hopeless. After three days and nights of cannonading by the French the fort had shot its bolt, and the white flag of surrender was raised. The terms of capitulation were generous. The French did not want prisoners, for it was difficult enough to feed their own people with the scanty crops of Canada and the modicum of supplies that managed to evade the British navy. So Montcalm decided to parole the troops and send them home. The British were to march out with their arms and baggage and retire south to Fort Edward, leaving to the French the fort and all its supplies, which included food for six thousand men for six weeks, manna for starving Canada. The soldiers retained their muskets, but, according to one who was there, they kept no ammunition.

Before the terms were finally completed Montcalm had a conference with the Indian chieftains, and secured their promise to restrain their young men from any action against the English. It seems hard to believe that after the experience he had had with Indian promises and his knowledge of the inability of the French to control the savages, he was still naïve enough to put trust in this pledge. He must have remembered what happened after the surrender at Oswego the year before. Certainly he should have taken more positive measures to see that the now defenseless British were amply protected. At the start of the siege he had reminded Monro of Indian cruelty in a letter which can be called nothing but threatening. "[I have] all the Indians from the higher parts of this country the cruelty of whom a detachment of your garrison have lately too much experienced. . . . I have it yet in my power to restrain the Indians . . . which will not be in my power . . . if you insist on defending your fort."

Now let Bougainville speak again, this time through a letter to his godmother, Madame Herault, written before the expedition started: "Your son shudders with horror at what he is going to be forced to witness. It is with great difficulty that we can restrain the Indians of the Far West, the most ferocious of all men and cannibals by trade. Listen to what the chiefs came to tell M. de Montcalm three days ago: 'Father, don't expect that we can easily give quarter to the English. We have some young warriors who have not yet drunk of this broth. Raw flesh has led them here from the ends of the earth; they must learn to wield the knife and to bury it in English hearts.' Behold our comrades, dear Mama; what a crew, what a spectacle for civilized man."

The moment the English marched out of the fort and retired to the barricaded camp, the Indians rushed in and tomahawked all the wounded left behind in the barracks and casements. Despite this most pointed warning Montcalm provided out of his force of six thousand regulars and militiamen a detachment of only four hundred to guard two thousand British with empty muskets from eighteen hundred murderous savages. Once the massacre started he undoubtedly did what he could to stop it, but his lack of precautions cannot but make one wonder. It is the one blot on an otherwise stainless reputation.

Some of the French officers had warned the British to make sure that the Indians got no rum or brandy, and strongly advised that they throw away all that they themselves had. Some probably followed this sound advice, but events proved that many did not. All the British had now been concentrated in the barricaded camp on the hillock. Seventeen wounded soldiers had been turned over to the French surgeon, and a guard of French soldiers placed over them, but before dawn on the day the English were to march away to Fort Edward the guard was suddenly withdrawn. The Indians immediately dashed in and finished off the wounded in the presence of the British and in full sight of several Canadian officers and a French guard, but no attempt was made to stop the slaughter.

The escort of four hundred Frenchmen had now arrived, and the column started to leave the camp. The Indians demanded plunder, and the French officers advised that all baggage must be given them, or the consequences would be dire. This was done, but the Indians were not appeased. As the column moved out of the camp they burst into it, snatching guns and clothes and applying the tomahawk to all that resisted, including a number of women and children who had accompanied the troops. Then a Christian Abnaki of the Penobscot Mission shouted the war whoop, and the whole maddened pack, hitherto mainly interested in plunder, turned to butchery. Montcalm and other French officers dashed up and did their utmost to quiet the savages, but only after a hundred or more British had been killed and hundreds carried off as prisoners. Many of the latter were recovered through the efforts of Montcalm, but about two hundred were taken north by the Indians. The remainder, often stripped of everything save their breeches, divided into two groups, one fleeing to the fort for protection by the French, the rest making the best of their way to Fort Edward, either by road or through the woods. The group collected at the fort were given protection at last and several days later were sent to Fort Edward under a heavy escort.

Father Roubaud wrote down in his story of the expedition:

The party of 400 of the French regulars, assigned to protect the
retreat of the enemy, arrived and placed themselves in line. The
English commenced to file out, misfortune to those who formed
the end of the line of march, or to stragglers whom indisposition
or some other cause separated by ever so little from the rest of the
body. There soon were many dead whose corpses lay scattered on
the ground and covered the outside of the entrenchments. This
butchery, which at first was the work of only a few Indians, was
the signal which turned almost all the rest into ferocious beasts.
They let fly right and left with great blows of their hatchets at
those who came to their hand. The massacre, however, was not of
long duration, nor as great as its fury made one fear; it amounted
to scarcely 40 or 50 men. [The best opinion today puts the figure
at about three times as many.] The patience of the English, who
were content to bow their heads beneath the steel of their execu-
tioners, suddenly appeased them, but it did not lead them to sense
or to justice. Uttering loud cries, they set about taking prisoners.
In the meanwhile I arrived. No, I do not believe that one can be
human and remain insensible to such sad circumstances. The son
snatched from the arms of the father, the daughter from her mother's bosom, the husband separated from the wife, officers stripped
to their shirts, without respect either for rank or decency, a crowd
of sufferers who ran hither and yon, some toward the woods, others toward those places that seemed to offer protection; such were
the pitiful sights presented to my eyes; the French, however, were
not passive and insensible spectators of the catastrophe. The Chev-
alier de Lévis ran wherever the tumult seemed to appear hottest to
try to calm it, with courage animated by a clemency most natural
to one of his illustrious blood. He dared death . . . a thousand
times. . . . Of what use could [a guard of] 400 men be against
some 1500 furious savages, who did not distinguish us from the
enemy?

Father Roubaud met a wild Huron Indian from the Far
West carrying a very young baby he had picked up some-

where, and he tried to secure the child. The Indian refused. Finally, after much dickering, the savage agreed to exchange the baby for a scalp, and the priest ran to one of the Abnaki and told him his need. The Christian Indian opened his war bag and told the Jesuit to take his pick. He seized a scalp and, followed by a curious crowd of Frenchmen and Indians, he again found his Huron and made the exchange. A little later the good father had the great pleasure of returning the baby to its mother. In later years Father Roubaud led a checkered life, abandoned his faith and married. As late as 1777 he was still trying to collect 6800 francs from the British government for ransom he claimed to have paid out of his own purse to the Indians at William Henry for 103 of their captive Englishmen. One would wonder how a Jesuit priest would have such a sum at hand, but both Montcalm and Colonel Monro seem to have attested to the truth of his claim. Toward the end of his life Roubaud returned to the Roman Catholic Church and died in a monastery in Paris.

Colonel Frye of the Massachusetts Regiment wrote a journal of the siege and its aftermath. He said that after the massacre started, when officers of the French escort were asked for protection, they refused help and advised the English to take to the woods.

Jonathan Carver, whose stories cannot always be trusted, wrote in later years that, when being robbed by the Indians, he sought the aid of a French sentry who called him an English dog and thrust him back into the hands of the Indians.

Montcalm blamed the whole affair on the English for having given rum to the Indians. In a report sent to the French Ministry he wrote: "I cannot conceal from you that the capitulation has unfortunately suffered some infraction on the part of the Indians. But what would be an infraction in Europe cannot be so regarded in America."

Bougainville was sent to Canada to report the capture as

soon as the capitulation was signed, and he missed the massacre. Hence the record in his journal is a hearsay one. Nevertheless he was an honest and very intelligent reporter and we
may be sure that he was certain of his facts. He wrote:

A great misfortune which we dreaded has happened. Apparently
the capitulation is violated and all Europe will oblige us to justify
ourselves. . . . At daybreak the English, who were inconceivably
frightened by the sight of the Indians, wished to leave before our
escort was all assembled and in place. They abandoned their
trunks and other heavy baggage. . . . The Indians had already
butchered a few sick in the tents which served as a hospital. The
Abnakis of Panaomeska [Old Town] . . . commenced the riot.
They shouted the death cry and hurled themselves on the tail of
the column which started to march out.

The English, instead of showing resolution, were seized with
fear and fled in confusion, throwing away their arms, baggage, and
even their coats. Their fear emboldened the Indians of all the nations, who started pillaging, killed some dozen soldiers and took
away 5 or 600 . . . a great number of English soldiers, hoping to
put them in a good humor, had given them rum, which despite all
our warnings they had kept in their flasks. Finally the disorder qui-
eted down and the Marquis de Montcalm at once took away from
the Indians 400 of these unfortunate men and had them clothed.
The French officers divided with the English officers the few spare
clothes they had, and the Indians loaded with booty [and some
200 English prisoners] disappeared that same day.

Would you believe that this abominable action of the Indians
at Fort William Henry had accomplices among those people who
call themselves Frenchmen; that greed and the certainty of getting
all their plunder from the Indians at a low price are the primary
causes of a horror for which England will not fail to reproach us
for a long time? Thank heaven our [French] officers are without
stain in this respect; several risked their lives on this occasion; they
shared all that they had with the unfortunate English, who said
that if they should ever besiege us and capture us, there would be

two terms of surrender, one for the French troops, and the other for the Canadians. These are frightful truths, dear Mama.

Bougainville was in Montreal when the Indians and the miserable party of English captives reached that town.

Meanwhile the Indians arrived [at Montreal] in a crowd with about 200 English. M. de Vaudreuil scolded them for having violated the capitulation. They excused themselves and put the blame on the mission Indians. They were told that they must give up these English, who were captured unfairly, and that they would be paid for them two kegs of brandy apiece. But this ransom was not greeted with enthusiasm. The Canadians bought the English plunder from them.

They did not spare the brandy, and this liquor, the god of the Indians, abounds in their camp. They swill it, and the English [prisoners] die a hundred deaths from fear every day.

At two o'clock in the presence of the entire town they killed one of them, put him in a kettle and forced his unfortunate compatriots to eat him. . . .

Will they in Europe believe that the Indians alone have been guilty of this horrible violation of the capitulation, that desire for the Negroes and other spoils of the English has not caused the people who are at the head of these nations [Canadian leaders of the Indians and the interpreters] to loosen the curb, perhaps to go even further? The more so since one today may see one of these leaders, unworthy of the name of officer and Frenchman, leading in his suite a Negro kidnapped from the English commander under the pretext of appeasing the shades of a dead Indian, giving his family flesh for flesh. That is enough of the horror the memory of which I would hope could be effaced from the minds of men.

The massacre at Fort William Henry was not intentional, but Montcalm failed to take the measures necessary to prevent it. His aide-de-camp Bougainville feared the worst, and in view of the close friendship and understanding existing between the two it is most unlikely that he did not communicate his fears to his general. Why Montcalm did not take the precautions he must have known were necessary is something we shall never learn. The whole affair clearly brings out the inability of the French to control their Indians or to utilize them effectively. You could persuade an Indian to go off to war with you; you armed him and fed him and pampered him. He was flighty and temperamental and gluttonous. When at last you gave him orders to fight, he did what he wanted to, not what he was told. Finally, once you had unleashed him, you lost him, and as soon as he had taken some scalps and plunder his only desire was to go home.

Such were some of the stories of the massacre at Fort William Henry, but one must also look at the event in its broader aspects. As the most advanced post of the British on the great colonial thoroughfare, it was the base for practically all action against the French. Its very existence meant that despite bungling, mismanagement, and inept commanders, the British were at last seriously threatening New France in the Champlain Valley. Some foresighted Frenchmen realized this, and Montcalm was one of them. His attack on the British fort was really a defensive act, an offensive raid aimed at removing a threat, not of occupying ground and advancing farther into the British colonies. The French were much too weak in supplies and transport to be able to move on against Fort Edward, as the Marquis de Vaudreuil expected them to do. The destruction of Fort William Henry, however, set the English back and preserved Canada for at least another year. There was always the hope of peace in Europe, and Montcalm was soon to realize, if he did not already, that only peace could save New France.

There was one final and grisly aftermath that needed a little time to make itself evident. After the massacre some of the Western Indians, still mad for blood and scalps, discovered fresh graves in the English camp. They dug the bodies up and scalped them. It was only later that they learned that they had been resurrecting victims of the smallpox! The disease went home with them and wrought havoc that fall and winter, for smallpox was a disease to which the Indian was most susceptible. Almost the entire Potawatomi nation was wiped out. Thus some of the victims of the campaign at last gained an indirect revenge.

Defeat at the Log Wall

THE BRITISH PLANS for the 1758 campaign called
for Jeffrey Amherst to capture Louisbourg, while James
Abercromby, the commander-in-chief in North America,
seized Ticonderoga and advanced on Canada north down
Lake Champlain. Fort Carillon became the major objective
on the mainland for 1758, and Abercromby was to lead the
attack in person. William Pitt, reinstated as British Prime
Minister after a brief eclipse, unfortunately took it upon himself to prescribe many of the details which should have been
left to Abercromby, whose hands thus became unjustly tied.
He might have done better if granted more latitude, but this
seems doubtful. The North American assignment probably
was beyond his capabilities.

James Abercromby was a Scot in his early fifties who had
seen a considerable amount of active service, and who had the
reputation of being a sound, if uninspired, officer. He was
made a major general in 1756 and sent to America to serve
under Lord Loudoun, from whom he inherited the command
when the latter was dismissed by Pitt. Loudoun was a good
man who deserved better than he got and whose plans for the
attack on Canada were sound, but he became the scapegoat
for the failure of the 1757 Louisbourg expedition and for the
loss of Fort William Henry.

Loudoun had planned a winter attack on Ticonderoga which was daring and yet sound in concept. It might very well have succeeded but for Captain Robert Rogers's failure to produce the needed snowshoes, which forced abandonment of the attempt. Abercromby assumed command early in the spring of 1758. His health was not of the best, and he had grown somewhat old before his time, slow and unaggressive. He was, however, seconded by a most able assistant. George Augustus, Viscount Howe, a brilliant young man of thirty-four, was approved of by both high and low. Pitt esteemed him highly, and after his death the tight-fisted and unsentimental General Court of Massachusetts Bay thought so well of his memory that they voted the quite material sum of £250 of tax money to build a memorial to him in Westminster Abbey. He was one of the relatively few British regulars — Bradstreet was another — who could break down the barriers and meet provincial officers on a common and friendly level. Lord Howe as brigadier was second in command of the Ticonderoga attack, and it appears that in effect it was intended that he should be the actual combat commander. The two leaders complemented each other not too badly and together formed a high command quite suitable for the purpose at hand.

A great army of British regulars and colonial militia assembled along the upper Hudson and then moved up the river and on to the head of Lake George. It had been planned that the expedition should start early in May, and thus catch Fort Carillon with only its winter garrison. As was usual, however, unexpected delays took place, the militia was late in arriving, and it was not until the end of June that the army had assembled near the ruins of Fort William Henry. There were some 6300 regular troops and 5900 provincials from Massachusetts, Connecticut, New York, and New Jersey. These militiamen of course were mostly raw and untrained soldiers, though some of them had seen service in previous campaigns of the war.

Captain Alexander Monypenny was Abercromby's brigade major, and his sailcloth-covered orderly book lies in front of me as I write. It tells many of the details of preparations for the advance. Equipment was lightened. The officers dispensed with their sashes, and were limited to one portmanteau, blankets and a bearskin, the last useful either as a mattress or as an extra covering. They also were permitted to take a small tent. Instead of being allowed the usual varying number of rations, based upon rank, each officer was restricted to the same ration as the soldier. The colors of the regiments were left behind. All friendly Indians would have a red ribbon tied around the muzzle of their guns for identification. All in all the orderly book shows a very considerable amount of thought and planning, and a reasonable adaptation of standard European practice to forest fighting. Salt pork, flour, dried peas, rice, and butter were to nourish the British soldier, and it is interesting to note that the salt was to be knocked off the pork before it was weighed for issue. Spartan fare indeed! Gambling by soldiers was frowned on most severely; any man caught in the act was to be given three hundred lashes without bothering to hold a court-martial.

The little book prescribed the assignment to the troops of the eight hundred bateaux and the ninety whaleboats. The latter had been bought on Cape Cod and Nantucket the previous fall and sent up the Hudson, and then had been hauled by soldiers on low-wheeled trucks over the portage to Lake George. Various camp activities were ordered while the troops were awaiting word to launch their boats. Some regiments turned out to early-morning target practice, while those who had been issued rifles were told to familiarize themselves with the new weapon. Hitherto the first use of rifles in the British army has always been said to have been in 1800, except for

Patrick Ferguson's private issue of his breech-loader to his own company in the American Revolution. Here in 1758, however, we find the rifle an article of issue, on a small scale to be sure, only ten per regiment, but an official issue to British regulars. The expedition which moved against Fort Duquesne that same summer also received a few. Some open-minded British officer — and he must have been one with powerful friends in the War Office — had evidently been much impressed with the American rifle as used along the Pennsylvania frontier, and had taken one home. A considerable number were made in England, following the American design exactly, and they now appeared in the hands of some of the troops in the campaign of 1758.

Lake George discharged its waters over two hundred feet of falls and rapids in the years before dams and power plants turned them into drab utility. Where they entered Lake Champlain nature had created the high and rocky peninsula the Indians called Ticonderoga. Its point reaches to within a quarter-mile of the Vermont shore, and high above the lake the guns of Fort Carillon decreed that none might pass without permission of the French King. The portage road from Lake George descended to almost the foot of the falls where the French had built a sawmill. Here boats and canoes were launched into Lake Champlain. The road then crossed the outlet on a wooden bridge, climbed the farther slope, and continued for about another two miles along the backbone of the peninsula out to Fort Carillon.

Montcalm's problem was where to make his fight. He had only about thirty-five hundred men, far too few to meet the British in the open field, yet nearly ten times what the little fort could hold. His decision was to take his stand on the Heights of Carillon, the highest part of the ridge, and about half a mile back from the fort. Here the ridge of the peninsula is only a quarter-mile wide. Its southwest slope

Capt. Monypenny's Map of
A B E R C R O M B Y'S DEFEAT
1 7 5 8
Copy of the map he sent home with his report
of the battle and of the death of Lord Howe

falls steeply into the lake, while the opposite and equally steep northeasterly side runs out into a flat plain almost a third of a mile wide before it reaches the shore of the lake. Across this narrow ridge, from one side to the other, sweating Frenchmen, officers as well as men, hacked down the virgin timber, and set up a wall of great logs, placed horizontally, two and three deep, and pierced with loopholes for musketry. Some of the logs were three feet and more in diameter, remnants of the primeval forest. The top of the wall was crowned with sandbags to a total height of from six to seven feet, so high that only the top of the Frenchmen's hats, and the flags with their golden fleurs-de-lis could be seen above it. The ground plan of the wall formed a great U, its sides crowning the steep slopes on either side of the ridge, and extending well to the rear. In front of the wall all trees and bushes were cleared away for a distance of about one hundred yards and an abatis built of the treetops, which were piled in an almost impassable hedge, the ends of their sharpened branches pointing toward the attacker. It was the predecessor of the barbed-wire entanglement of modern wars, and equally effective.

This great wall, raised in less than two days by the exertions

of perhaps three thousand men, was practically impregnable
to an attacker lacking artillery, but a few cannon could have
knocked much of it down in short order. The line of the
wall zigzagged across the peninsula so as to furnish salients
from which the attackers could be enfiladed. It was hurriedly built, too low in places, and in others exposed to
enemy fire from the flank, but, considering the time and the
manpower available, its construction was a mighty feat. Montcalm placed one battalion in Fort Carillon as a reserve and
to man its guns, while the rest of his force, except for small
detachments sent out to harass and delay the enemy, lined the
wooden wall with their muskets. They did not, however,
have any cannon on the Heights of Carillon.

Abercromby embarked his army on 5 July and proceeded
down Lake George, a great flotilla of almost nine hundred
boats spread in ordered columns across the narrow lake. The
British rowed to the foot of the lake, making a short halt during the night and reaching the outlet of Lake George on the
morning of the sixth. The small French outpost at that point
withdrew without offering any resistance, and the expedition landed on the west side in heavy woods, although the
portage road to Lake Champlain lay on the opposite shore.
The advance party moved downstream through the virgin
forest, not quite sure just where it was going. After advancing
for a mile or so the British floundered into contact with a
French detachment which also had gone astray.

There was a brief interchange of shots, and most of the
French were killed or captured, but a heavy price was paid for
this petty victory. Lord Howe, pushing forward at the head
of the detachment, where a senior officer had no right to be
in such a situation, fell dead almost at the first shot. Everything collapsed into confusion, some of the troops continued to advance, while others returned to the landing
place. Firing broke out toward late afternoon, but there was

no enemy, it was merely British firing at other elements of their own forces.

In short, all was chaos, and night fell upon a scared and disorganized army. Had the French been able to turn a pack of Indians loose upon them in the woods that evening there might have been a fearful slaughter, but Montcalm had less than a score of redskins in his little army. Daylight restored courage, and all the troops were drawn back to the landing place, moved over to the eastern shore, and the expedition advanced down the portage road without meeting any opposition, even at the sawmill where the crossing of the little river offered the French an excellent chance to fight a delaying action. All the advance elements of Montcalm's forces fell back upon their main defenses on the Heights of Carillon, followed by light elements of the British who approached the log wall but remained at a discreet distance from it. Abercromby's main army camped that night on the open ground north of the little river, perhaps a mile and a half from the French defenses.

Up to this point matters had not gone too badly. The British had achieved a major logistical success in bringing so great an army up to the immediate vicinity of their objective, the losses had been small, save for that of Lord Howe, and their enemy was penned up on a peninsula with the lake at his back. Here was opportunity for annihilation of the French, given a proper leader. Such, however, was now lacking, and incompetent command proceeded to bring disaster upon the British.

Lieutenant Colonel Eyre led one of Abercromby's regiments, and he was a most competent engineer officer. Montressor, the senior engineer, was ill, and, instead of sending Eyre to reconnoiter the position and suggest plans for the attack — one of the duties of an engineer officer in those days — the British general, perhaps because of a coolness then apparently existing between the two, bypassed that excellent officer and sent a junior engineer lieutenant instead. This young officer proved his incompetence by reporting that the defenses were weak and could be taken by a frontal infantry attack. Later in the day he was to pay for his poor judgment with his life.

Abercromby had left most of his artillery train on their barges, although nearly forty-eight hours had elapsed, but a few cannon had been advanced to a point within perhaps half a mile of the French defenses. Less than an hour could have had them pounding away at the log wall, and they could have promptly knocked down parts of it. But Abercromby, misled by his engineer's lack of skill, scorned to use his guns and ordered a frontal attack by his infantry. Had he taken the trouble to look at the French defenses himself, he might have chosen another course of action, but there is no evidence whatsoever to show that he at any time went within a mile of the log wall, and considerable reason to believe that he remained in the vicinity of the sawmill throughout the day. His sole leadership throughout the entire action seems to have been merely the ordering of another attack as soon as he learned of the failure of the previous assault.

Montcalm manned his great log wall with seven battalions of French regulars, La Reine, Béarn, Guyenne, Royal Roussillon, 1st Berry, Languedoc, and La Sarre, troops that he knew and in whom he had confidence. On the flat plain on his right he placed his small force of Canadian regulars, soldiers of La Marine Regiment, and his militiamen, expecting little of them, but hoping that they and the guns of Carillon would cover that flank. On his left the slope fell sharply to the water and there was room only for a handful of French volunteers on the narrow strand. The 2nd Berry was held in reserve in the fort along with a small body of gunners to man the cannon on the ramparts. Some three thousand men armed with muskets stood behind the great wooden wall and through its loopholes they could fire almost without risk upon anyone who dared to cross the open ground in their front. Another five hundred guarded the flanks, but their defenses were less secure, and they were less apt to be assailed. Provided that the French had sufficient powder and ball, and that the British failed to use their artillery, the position could be held indefinitely against charging infantry, however well led.

Governor Vaudreuil had planned to send an expedition in the early summer of 1758 up the St. Lawrence and on by way of Oswego to the Mohawk Valley, partly to overawe the Iroquois, but also to do as much damage as possible to the English settlements in that region. Late in June, Brigadier Lévis had led a party of four hundred regulars, four hundred troops of La Marine, and eight hundred Canadian militia off on that mission, regardless of Montcalm's warnings of an English move down the Champlain waterway. At last Vaudreuil appreciated the British threat and recalled the expedition, too late to get most of the troops back. By marching night and day, however, Lévis managed to get the four hundred regulars to Ticonderoga the evening before the battle, and this reinforcement was a very material help to Montcalm.

The French actually were in a most precarious condition, their backs to the lake, only five days provisions on hand, and a mighty army hemming them in. Of all the possible courses open to Abercromby he picked the one least likely to succeed. The correct solution is always easy by hindsight, but even at that time a little thought would have brought the British commander to the realization that an immediate infantry attack was not the best course of action to take. He believed that reinforcements, perhaps six thousand in number, were on the way. Even so, had he merely advanced to the lake shore a little north of the fort and put some artillery in position, he would have secured command of the artery by which the reinforcements must come, and he would at the same time have cut the troops on the peninsula off from their supply base to the north. Starvation would soon have forced their surrender. His other alternative was to bring up artillery and blast the wooden wall to bits. Either of these plans, or even both at once, were perfectly practical to a force as large as his, and the fort would have fallen in a few days almost without bloodshed. Instead, the British leader ordered execution of the worst possible plan, a frontal infantry attack, unsupported by any artillery, against a very strong defensive position. Abercromby must have lost his wits that day. His only possible excuse was fear of an immediate arrival of heavy reinforcements, and hence a belief in the need for speedy action.

Sir William Johnson, His Majesty's Superintendent of Indian Affairs, had promised to bring a considerable body of Iroquois to assist Abercromby as guides and scouts. At that particular time, however, the Five Nations were torn by internal dissensions into pro-French and pro-British groups, and it was with great difficulty that Johnson managed to persuade any Indians to come on the expedition. He at last got some volunteers together at Fort Johnson on the Mohawk River, but, despite his efforts to prevent it, they secured rum from the Dutch traders of Schenectady and proceeded to get completely drunk, as only Indians could. Sir William wrote that "liquor was as plenty among them as ditch water." This carouse further delayed the departure of Johnson's force. They finally joined Abercromby at Ticonderoga on the morning of the battle, some four hundred in number, too late to serve their most useful purpose as scouts during the advance from the landing place, when their presence might well have saved the life of Lord Howe. With Howe alive the chances are excellent that the fort would have fallen, and the whole course of the last of the French wars would have been materially changed. Sir William led his Indians, presumably at Abercromby's order, to the slopes of Mount Defiance, and during the day they delivered a random long-range fire against the extreme left of the French lines. Their total bag, as reported by Montcalm, was one officer wounded. Sir William gained little glory in this year of 1758, but he was to more than make up for it in the campaign of the following year.

Early in the battle the British attempted to send barges armed with cannon down the river flowing out of Lake George, and thus get around the French left flank. The cannon of the fort took them under fire, sank two, and drove the rest away.

The initial British attack was made in the worst possible way, an uncoordinated attack by several regiments in long lines three deep. The only hope of a successful assault on so strong a position as this would have been the carefully co-ordinated simultaneous advance of several columns with narrow fronts and great depth. The slaughter would have been great, but the log wall might have been carried at one place at least. Instead each regiment attacked in a long thin line as soon as it was ready, regardless of the movements of its neighbor. The forces on the right moved forward before the center brigade was formed, and the assault had proceeded for some time before all the troops concerned were up to the line upon which they were supposed to form for the attack. The men at once got snarled in the abatis, some could neither advance nor retreat and merely awaited slaughter, while the Highlanders tried to hack their way through with their broadswords. Eventually a few soldiers would break through the sharpened treetops, then dash toward the wall, shrouded in the smoke of musketry, and fall dead or wounded. The hot July sun had rapidly dried out the leaves and small branches of the felled trees in the abatis, which caught fire at several places. Brave Frenchmen dashed out from behind the wall carrying pails of water brought up from the lake and put the fires out before they became serious.

Almost three-quarters of the Regiment of Berry were young recruits, and their first battle was more than their morale could endure. At one time in the conflict their courage left them and they fled from behind the log wall in utter confusion. Before the British could grasp the initiative, the reserve companies of grenadiers rushed up and plugged the gap, just in time to save the day.

The battle started somewhat after noon and lasted over six hours. The British attacked with the greatest of bravery at various places along the French lines, but never gained their objective. Time and again they tried, as the sun sank lower in the west, throwing their lives away uselessly, but it was all in vain. Perhaps the most gallant assault of all — and all were most gallant — was that of the 42nd Highlanders, the Black Watch, on the right of the French defenses.

Then it was that Duncan Campbell received his death wound and met the fate he had dreamed of many years before. Campbell was the Laird of Castle Inverawe in the western Highlands. Late one night in the 1740s a fugitive knocked at his door and begged asylum, saying that he had killed a man and was pursued. Campbell swore on his dirk to shelter him and hid him in a secret place. Soon the pursuers arrived, and told the laird that it was his own cousin that had been killed. That night and for other nights the murdered cousin came to Campbell in his dreams and begged revenge, but the laird had sworn on his dirk. Finally the ghost appeared for the last time and bade him farewell until they should at last meet at Ticonderoga, a name that meant nothing to Campbell. Later he became a major of the Black Watch and went with it to the wars in North America. Then to his horror he learned that he was to take part in the attack on Ticonderoga, and the night before the battle the ghost again appeared. Such is the legend of Inverawe, immortalized in a poem by Robert Louis Stevenson.

The assault by the Black Watch was the last major effort of the British. Over half of that regiment were lost that day, 499 men in all. When this last attack was made the Canadian militia on the flats were ordered forward to assail the Scots on the flank, but, undependable as militia usually turned out to be, they failed to advance. Two of their officers charged forward alone, unsupported, and one fell wounded. Earlier in the day the French had been forced to fire on a body of their own militia that was running away to the boats. One of the group was wounded and the fugitives returned to their lines, where some hid under their abatis while others cowered behind stumps. The militia earned no glory in this battle, though Montcalm later wrote, "Nevertheless . . . I have considered it for the good of the service to praise them." It was the French regulars and the stout log wall that saved New France on that bloody day.

At last, just as the sun was dropping behind the Adirondacks, the British gave up and retreated back as they had come. Soon the retreat became suspiciously like a flight, so hurriedly did the withdrawal take place. The army reembarked and headed back up the lake, abandoning many provisions, baggage, and burned boats to the exultant French.

Despite his heavy losses Abercromby still vastly outnumbered the French, and he still had all his artillery to use. A renewal of the attack, after cannon had smashed down the wall, would almost certainly have succeeded, but Abercromby was not one of those who could salvage victory out of initial defeat. His losses were very great, 1610 killed, wounded and missing, almost all from the 6367 regular troops, while the

French lost 377 out of their total of about 4000 in their defense of the log wall. From the point of view of numbers
engaged and losses sustained this was by far the greatest battle that had yet been fought on American soil. Only the Battle of Long Island in the Revolution was to exceed it until the
mighty conflicts of our Civil War set new records in death and
suffering.

It is hard to account for Abercromby's actions on this unfortunate day. Although no military genius, Abercromby had
the reputation of being a sound and experienced officer. A
senior British officer, when he learned of the battle, expressed
sorrow for the defeated general, and wrote that he could not
understand how it had happened, it was not at all what he
would have expected of Abercromby. There is, it would seem,
one quite possible solution. A month before the battle, Abercromby was laid up for several days with a violent stomach disorder, and later, two weeks before the battle, he was struck
again. Did the general perhaps suffer from some chronic
stomach ill that hit him again on the day of battle and rendered him incapable of effective thought or action?

A few days after the battle Montcalm was reinforced by
two thousand Canadians and six hundred Indians, but they
came too late and succeeded only in consuming precious rations. The British for their part reoccupied their old camp
at the head of Lake George and devoted the remainder of
the summer to doing nothing, except for firing a *feu de joie*
when they learned that Amherst had captured Louisbourg. A
most inglorious summer for the British forces on the American soil, but two less-known leaders, both far exceeding Abercromby in competence, were to retrieve the reputation of
their country and to deal vital blows to the cause of New
France later in that summer of 1758.

Montcalm caused a great wooden cross to be erected at the

center of the lines that his troops defended, and it was blessed by Abbé Piquet. Today a replica of that cross towers above the entrance road to restored Fort Carillon, flanked on either side by posts bearing the arms of France and two commemorative inscriptions written by Bougainville.

SEVEN

Amherst Planned Well

F OR THE CAMPAIGN of 1759 Pitt had planned assaults on Canada from three directions. Wolfe, who had shown his capabilities at Louisbourg the year before, was to move up the St. Lawrence, amply supported by the navy, and assail Quebec. Another expedition, much smaller in size, would reestablish Oswego, abandoned since its destruction by Montcalm in 1756, and, if at all possible, cross Lake Ontario and capture the vital French post of Niagara. Meanwhile Amherst, the commander for North America, would with a very considerable force advance up the Hudson-Champlain Valley, seize Fort Carillon at Ticonderoga and the other French forts in the valley, and reach the St. Lawrence between Montreal and Quebec, thus severing the lifeline of Canada. This last undertaking might well have been accomplished by an energetic and driving commander, but Amherst, competent general though he was, was hardly a driver, and one thing or another delayed his start until late into the summer. Then his natural caution and policy of slow and sure further delayed his advance. The end of the year was to find him still far to the south of the St. Lawrence.

Amherst reached Albany, the assembly point of his army, by mid-May, but the colonial troops did not start coming in for some little time, and it was well into June before the bulk of them had arrived. Then, just to cause further delay, the

Hudson suddenly rose in unexpected freshet and greatly impeded the forwarding of supplies and munitions. Bateaux and barges could usually be poled along the stretches of the Hudson above Albany, but now the high and fast-moving waters prevented this, and the men had to fall back on the slower and more laborious use of oars.

While the regulars are at last marching north toward Lake George and the sweating colonials are manhandling the barrels of provisions, the kegs of powder and the cannon and their shot aboard the boats, we shall leave them for the moment to their toil and go back a few months in time.

In 1758 General Abercromby had bullheadedly sent his great army in a bayonet charge against the strong defensive works on the Heights of Carillon, works which he had never seen. He had acted on the advice of a young and untried engineer who had viewed Montcalm's lines only from a distant hilltop. This year Amherst would take no such risk. Early in March, while the snow still lay heavy in the Adirondacks, Lieutenant Dietrich Brehm of the 60th, the Royal Americans, had been sent from Fort Edward to reconnoiter Carillon and its defenses. He had been asked to find the answer to a number of specific questions, questions which proved Amherst to be a far abler general than Abercromby. Robert Rogers was sent with a party of over three hundred of his rangers to escort Brehm and guard him while he explored the defenses of the place. The engineer lieutenant was a good officer who knew his trade (eventually he would be a colonel of his regiment) and he was able to examine all the works in considerable detail, as fear of the rangers held the fort's small winter garrison within its walls. On snowshoes Brehm prowled the main defensive line by moonlight. He found it much stronger than when he had seen it the year before, and its location was somewhat different, about a hundred and fifty yards farther from the fort, it seemed to him. At its lowest

point the great log wall was seven and a half feet high, and
the sharpened tree branches of the abatis that had so impeded Abercromby's men in 1758 were now firmly staked to
the ground. For a quarter of a mile in advance of the lines,
and all the way from the shore of Lake Champlain clear
across the peninsula to the outlet of Lake George, every tree
and bush had been grubbed away so that there was no cover
whatsoever for an attacking enemy.

Brehm climbed Mount Defiance, which the French called
Rattlesnake Mountain, and reported that light howitzers and
mortars could be gotten to the summit. He said that the main
lines of the French looked from this mountaintop like a rail
fence surrounding part of a field.

The engineer officer then crossed to the eastern or Vermont
shore of Lake Champlain and viewed the fort from the
heights that seventeen years later would be christened Mount
Independence. Meanwhile Rogers's men took a few prisoners,
who gave much detailed information about the structure of
the fort, the height and thickness of the walls, the number of
the guns. Thus by the end of March Amherst had quite
clear and precise knowledge of the condition of the fort and
its defenses, and was able to plan well in advance his method
of attack.

Now let us return to the army struggling up the Hudson
Valley, some fighting the swift waters in bateaux, while
others slogged, slipped and splashed up the crude road,
made even worse by rains, marching feet and lumbering ox
teams. An army such as Amherst led required a vast amount
of supplies, barrels of pork and beef and bread and rum,
spare clothing, and tents, as well as the heavy cannon and
their powder, shot and shell. His eleven thousand men,
half regulars, half provincials, would need, for a campaign
which would probably last for some four months, nearly thirteen thousand barrels of meat and bread. It would have re-

quired one thousand bateaux, eight hundred wagons and a thousand oxcarts, along with at least six weeks of good weather, to move this vast mountain of supplies. But fortunately a considerable portion of these provisions were already at Fort Edward, left over from the unhappy campaign of 1758, and they had only to be hauled over the portage road from the Hudson to Lake George. This was no easy thing, however, for the rough road was also choked with long convoys of wagons carrying part of the vast number of bateaux the army would need to go down the lake. And then there were the Nantucket whaleboats the scouts would use, some carried on men's shoulders, fifteen men to a boat, and others on wheeled trucks dragged along by plodding soldiers. It was indeed a busy road that spring.

Pitt had given Amherst almost complete discretion as to the methods of executing his mission. The general had promised the minister that he "intended to make an eruption into Canada with the utmost vigour and dispatch," but unfortunately he was somewhat lacking in these qualities, particularly the latter. Safe and sure was Amherst's motto, as he would have been the first to admit. The colonial troops slowly draggled in and the general waited, perhaps with more patience than was desirable. There was much to do at Lake George before the army could hope to embark, and there was no real reason why at least some of the essential work should not have been started while the provincials continued to trickle into camp. To be sure, there was some risk from French and Indian raiders, but Amherst could easily have sent ahead to the lake enough of a force to hold the place in safety while the water transport was being readied. Instead he played it safe and accordingly was at least a month late in getting his campaign under way.

Part of the army was started north by early June, and by the twenty-first of that month the British at last had gotten some six thousand men to the southern end of Lake George. A strong stockaded post had also been built at the midpoint of the portage (near the Glens Falls of today), both for security and as a staging point for supplies. There were also two other stockades or blockhouses to guard the road, one four miles north of Fort Edward, the other three miles before Lake George was reached. Patrols from these three posts could maintain constant observation over the road to the lake. Spruce beer was brewed, and troops were given special training suitable to wilderness fighting, while the rest of the boats and supplies were hauled north over the wretched road. To avoid risk of Indian ambush both sides of the roadway were cleared of all trees and bushes for a distance of thirty yards. Four hundred colonial axemen made short work of this job, and must have greatly impressed the British regulars with their skill. Frequent heavy rains kept the road soft and muddy, and there must have been many washouts to repair and miry places to corduroy with logs.

Early in July the British general suddenly realized that he had no way to carry his heavy siege cannon down the lake, and he ordered construction of a radeau, a great slab-sided scow-like vessel. I have found no record of the size of this odd affair, but the radeau Amherst built a little later that year on Lake Champlain was eighty-four feet long by twenty wide and carried six 24-pounders, the same guns he was now transporting, so it is probable that this Lake George radeau was of about the same dimensions. In the fall of 1758 Abercromby's men had built two radeaux at the head of the lake and sunk them for safekeeping. The larger of the two was fifty feet long by nineteen wide and six feet deep. It seems most odd that these were not raised and utilized by Amherst, but they apparently were not, for there is no mention of them in any of the journals of this campaign.

Captain Joshua Loring, a New Englander who held a

commission in the Royal Navy, had been directed by Amherst to raise, rerig and equip the sloop *Halifax,* built the
summer before and in the fall sunk in the lake for safekeeping. Only thus could a vessel be held safe from damage by
ice or the torch of a party of raiders. And even then there
was always a risk that the enemy might locate and destroy
the sunken warship. The *Halifax* was a fair-sized vessel armed
with fourteen cannon. Amherst used her to carry his artillery
ammunition and filled her hold with powder, shot and shell
to a total weight of over a hundred tons. The general noted
in his journal in mid-July that he had tried out the "flat bottomed English boat," which carried a 3-pound swivel gun at
its bow. This almost certainly must have been a craft similar
to the ones that we know Wolfe took to Quebec — sectional
knockdown "foldboats" which, when assembled, were held
together with brass bolts. They were a success both at Quebec
and on Lake George, each holding some seventy or more
soldiers, yet having a relatively shallow draft. Work meanwhile was continued in bringing the bateaux overland across
the low divide between the Hudson and St. Lawrence water-
sheds, repairing the damage they received in transit, and
completing the sloop and the radeau. Amherst seems to have
been both patient and somewhat fatalistic, for his journal
says on 17 July: "As I can't cross the lake till the whaleboats
and the artillery are ready, I may as well keep adoing other
things [he was building a new fort at the head of the lake]
— as I lose no time by it."

At last on 21 July "at peep of day" the army took to its
boats and got under way to the north, a full month after it
had first arrived at Lake George.

The defenses of Carillon had, as we learned from Lieutenant Brehm's report, been rebuilt and considerably strengthened since Abercromby's futile attack of the previous year.
Brigadier Bourlamaque had a force of about the same size as

had Montcalm in 1758, some four thousand in all, but this year Governor Vaudreuil had regretfully realized that the Ticonderoga frontier could no longer be held with the forces that he had available, and he ordered the brigadier to abandon the fort once the enemy had appeared in strength. A delaying force of about four hundred was to be left to stall the British advance for as long as was possible, and then to blow up the fort and make its escape. The French King had failed to furnish enough men and supplies to hold the frontiers of New France, but he was hard pressed in Europe and his troops had to be rationed out to several theaters of war, of which Canada appeared to be of lesser importance. Thus, Fort Carillon was, although Amherst did not know it, ripe to fall to the British once they had landed in force and invested the place.

More than four hundred bateaux and almost half as many whaleboats carried Amherst's men down Lake George accompanied by the little *Halifax*, the radeau *Invincible*, carrying the siege artillery, and the "English flat bottomed boat." Abercromby had left his regimental colors behind, but this year they were taken along, and the narrow waters of the lake must have presented a colorful spectacle. Flag signals had been prescribed for all the necessary maneuvers, and the flotilla advanced in regular columns with military precision. But with nightfall came discomfort, as the boats rested on their oars through the hours of darkness, while high winds and violent waves made keeping position impossible. Many an unhappy man huddled shivering in his drenched regimentals and prayed that daylight would come. Constantine Hardy of Ruggles's Massachusetts regiment noted in his journal: "July the 21. They all imbarct to set out for Tiantaroga and we got with in three or four miles of the landing place and then lay down our ores all night and a teedious night we had." When dawn at last came it must have taken both time and violent language to get the columns re-formed and lined up again in proper order.

At about nine o'clock on that morning of 22 July the army started landing at the foot of Lake George, while an advance party of rangers and light troops was promptly sent forward down the portage road to the sawmill and the bridge. There they made contact with French outposts, which at once fell back after delivering a slight scattering fire. The French had attempted to block the portage road between the two lakes by felling trees, but colonial troops, axes in hand, made short work of these obstructions. The army advanced to the sawmill, crossed the river, took up position on the higher ground beyond and settled down for the night. Ticonderoga, particularly since Abercromby's defeat, had been a place of ill omen to the colonials — "Boges" they often called it. William Amherst, the general's brother and aide-de-camp, noted in his interesting diary that the provincials were full of spirit and no longer feared the place as being enchanted.

Amherst had promptly pushed his artillery forward and by dark of this first day had several pieces across the river at the sawmill. At daylight next morning, the twenty-third, the British pushed ahead, brushed aside very light resistance and found the enemy's main lines abandoned. This was indeed an unexpected stroke of fortune, for Amherst was thus presented by the enemy with a complete set of lines already built, exactly what was needed as a base from which to commence siege operations against the fort itself. The British general could hardly believe his luck, and it was a complete mystery to him why Bourlamaque had not either tried to destroy the lines or to defend them. The troops at once filed into the long line of log walls and started building new firing platforms on the outer side, while Amherst in his safe, sure, conventional manner started digging saps, establishing advanced trenches and preparing batteries to open fire. His attempt

against Fort Carillon was to be the very antithesis of Abercromby's. He had secured precise knowledge of the fort and
its surroundings, had brought his army safely to it, and practically without any loss at all. Now he was to invest the
place and proceed with formal siege operations, which under
the circumstances could not help but be safe, sure, and certain.

Bourlamaque had planned to delay the British advance by
attacking their forward elements before they reached the log-
wall defensive line, and had designated a force of three hundred mission Indians and some regulars and volunteers to
advance against them before they reached the line. The Indians, however, refused to move forward to the attack, just
as they had so often refused in other battles of the war, and
the soldiers alone accomplished little or nothing. William Amherst was scornful of Bourlamaque's Indians: "The cowardice of these barbarians is so great. . . . Their whole depend-
ence is upon a tree or a bush. You have nothing to do but
advance & they will fly. They never stand an open fire or
an attack." Thus the French brigadier's plan to delay the
British deployment collapsed and he was forced to abandon
all hope of holding his best defensive position for even a day.

Amherst's initial plan, a sound one, had been to get troops
with artillery around the fort and on the shore of Lake
Champlain between Carillon and Crown Point, thus prevent-
ing any relief either of men or of supplies coming from the
north. As soon as it became evident that the French were
starting to withdraw — and this had become apparent by 23
July, the day after the landing — Amherst gave up this plan
and concentrated his forces on the fort alone. This perhaps
was a mistake, for had he adhered to the original plan he
might well have gobbled up all of Bourlamaque's force. Amherst's objective, however, was the fort, not Bourlamaque's
little army, although in the broader strategic sense the latter
was far more to be desired.

The men were kept well under cover while the siege batteries were being prepared. The fire from the French fort was
very heavy but the damage was of the slightest except that
Roger Townshend, Amherst's close friend and chief staff
officer, was cut in two by a cannonball. Work on the
trenches and batteries went on for another two days, difficult
work because there was little dirt and much ledge in the area
around the fort. This required the construction in many
places of communication trenches on top of ledges by means
of fascines, gabions or sandbags instead of the easier and safer
method of digging. By this time the British had with great
difficulty hauled up into position a 13-inch mortar, a clumsy,
unwieldy weapon of great weight, but possessed of tremendous firepower. In fact, it was almost an axiom in colonial
America that if a 13-inch mortar could be gotten within
range of a frontier fort, the fort was practically certain to
surrender.

Sam Merriman, of Deerfield in Massachusetts, confided
to his diary: "July the 25 . . . No firering upon our side,
thee enemies fire is very havey. The armi hath entrench
within 30 rodes of the French fort our English went to the
fort & fired at the sentry upon the wale. Some of our men
went into the French garden & fetch a armfull ful of cabbage
to Genl. & he gave them tow dollars. . . ."

On this same 25 July the British got whaleboats and the
"English flat bottomed boat" into Lake Champlain north of
the fort. The next day Rogers and some of his men were to
use these craft to make an attempt to cut the log boom which
the French had stretched across the lake. There is reason to
believe that this boom may also have been intended to serve
as a floating footbridge which might have allowed a possible
French withdrawal by land along the eastern shore. Merriman's journal continued: "July the 26, 1759 . . . our English never fired one cannon att the enemie till they im bark,

then the fire was vary hot & took 20 prisoners . . . soe the sege was over a gainst Ticontorogue, with grate rei-joceing. . . ."

What had happened was that Bourlamaque had with-drawn most of his men once the British had crossed the river at the sawmill, and had left only four hundred under the able Captain Hébecourt with orders to hold out as long as they could, then blow up the fort and get away.

The withdrawal of the major part of the garrison must have been obvious to Amherst, but he continued his siege prep-arations in order to make absolutely certain. The batteries of heavy cannon were almost ready to start smashing down the walls of the fort when, at nine in the evening of 26 July, three French deserters came into the British lines and re-ported that the garrison was leaving. Hébecourt had timed his actions perfectly. The deserters also reported that a lighted slow match had been left which shortly would blow up the powder magazine. Amherst offered one hundred guineas to any of the three who would guide the British to the fuse so that it might be extinguished. He found no taker, however, and two hours later there was a great explosion, followed by a raging fire, which continued unchecked for several days, while cannon left loaded for this purpose were discharged from time to time by the flames. John Hurlburt was another colonial who kept a journal that has survived. "July 27, . . . We never fired one gun but they fired canon and flung bums. When the French marched from the fort, Rogers fell upon them and killed a great many of them and took a hundred of them. [This is considerably exaggerated.] Cabbage is very plenty and all sorts of greens which they got in the French garden. They had a fine garden large anuf to give the whole army a mess. We have not lost one man nor had one man wounded in our regiment. In the whole loss of men was 16 killed, one colonel, one ensign, belonging to the 17th regiment and 50 wounded in the siege of Ticontaroga. They had in the fort a fine stable of horses over the magazine which they blew up and killed about fifty. The[y] burnt up a great many guns and they left 16 canons and six mortar pieces." French soldiers during the last hour or two before they left broached some brandy kegs and drowned their sorrows. Quite a number of drunken Frenchmen were gathered up by the British that night and early morning.

Thus fell the great French fortress against which Abercromby had thrown away the lives of hundreds in a hasty and ill-planned attack. Now Amherst in a slow, almost dilatory campaign, after careful planning and preparation, had seized the place practically without loss. It is true that the French withdrew once the British had landed and started siege operations, but so might Montcalm in 1758 had Abercromby played his cards correctly.

The woodwork of the fort, the barrack floors, the roof timbers and the wooden facings of parts of the outer walls burned merrily for several days, despite the violent activities of bucket brigades of soldiers who passed their water-filled camp kettles up from the lake. The flames did not entirely die down until the end of the month. Examination then showed that the structure on the whole was surprisingly little damaged. The bastion which had held the powder magazine and the unfortunate horses was destroyed, as well as part of the east curtain wall; but the rest of the fort, save for the woodwork of the barracks, had suffered much less than would have been expected. Amherst, who evidently had no high opinion of the engineer officers, wrote: "I will repair the fort upon the same plan as the enemy had built it which will save great expense & give no room for the engineers to exercise their genius."

Early in August the bulk of the British army moved on to Crown Point, where Bourlamaque had also blown up Fort

St. Frédéric as he withdrew to a new position at the northern
end of Lake Champlain. Amherst now suddenly realized that
the four little French warships on Lake Champlain held
unquestioned control of the lake, and that he could not advance until this fleet had been at least neutralized. The commander of these puny warships bore the odd name of Dolo-
boratz, a name so unusual that he must have been the same
man who captained a privateer out of Louisbourg in 1744,
had been captured by the British and clapped into Boston
jail. One of these vessels, *La Vigilante*, was a schooner, but
the other three, all bearing names of freshwater fish, were
chebecs carrying lateen sails, precursors of the row galleys
Benedict Arnold would lead to battle at Valcour Island seventeen years in the future.

Accordingly Amherst settled his army down at Crown
Point, started to build his naval force, and meanwhile set
his men to work on a new and mighty fortress, one which
would cost Britain vast sums and serve no useful purpose.
Amherst certainly could exercise patience at least as well as
the next man, and he was not to move from Crown Point,
save for an abortive advance of about a week, during the
remainder of the campaign of 1759. Had he taken a shade
more risk and employed a quarter of the dash of a Montcalm,
he probably could have cut Quebec off from Montreal and
caused the fall of Canada a year earlier. But we must not be
too critical, for Amherst planned well, knew what he was
doing, and ultimately, if somewhat belatedly, he achieved his
purpose with a minimum loss of men.

In the late spring of this year of 1759 Admiral Charles
Saunders had found no difficulty in leading a British fleet
up the broad St. Lawrence, thus confounding the French,
who had long believed that its shoals and swift currents were
the best defenses of Quebec. Wolfe, after delays, false attempts and despair, at last gained the Heights of Abraham

and the capital of New France fell to Britain. In July Brigadier John Prideaux brought his expedition to the walls of Niagara, catching the French entirely unaware of his approach. He lost his life in the siege, but Sir William Johnson assumed the command and that vital citadel of the French *"pays d'en haut,"* the Far West, hauled down the lilies of France.

Thus the year 1759 ended with two of Pitt's objectives accomplished: the capture of Quebec and of Fort Niagara, the key to the heartland. The third, and in many ways the major, attempt had produced only partial success. On the other hand it was obvious that, barring a miracle, the days of New France were fast approaching their end. On the east the capital city had fallen to the enemy, while in the west the French had lost all hold on the Great Lakes. From the south Amherst, although partially balked in his drive up the Champlain Valley, held all that great waterway with only the minor French defenses on the Richelieu River between him and the St. Lawrence. Next year's campaign would see the fall of Canada, but the tide of war had already passed by Ticonderoga, and the role of this vital key to the Hudson-Champlain Valley had been played out in this year of 1759. The repairs to the fort were completed, and a small housekeeping garrison installed, but it would be many years before Fort Ticonderoga would again appear in history.

EIGHT

"In the Name of the Great Jehovah . . ."

THE WAR MOVED northward, Montreal fell and Canada became part of the British Empire. There was now little if any need for forts on the Champlain waterway, but the King nevertheless decided to maintain Fort Ticonderoga and Crown Point, the great new fort that had occupied Amherst's time in the late summer of 1759 when he might have been pushing on toward the St. Lawrence. Small garrisons were moved into the two forts, and history became silent. Life on the lake, unless one was a keen sportsman, must have been one of deadly monotony, particularly when the heavy snows of a northern winter buried the countryside. The commander at Crown Point ran a farm, as probably did his counterpart at Ticonderoga. The latter certainly kept cows and sheep at one time.

A glimpse of happenings at the fort is given us in the winter of 1764. Private James Cahoon burst one day into the officers' mess at Crown Point, where Colonel Beckwith, the senior officer on the lake, had his headquarters. Cahoon blurted out a plea for justice, stating that he had found the commander at Ticonderoga, Captain Charles Osborne, in bed with Mrs. Cahoon. Imagine the sensation in the officers' mess! The soldier went on to say that, when he told his captain that he really did not think that it was right, he was put in the "clink" for ten days. Beckwith at once called on Osborne for an explanation, and received a lengthy letter in reply. This stated that Cahoon was no good and a drunkard as well, and that his wife was Osborne's washerwoman and cowherd. She had slept in the milk room since her husband's bad behavior had forced their ejection from the married quarters and had relegated him to the common barracks. The letter meandered on at a very considerable length, but nowhere at all did it make any denial of Cahoon's charge. There was a further interchange of notes which added but little to the facts and our knowledge of the incident comes to an end. Silence closed in on Fort Ticonderoga for another decade.

The French had left a damaged fortress, its walls partly of great squared timbers and partly of stone. Amherst's men had repaired the destruction resulting from the explosion of the magazine and replaced some if not all of the wooden walls with stone. But these walls were really only thin stone facings covering steep banks of earth and clay, and each bitter winter the frost crept in a little deeper behind the stonework and exerted its destructive forces on the roughly built masonry. Stone walls require maintenance and repair, particularly in our northern climates. Little or no work of this nature was done at Ticonderoga, and the fort gradually but steadily fell into decay. By the early 1770's the walls had collapsed in places, the parapets which sheltered the cannon on the ramparts had disintegrated into a mass of dirt and rotten wood, while the stone barracks that once held a garrison of four hundred men were now in sad repair. Amherst's great fortress at Crown Point had been almost entirely destroyed in the spring of 1773, when a washerwoman's fire got out of control and ignited the tarred wooden facing of its walls. Headquarters had at once been moved to Ticonderoga and a handful of men and a sergeant left behind to keep watch on the ruins.

By the spring of 1775 Captain William Delaplace of the 26th Regiment was in command, with only one officer, Lieutenant Jocelyn Feltham, to assist him. The garrison was composed of forty-two men, and half of these were "old, wore out & unservicable" or otherwise incapacitated. Then there were two dozen women and children. Had Fort Ticonderoga been repaired and restored to battle readiness, it would have required a garrison of at least four hundred. Now with its walls in ruins it had but a score of able-bodied men to hold it safe for Britain.

On 19 April 1775, 120 miles to the eastward, Lord Percy's battered column of British fell back from Concord and Lexington through the Middlesex countryside into Charlestown. They were ferried over to Boston, then a peninsula connected with the Roxbury mainland by an exceedingly narrow neck of land soon to be guarded by ample earthworks. Minute Men from the villages north and west of Boston had harried the steps of the retreating troops, and then, reinforced by eager volunteers from much of eastern New England, they sat themselves down in a tight ring around the town. All was in utter confusion among the provincials; no such development had been foreseen, and there was no effective higher command. No one knew quite what to do. They had the lion by the tail for the moment, but they must watch to keep away from his teeth. A major British eruption from Boston must be prevented at all costs, and eventually General Gage's army must be persuaded to quit the town. The one essential tool which would achieve both of these objectives was to a very large extent lacking to the provincials. This was artillery, and especially heavy artillery. Accordingly every endeavor was soon to be directed toward eliminating this vital deficiency.

Benedict Arnold, captain in the Governor's Footguards of New Haven, led his company to Cambridge five days after the Concord fight. As a boy he had run away to the last of the

French and Indian wars, had deserted after a short period of service, but had enlisted again the following year. Possibly he had been at Ticonderoga after its capture, certainly he had heard much about it. On the road to Boston, Arnold met Colonel Samuel Parsons, who was returning to Connecticut from the encircled town. The colonel must have told the future traitor of the need for cannon and Arnold spoke of the great number of them that were available at Ticonderoga to one who had the courage and energy to take them. Real rebellion such an action would be, an action going well beyond the initial plan of the patriot leaders, who still hoped to avoid war and separation from Britain. Two trains of action were ignited by the chance meeting of these men, and two expeditions against the fort were shortly conceived. Arnold, immediately upon his arrival at Cambridge, contacted the patriot authorities in that town, while Parsons assembled a small but influential group in Hartford.

Concord Fight had exploded some three weeks before the second Continental Congress was due to convene, but the Massachusetts Provincial Congress was actively in session. This latter body initially assumed effective control of the siege of Boston and its accompanying military problems until the Philadelphia congress could organize and take over the reins. Purely military matters were delegated to its Committee of Safety, and it was to this body that Arnold went on 30 April with his story of the great store of ordnance up on Lake Champlain at Ticonderoga, eighty iron cannon and twenty of brass, from 4- to 18-pounders in size, as well as a dozen large mortars. An exaggeration indeed, but actually on the low side when the spoils of Crown Point were later added. The committee showed great interest, and on that same day wrote the New York Committee of Safety that the capture of the fort at Ticonderoga had been proposed to them, but that they hesitated to infringe on the rights of New York. Further thought evidently erased their qualms and fired them to action, for on 3 May the committee gave Arnold a commission to raise a force of four hundred men, appoint his officers and proceed to take the fort. The day before they had anticipated their action by giving him an order for powder, ball, flints and horses, as well as a war chest of £100.

Here we suddenly encounter a fascinating sidelight and a fine example of the might-have-been. Arnold's commission was issued by Dr. Benjamin Church, chairman of the committee, and Church was a spy in General Gage's pay. He had been such for at least a number of weeks before Lord Percy's column was chased back into Boston. Thus on 30 April a British agent knew of the possibility of a raid on Ticonderoga, and two days later he himself authorized it! Why was the commander of the fort not warned? Here was vital information regarding a strategic point about which Gage had recently shown concern. Surely the general would have expected to be informed and, if he had been, would have attempted to alert the fort. The answer probably is that Church's reports to the British general had, in order to maintain the utmost secrecy, to pass through slow and perhaps devious channels. Thus, if information of the impending attack ever reached Gage, it had come too late to allow a warning to be gotten to the lake.

John Brown, a young lawyer of Pittsfield in western Massachusetts, had been sent to Canada in February of 1775 by the Massachusetts authorities to sound out the feelings of the Canadian people. In March he reported on the conditions he had found, conditions not favorable to the American cause. At the same time he strongly urged that the fort at Ticonderoga should be seized the moment that hostilities had broken out. Brown had broached the idea of this seizure to some "people on the N. Hampshire Grants" — the Green Mountain Boys, whose leader was Ethan Allen, originally of Connecticut. It is hard to summarize the character of this man in a few words. For our purpose it perhaps is sufficient to say that he was a born leader, one exceedingly vocal both in word and in print, deeply involved in land speculations in the regions immediately east of Lake Champlain, and a man whose blasphemy approached the majestic. He was boastful, egotistical, abounding in rashness and in energy, and a bitter hater of the Yorkers who claimed the lands of the settlers in the Green Mountains of what later became the state of Vermont. An almost ideal leader for these turbulent folk of the Hampshire Grants.

The Green Mountain Boys were settlers in the southern and western parts of today's Vermont. They held their lands under grants made by New Hampshire, a province which claimed title to all the land within its latitudes as far west as twenty miles east of the Hudson. New York in its turn held that it owned eastward to the Connecticut River. Both provinces issued land grants in the contested region. An appeal to London met with a decision favorable to New York, and this province then attempted to force settlers who held under a New Hampshire grant to pay for their lands a second time. New York's attempts to collect, or in default of payment to evict the settlers, brought on a form of guerrilla warfare between the Green Mountain Boys and agents of the New York grantors which, starting in the mid-1760's, became increasingly violent. Thus these settlers in the Hampshire Grants had to fight the Yorkers at the same time that they were conquering the wilderness. Only the hardy could endure such an existence.

The struggle for the land blew hot and cold, as New York sent surveyors and agents to evict the settlers, who turned out like hornets and thrust the intruders back across the borders. Harsh words, threats, whippings and house-burnings abounded, but practically no blood was shed despite dire threats by both sides. From the point of view of the Green Mountain Boys it was all great fun, in spite of the seriousness underlying the contest.

Eventually two Vermonters lost their lives in a bickering when a Yorker judge tried to open court in the disputed lands, but aside from this unfortunate affair the strife appears to have been carried out, at least by the Vermonters, on very much of a Robin Hood basis. The result, however, was that the Green Mountain Boys, known to the New York authorities as "The Bennington Mob," because that hamlet served as their capital, had little respect for any law, did as they wished and followed only their own leaders. And so we have a few hundred lawless frontiersmen inhabiting the region between Lake Champlain and the Connecticut River, with loyalty only to themselves, experienced in border warfare and ready to take on the devil himself if the spirit moved.

Thus by May Day of 1775 three groups had their eyes on the old French fort, the Massachusetts Committee of Safety, an unofficial but nevertheless powerful group in Connecticut, and the unruly inhabitants of the Hampshire Grants, whose leader was the formidable and energetic Ethan Allen.

The British also appreciated the importance of the forts on the lake, despite the lack of attention they had given them over the years since the Peace of 1763. In 1767 Governor Carleton had declared that the Lake Champlain forts must be kept in repair, but nothing was done. As the troubles with the colonies became increasingly apparent a more positive interest in Ticonderoga developed. Crown Point's destruction had left the fort at the outlet of Lake George the only habitable place and its capacity was most limited. A garrison of only fifty was all that could be sheltered there in winter. In 1774 Captain Montresor, Gage's senior engineer officer, was ordered to the lake to make plans either for repairing one of the two forts or for building an entirely new structure. His report on Ticonderoga was discouraging. "It's ruinous situation is such, that it would require more to repair it than the constructing of a new fort, . . . in many places there are very capitol breaches." Montresor advised building an entirely new fort at Crown Point. The excellent General Haldimand was then in command in America during Gage's temporary absence in England. After receiving the engineer's report he wrote Lord Dartmouth, Secretary for the Colonies, that if it was feared that the New Englanders were heading for trouble, it might be an excellent idea to have a couple of regiments camped in their rear on Lake Champlain, and that they could be sent there under the pretext of their building a new fort. A sound idea, indeed, but one not followed.

In early November of 1774 London at last ordered that the forts should be repaired, but Gage did not receive the instructions until winter had closed in on the Adirondacks, and work would be impossible for months to come. The American commander accordingly took a leisurely approach to the matter, and no action was started. Captain Delaplace at Ticonderoga, however, was warned to be on the lookout for trouble. It was on 19 April that General Gage, having sent the troops off to seize the military stores at Concord, sat down and wrote Carleton in Canada, directing him to send a regiment to Ticonderoga or Crown Point with all dispatch. The letter was a month in reaching the Canadian governor, and it arrived too late.

Colonel Parsons, ruminating on what Arnold had told him of cannon at Ticonderoga, reached Hartford, Connecticut, on 27 April, and the very next day he met with a small group of prominent men, most of them members of the Governor's Council or of the Assembly. This unofficial gathering took upon itself the authorizing of the dispatch of the nucleus of an expedition against the fort, and they withdrew funds of the Province for its use, they themselves going bond for its authorization or repayment. On 28 April, Edward Mott, just appointed captain in the 6th Connecticut Regiment, reached Hartford and was directed by this same group of citizens to push on and catch up with the party dispatched the day before. There is one statement on record which says that this self-constituted committee of citizens had been joined in its deliberations and decisions by "Mr. Hancock and Mr. Adams." This is quite possible, for both John and Sam Adams were in Hartford at least on 30 April, and Hancock had preceded them. None of these men, however, could have known of the action of the Massachusetts Committee of Safety in commissioning Arnold to seize the fort.

On the way northward the Connecticut contingent picked up John Brown and some forty Massachusetts men to add to their initial party of sixteen. Meanwhile the leaders of the Green Mountain Boys were conferring as to their future actions in a meeting at the Catamount Tavern in Bennington, where a stuffed catamount snarled constant defiance at York Province from the top of a tall pole. The Connecticut men dropped in at the ideal moment, and plans were soon under way to make the venture against Ticonderoga. The combined party then went on to Castleton, where they assembled at the farmhouse of Richard Bentley, and completed their dispositions. After the meeting had broken up, and Ethan Allen had gone on ahead to spy out the land, another small party was sent off to Skenesboro to capture Major Philip Skene, the great Tory landholder of the region, and, if possible, to secure boats with which to cross the lake. Then late in that evening of 8 May, Benedict Arnold, colonel by grace of his Massachusetts commission, stormed into the farmhouse, accompanied only by a servant, and demanded command of the expedition. He must in some way have heard of what was afoot in the Hampshire Grants and, abandoning attempts at

recruiting his authorized force of four hundred, rushed ahead
to get into the adventure before it was too late. His demand
was laughed at by the hardy frontiersmen, who would follow
leaders of their own choice or none at all. Nevertheless Arnold was allowed to join the force, and, determined to make
the best of it, he bided his time and went along. One can
easily see how little appeal the brash demand for command
by a Massachusetts officer would have to the Bennington
boys who formed the major part of the little army, and one
might wonder why Arnold was accepted at all. There was a
reason, and a good one. Allen had no authority at all for his
undertaking, and technically the entire group, both Green
Mountain Boys and Connecticut men, was engaged in a
highly irregular activity for which, if things went badly, its
members might receive the harshest of treatment as bandits
and outlaws. Arnold, however, had a proper commission
from the Massachusetts Provincial Congress, which, even if
most irregular and revolutionary in British eyes, was at the
moment the supreme authority in the land, in practice if not
in law. He thus had something which might well stave off
the gallows if the worst came to the worst. And so Arnold
was accepted and granted a certain, if still dubious, standing,
although formal command was refused him. Later, when he
had caught up with Ethan Allen, his position might be clari-
fied, and we have his statement that it was.

The late hours of 9 May saw waiting at Hand's Cove on
the shore of Lake Champlain a motley body of some two
hundred, mostly Green Mountain Boys, with some two score
from Massachusetts and a handful from Connecticut. The
lake was still to be crossed, and the expected boats had failed
to appear. Dawn was not many hours away. At last a couple
of scows were located and the ferrying of the party commenced. It was almost daylight before some eighty men had
been landed on the New York shore, and it was now too late

to wait for any more. Just what agreement had been reached
between Allen and Arnold we can never know for sure, but
after the crossing Arnold made a new demand for command
and the right to be first to set foot in the fortress. This was refused, but, according to Arnold's statement, Allen conceded
him a joint authority, and the two leaders, marching side by
side, led the party onward into our country's history.

It was just turning light as the men, marching in column,
three abreast, approached the fort. The provincials passed
by the great well and up the slope to the base of the east
curtain wall. A small portal and a tunnel here penetrated
into the basement of the eastern barrack building, then up a
flight of stone steps onto the parade ground. A sentry posted
at the entrance snapped his firelock at the leader of the intruders but the gun misfired, and the sentry turned and fled
into the shelter of a bombproof on the north side of the
parade ground. The Green Mountain Boys poured up the
steps and then on up onto the walls and into the barracks,
startling the garrison from a sound sleep, overpowering them
with ease in their beds, and at once starting their search for
plunder.

Allen, Arnold and a few others stormed across the courtyard, where they were accosted by a second sentry who
pricked one of the Boys with his bayonet and then was struck
down by the flat of Ethan's sword. Allen demanded to be
shown the commander's quarters and the cowed sentry
pointed out a stairway which led up to the second story of
the western barrack. The Vermonter dashed up the steps,
closely followed by Arnold. "Come out, you old rat," roared
Ethan, mad with excitement. Almost at once the figure of a
British officer appeared at the top of the stairs, fully dressed
except for the breeches held in his hands. This was Lieutenant Feltham, Captain Delaplace's only officer. The assailants
paused for a moment, as Feltham talked and tried to stall for

time, hoping that the garrison would come to his aid. But they were already overpowered. Allen became impatient, breathed threats of no quarter, threatened Feltham with his sword, shouted that he had orders from the state of Connecticut to take the fort, and that he exercised a joint command with Benedict Arnold, who had similar orders from Massachusetts. Arnold seems to have remained calmer and attempted to restrain Allen's violence with some little success, but the situation was tense. Vermonters in the courtyard were threatening Feltham with their fowling pieces, when Delaplace, fully dressed at last, appeared in the doorway at the head of the stairs. He asked under what authority the leaders were acting. Allen, now somewhat calmer, cried, "In the name of the Great Jehovah and the Continental Congress." There was nothing that Delaplace could do but surrender, and so the old stone fortress passed into the hands of the Green Mountain Boys without bloodshed.

The question of who really was in command at the fort's capture perhaps deserves a little more consideration, as it has been argued over the years. Arnold wrote to the Massachusetts Committee of Safety just after the capture that he and Allen had agreed to issue orders jointly, while Allen at the same time wrote the Albany Committee that Arnold entered the fort by his side. In a letter to the Massachusetts body, however, Allen made no mention whatsoever of Arnold, while in his *Narrative,* printed in 1779, he made it appear that he and the Green Mountain Boys alone took part in the capture. That left the matter open to argument for many years, Arnold on the whole faring poorly because of the taint of his later career. Thus for a century and a half all credit, practically speaking, was given Allen, and Arnold was portrayed merely as a bystander. Then some thirty years ago a letter was found among the papers of General Gage which brought forth new evidence. This was a complete report of the capture written by Lieutenant Feltham. We cannot be sure to whom it was sent, presumably to General Gage, and it certainly found its way into his hands. The letter was written a month after the capture, but the writer's memory was evidently clear and fresh. Its careful relation of the affair agrees closely in all major points with the tales told by the other reporters. Feltham specifically stated, "I was inform'd by one Ethan Allen and one Benedict Arnold that they held a joint command." This is clear, specific and agrees entirely with Arnold's claim.

Thus we have three stories, two of which agree as to the joint command, one of them by an arrogant, self-seeking and jealous glory-hunter, who soon was to become one of the famous traitors of all time, the other by a British officer who presumably had no reason to distort what he saw and heard. Opposed to them is the story told by Ethan Allen.

Regardless of the technicality of who held the theoretical command, it was Allen alone who held the practical leadership. He had the intent and the men needed to capture the fort without the help of Arnold, while the latter was powerless without Allen's men. The Vermont leader merely made the wise decision to assure his project a better legal status through his concession to Arnold. After the capture Allen secured from Mott, chairman of an informal and self-constituted committee, an ex post facto commission authorizing him to take the fort. Thus it is obvious that he wished as much legal justification as possible for his actions.

And so we should agree with the historians of the past and say that Allen was the commander of the band that captured the old French fortress. But we must also grant Arnold his modicum of credit, for it was his talk with Colonel Parsons on 26 April that started the Connecticut party on its way, and the arrival of these men in the Hampshire Grants was undoubtedly the straw that caused the hitherto hesitant Green Mountain Boys to decide to act.

One final word might well be added. The capture of Fort Ticonderoga was no great military victory. A ruined fort, its ramparts rotted away and its walls already breached, and garrisoned by only some two score men, and only half of these considered effective, was surprised while all were asleep, save dozing sentries, by a rush of a wild crew of at least double their numbers. Even if the commander had shown due vigilance (he had been warned of trouble) there would have been little that he could have done to ward off a determined attack. Allen had more men still on the Vermont shore, with others available on call, while the British could expect no help for many days to come. Allen's seizure of the fort was, however, a most daring and courageous act, the first really overt military act of the Revolution. Lexington and Concord had been defensive measures against a British offensive, but here at Ticonderoga the patriots determinedly and with planned intent seized a possession of the British King. This was revolt.

NINE

Britain Loses the Waterway

BY SUNRISE of that tenth day of May the fort was secure, the garrison disarmed and safely confined. But all
was far from quiet as the Green Mountain Boys dashed
hither and yon after plunder, breaking into the magazines
and storerooms on a wild rampage. The captors were joined
by late arrivals from further ferrying operations who, although they had missed the mad rush into the fort, were
not, if they could help it, to be cheated out of their share of
the loot. At such a time and with such men there could be
no discipline, but Arnold, with experience behind him both
as a soldier and as master of a ship, tried nevertheless to restrain the looting. His attempts were hopeless and achieved
nothing beyond arousing the animosity of the Vermonters.
According to one story a few surreptitious musket shots were
directed at Arnold, but without luck. The future traitor
became for a short period a useless supernumerary, while
Allen styled himself the commander of the fort, as indeed
he was.

A party under Seth Warner, who had been too late for the
capture, at once took off for Crown Point, but contrary
winds held them up, and it was not until the next day that
the ruins of Amherst's great fort and its garrison of eleven
were taken. There were many more cannon here, but little
else. At about the same time another detachment of Allen's

men descended on Fort George at the head of the lake of that name, and it was seized without bloodshed. The British now had no hold on the Hudson-Champlain waterway south of St. Jean on the Richelieu River just north of the outlet of the lake.

Arnold's period of disgruntled inactivity was of short duration, for on the thirteenth Skene's schooner dropped anchor at Ticonderoga. The party that Allen had sent to Skenesboro from Castleton four days previously was on board, but much more important to Arnold were the recruits his officers had raised along the road from Boston. With the addition of these men Arnold now had about a hundred who would follow his orders, as well as a sailing ship, something of no use to the landlubbers of Vermont, but of the utmost value to an energetic man who once had sailed the seas.

Arnold fully appreciated the vital importance of the command of Lake Champlain, and all that stood between him and that command was a single sloop of the British King, then tied up at St. Jean. On 15 May he put some of his men in bateaux and headed north, leaving the schooner behind, presumably to improve its armament. They had the luck to capture a bateau carrying the mail south from Canada, and the catch included not only a British ensign but also a current list of the location of all the troops in Canada, only some seven hundred all told. The next day the schooner — later if not already named the *Liberty* — caught up with the bateaux, and Arnold climbed on board. But before long the wind dropped and the lake became a dead, flat calm, so the bateaux resumed the advance over the last thirty miles. By sunrise of 18 May the party was hidden in a mosquito-infested swamp only half a mile from St. Jean, while one man scouted ahead to spy on the village. There were only fourteen soldiers there, he reported, and the sloop's crew of seven. All quickly surrendered upon the appearance of Arnold's men. The vessel was a real prize, seventy tons in burden, almost sixty feet long, and armed with two brass 6-pounders, quite sizable guns. Within little more than a year this sloop, renamed the *Enterprise* and armed with twelve guns and a crew of fifty men, would take her place in the battle line at Valcour Island.

Arnold promptly loaded his little fleet with his men and his prisoners, taking along four bateaux he found at St. Jean and destroying five others. He put on board all the usable supplies of food and munitions that he could locate and set sail south for Ticonderoga. Not only did Arnold now have absolute command of the lake, but the British did not have a single boat that would float. Until the enemy could build a fleet sufficient to contest the waters of Champlain, it would remain an American lake.

As Arnold was working his way southward he suddenly sighted a fleet of four bateaux carrying Ethan Allen and ninety of his men. The Vermonter, probably not wishing to be outdone by Arnold, had been seized with the idea of occupying and holding St. Jean, a rather useless proceeding now that the Americans controlled the lake. The Green Mountain Boys must have come off in a great hurry, for they were much exhausted, ravenous and without rations. Arnold tried to dissuade Allen, telling him that to hold St. Jean was "a wild impracticable scheme, and provided it could be carried into execution, of no consequence, so long as we are masters of the lake, and of that I make no doubt, as I am determined to arm the sloop and schooner immediately." Allen stuck to his idea, and, after receiving some food from Arnold, continued north.

The Green Mountain Boys and their leader arrived at St. Jean without trouble, learned that a party of British troops was moving toward the village, and set out to ambush it. At the last moment, however, Allen's people lost courage and decamped, crossing the Richelieu River and then bedding down for the night. Next morning they were awakened by a volley of grapeshot from six British cannon, accompanied by musketry. They fled to their bateaux and escaped, leaving behind three of their number.

It is a bit difficult to decide which party should have been the more ashamed of its performance that morning, the Americans for allowing themselves to be caught unawares, or the British for their terrible marksmanship. The river was evidently between the two parties, but even this does not excuse the British artillerymen. Allen, who was loud in proclaiming his successes, had nothing to say about this adventure either in his reports to his various correspondents or in his later pamphlet. He did, however, write the Continental Congress: "Provided I had but five hundred men with me at St. Johns, when we took the King's sloop, I would have advanced to Montreal."

On 22 May, Allen's party was back at Crown Point, while Arnold was at Ticonderoga, but moving to the more northern fort the next day. Arnold now had about a hundred and fifty men under him, whereas Allen's men had been steadily drifting homeward. Within another week all the Green Mountain Boys were gone, and Allen no longer had any command at all.

By the end of May, Arnold was in unquestioned charge of the lake frontier. He had a hundred and fifty men at Crown Point, believing this to be the best place to make a defense against the counterattack he was momentarily expecting from Canada. He seems to have forgotten the enemy had no boats. He had armed his prizes, and with them he would hold the lake until the British should succeed in building a fleet at least as powerful as his. Arnold had moved ten mortars, howitzers and cannon to the head of Lake George for the use of the province of New York. The records do not tell us just what else he was doing the first half of June, but it is safe to assume, knowing his driving energetic personality, that he was furiously busy. Sometime during these spring days he worked up a plan for an attack on Canada. From the dispatches he had captured when on the way to St. Jean he knew the exact strength of the British regulars in Canada — about five hundred and fifty, allowing for those captured during the last few weeks — and he believed that an army of two thousand men could take all Canada. His plan was well thought out, and accompanied by a list of all the supplies needed. Had it been possible to send off an expedition as he specified that spring, it is quite probable that it would have succeeded. But it was neither possible nor considered desirable. Only a mob of undisciplined and untrained soldiers could have been assembled, and supplies of all sorts were practically unavailable. Moreover the patriot leaders were most conscious of the vital need of preserving the friendship of the Canadian people, and they feared that such an expedition might antagonize them.

Connecticut became nervous over its part in dispatching the nucleus of the expedition that took the fort and disclaimed all responsibility for the seizure, stating that it was done solely by private parties acting without authority. New York Province made a similar disclaimer. Late in May the Continental Congress decided to withdraw the guns to the head of Lake George and to abandon the forts, at the same time making a careful inventory of their contents so that all could be accounted. for to the King when the present troubles were over. The thought of complete independence was still far from the minds of most men.

Southern New York was quite content with the abandonment of the lake forts, but Albany most certainly was not and protested volubly to the Congress. New England naturally felt the same way with its memories of invasions by Frenchmen and bloodthirsty Indians less than a score of years before. Connecticut did more than protest, for this province early in June ordered Hinman's regiment to march to the lake and reinforce the small garrison of Arnold's men who still remained.

Meanwhile, Ethan, a leader without followers, went to Philadelphia early in June to try to persuade Congress to authorize a regiment of five hundred Green Mountain Boys. This accomplished, he returned home to get the regiment recruited, but when the officers were selected by a convention of Vermonters, Allen, to his great chagrin, was left out entirely. He claimed that this was because the electors were all older, more staid citizens, and not the younger, rowdy crew he had led against Ticonderoga. Ethan next undertook some unofficial scouting into Canada to try to learn the feelings of the habitants. Finally in the fall, when the American army had moved down the lake and was besieging St. Jean, he attempted a foolhardy attack on Montreal with a party of Americans and French Canadians, mostly the latter, who had been promised pay and plunder. Allen was captured and taken to England. Later he was released but he never again took any part in the Revolution.

And so a brilliant actor passes from the scene. His daring capture of Ticonderoga was an act of great importance, but one which he could never again approach. Schuyler doubted his dependability, and after Allen's return from captivity Washington did not see fit to give him employment. A great historian of this period wrote of him: "brilliant, versatile and headstrong [he] lacked steadiness." Perhaps so, but let us always remember that it was he who first dared to take offensive action against the British King.

Congress gave heed to the pleas for retention of the forts, and voted to put them under the jurisdiction of New York. Meanwhile Hinman was marching his Connecticut regiment northward, arriving at Ticonderoga about 17 June, while the battle of Bunker Hill was being fought at Boston. The problem of command now raised its ugly head again. Arnold had only some two hundred men, while Hinman had a thousand. At about this same time there arrived at the lake a committee from the Massachusetts Congress, charged with examining the situation at the captured forts. Whether or not they actually had the authority, they nevertheless proceeded to order Arnold to serve as second under Hinman, and that violent, egotistical and ambitious man blew up, vowing that he would serve under no man.

The story now becomes somewhat clouded, but of the utmost interest, because it seems to give us the first inkling of Arnold's ultimate treachery. The facts are scanty, perhaps reported with bias, but nevertheless they contain a hint of possible treachery. It is all based on Edward Mott's letter to the governor of Connecticut, written a week or two after the event (and we must remember that Mott was an adherent of Ethan Allen in the contest for command when the fort was taken). Undoubtedly Mott was a hostile witness, and, were it not for Arnold's great treachery at West Point years later, we perhaps should give his story no credence. After hearing the committee's directive Arnold resigned his commission in a rage and retired to the little fleet which was manned by his followers. A bit of a mutiny, or at least a threat of one against Hinman's men, followed. Somebody, we do not know whether it was Arnold, some of his men, or conceivably someone inspired by Arnold — "they" is all the report gives — threatened to sail away and take the boats back to the British. Was this an idle threat, or was the idea in Arnold's mind as a possible course of action? We shall never know, but this hint, intangible as it is, when coupled with the traitor's later action, cannot but make one wonder. In fairness to Arnold it must be noted that as yet there was no real war with Britain, the provincials at this time were planning to account for all they had taken, and the act of returning the warships was really not treachery to the cause because that cause was still intangible and in its infancy. Nevertheless the incident offers a fascinating hint as to what may have been going on in Arnold's mind even at this early date.

The members of the Massachusetts committee attempted to go on board the vessels, and some of Arnold's men fired off a few swivels and some muskets at them. They probably fired over their heads as a threat, for no one was hurt. Eventually Mott, Judge Duer and two officers climbed into the ships, and were promptly confined and closely guarded for most of the day. Arnold apparently was no longer aboard, or perhaps he was sulking in the cuddy. Anyway Mott tried to argue with the crews and convince them that they were on the wrong course. His arguments apparently met with some success, and the prisoners were released by evening, unharmed.

Arnold now left the lake and headed back to Massachusetts to struggle over the settlement of his accounts, and then, before many months had passed, to start on his famous march through the Maine wilderness to Quebec. His men either joined Hinman's regiment or went home, and all became quiet on the lake. The British had moved some four hundred regulars to St. Jean and had started to build defenses there to prevent an American advance into Canada. Neither side, however, chose to take the initiative.

The Continental Congress had at last assembled and gotten down to its work of organizing the rebellion. On 27 June General Philip Schuyler, an Albany patrician, was ordered to the northern command. The orders given the new major general were edged with "ifs" and left much to his judgment. "Resolved, that if General Schuyler finds it practicable, and that it will not be disagreeable to the Canadians, he do immediately take possession of St. Johns, Montreal, and any other parts of the country, and pursue any other measures in Canada, which may have a tendency to promote peace and security of these colonies."

A man of the highest character and of considerable ability, Schuyler was no stranger to the military life, for he had seen much service in the last French and Indian war. A captain at General William Johnson's defeat of von Dieskau in 1755, he had been with Bradstreet in the battle of the bateaux near the Oswego portage the next year. He was a staff supply officer with Abercromby in 1758 and with Bradstreet on the Frontenac expedition later that year, and ended the Seven Years War as a supply officer based in Albany. This was more, and more varied, service than many a British regular had seen. Schuyler had a high sense of duty, was free from jealousy and ambition, and was anxious to serve his country; but his health was poor, and he was sometimes leisurely in his actions, certainly in that respect not to be compared with the driving Arnold. His abilities may not have been of the highest, but what he had he gave to his country without stint, and asked for no reward.

At ten o'clock in the evening of 17 July Schuyler reached the head of the portage at the foot of Lake George to find only a single sentry on duty. The soldier left the general and went off to wake the rest of the guard, and Schuyler walked on until he met a second guard who allowed him to approach to close quarters, while the rest of the guard lay deep in slumber. "With a pen knife only I could have cut off both guards," he wrote Washington the next day. The following morning Schuyler received further unpleasant shocks when he found that Hinman's men, although they had been at the fort for a month, had done nothing. "No orders," said Hinman in explanation. Both forts were in ruinous condition, but the Connecticut colonel had not had sufficient initiative to undertake any repair work.

Schuyler was never to be a leader of men in battle. His fate was to remain in the rear as a planner and a provider of necessities for the fighting men. In this last capacity he was most effective, and this he proved once he had reached Lake Champlain. There was much to be done, forts to be repaired, hospitals established, wood to be cut and sawed for the boats that must be provided. Moreover, the relatively few troops on the lake were sick, half starved, without proper clothing and equipment, and almost on the edge of mutiny. Schuyler at once set to work, on the one hand constantly beseeching the authorities at Philadelphia for the essential supplies, and on the other making the most of what he already had on hand. The sawmills were put in shape, and preparations made for building vessels of larger size than bateaux. Tools, however, were in very short supply.

There were also many sick — a hundred men out of the total of five hundred stationed at Ticonderoga. Those who were healthy lacked shirts, shoes, underclothes, blankets, even muskets, but gradually conditions improved as July passed into August. By the middle of the latter month additional troops began to arrive — Waterbury's Connecticut regiment and the first four companies of New York troops. By now Schuyler's letters to the Continental Congress had taken on a more cheerful tone, although there were still great shortages of essentials. Early in August he had launched a sixty-foot flat-bottomed boat said to be capable of carrying nearly three hundred men, and with an armament of five 12-pounders. Soon a second such craft was in the lake, but due to a shortage of carpenter's tools, gun carriages could not be made, and only one of these new boats received its armament. Hospital arrangements were improved, and everyone became more cheerful. It was a real change from the discouraged and almost mutinous condition that had existed when Schuyler took command.

Late in August an unknown officer wrote home: "There is the greatest plenty of salt and fresh provisions here; the men have as much as they can use; a gill of rum and as much spruce beer as they can drink every day; so that they have no occasion to drink the lake water, it being reckoned very unhealthy." By now there were seventeen hundred men at Ticonderoga and another seven hundred at Crown Point. Bateaux were being put together at a great rate. It was time to think of starting the offensive against Canada.

The attitude of the French Canadians, of course, was of the greatest importance. Would they stand by the King, or would they take the American side? That was a question upon which much depended, for if any American advance into Canada should alienate the habitants, it would do great damage to the cause and might be fatal to any invasion. Rumors and reports had drifted south over the border, most of them to the effect that the French Canadian people, except for most of their noblesse and the clergy, favored the cause of the patriots. To seek confirmation, Schuyler shortly after his arrival dispatched John Brown to determine what he could of the military dispositions opposing an advance into Canada, as well as the feelings of the Canadian people. Accompanied by three men, Brown made an arduous journey northward, was discovered, pursued and nearly caught, but made his escape and returned safely to Crown Point, reporting that the Canadian habitants were generally favorable and would furnish supplies to the invaders. Further scouting parties kept Schuyler well informed of the British military preparations at St. Jean.

There was considerable intercourse back and forth over the border and from one source or another Schuyler had a pretty fair idea of the British strength and conditions. Most of the regulars were at St. Jean, probably well over four hundred of them, and they were busying themselves at putting up a stockaded fort and completing two vessels, the frames of which had been made at Chambly, knocked down and carted by the rapids and on to St. Jean for final assembly and planking. One of these would probably be finished before mid-August. It was reported to be fifty-two feet long on the keel and carrying sixteen guns. Then there were about one hundred regulars at Chambly, eighty at Quebec, and, report said, only a score at Montreal. But at the latter city Guy Johnson was believed to have five hundred of his Indians, a dubious factor, perhaps neutral, perhaps pro-British. The true feelings of the French Canadians were yet to be determined. Only an actual invasion could answer this most important question.

The two newly constructed British vessels now being completed at St. Jean, small as they were, could regain the command of Lake Champlain once they sailed into its waters. Schuyler fully realized this. If he could get in position on Isle aux Noix before these little warships could sail south, he could, by placing a boom across the Richelieu and planting cannon to cover it, prevent the British from entering the lake and retain for his own use the vital Champlain waterway. Thus the report of the near completion of the ships at St. Jean was a spur to expedite his advance northward.

Schuyler seems to have been somewhat dilatory in his actions that summer. He perhaps was over-patient with the shortcomings of his subordinates, for he was never the demanding, driving type of commander. His supplies were undoubtedly insufficient for an advance into Canada, and no such move could be made until a backlog of food and supplies had been accumulated. Despite such shortages outposts could easily and without material risk have been advanced farther north toward Canada. It is interesting to inquire why Schuyler did not take up some position farther down the lake than

Crown Point. With his command of the lake he could have safely established himself almost anywhere he wished. Both Ticonderoga and Crown Point were in a ruinous condition, but an excellent stone house, its walls pierced with over two score loopholes, was standing at Pointe au Fer, only thirty miles from British-held St. Jean. A little work of digging trenches or throwing up earthen embankments would have made this place into a strong outpost, one which could have kept closely in touch with both the Canadian habitants and with British activities at St. Jean. Or Schuyler could equally well have occupied Isle aux Noix in the Richelieu River, still closer to the future scene of action.

By the end of August there were enough supplies at the two forts for the seventeen hundred soldiers assembled there, and Schuyler decided to start his move northward. His able second in command, Brigadier General Richard Montgomery, a former officer in the British army, started down the lake with a force of twelve hundred men and four 12-pound cannon to take a temporary station at Isle aux Noix prior to an assault on St. Jean. The island was only about a dozen miles south of the British post. Schuyler followed shortly with the rest of the army, reaching there on 4 September. The Americans made their base at Isle aux Noix, put a boom across the river and placed artillery to cover it. The effective army consisted now of but some one thousand men. On 6 September an advance was made against St. Jean but no attack was undertaken, although a minor skirmish developed, followed by a withdrawal to the island. Soon another seven hundred were added to the invading army, and an unsuccessful attempt was made to cut off the communications of St. Jean with Montreal. Many of the Americans had become sick, including Schuyler, who at last on 16 September was forced to give in, and be carried back to Ticonderoga.

This left Montgomery in command. The short and unsuccessful foray against St. Jean was to be Schuyler's only active military service in the Revolution.

The day after Schuyler's departure Montgomery successfully invested St. Jean, and started a siege which was to continue for six weeks before the post fell. The fort at Chambly, well to the north, surrendered its pitifully small garrison some two weeks earlier. The fall of these two places left the road open to Montreal, and that city surrendered on 13 November, but General Carleton, the Canadian governor, managed to escape just before the capitulation. And so the western assault on Canada succeeded with the fall of one of the only two important cities in the land. The eastern attack, that of Benedict Arnold up the Kennebec and over the mountain chain between Maine and Canada, by this time had stalled in front of Quebec, and was to remain so until Montgomery brought reinforcements to its aid. Then, on the last day of 1775, the Americans attacked the city during a blinding snowstorm, failed and fell back with Montgomery dead and Arnold wounded.

Ticonderoga Becomes the Northern Bastion

LITTLE IS KNOWN of the happenings at Ticonderoga that winter of 1775-1776. The war had moved north from the old French fort, and for the next few months Ticonderoga was to become a backwater, a point on the line of communication to Canada, garrisoned by only a few dozen men at most. Schuyler was there in November, building heavy sleds to move cannon or ship timbers. Homesick soldiers drifted back from Canada, claiming various illnesses and disabilities which would justify their discharge. Schuyler noted that it was amazing how once released from service they perked up; nine times out of ten the invalids at once made a complete recovery and started briskly on the homeward trail.

Late in November all the vessels were assembled at Ticonderoga, two schooners, a row galley and the sloop *Enterprise*, so poorly designed and built that she could never work up to windward and was practically unmanageable. Late in November Congress sent a committee, consisting of Robert Treat Paine, John Langdon and Robert Livingston, up to the lake to look the situation over. They advised the abandonment of Crown Point and concentration of all activities at Ticonderoga.

Meanwhile the Continental Congress had directed Henry

Knox, Washington's artillery officer at Cambridge, to proceed to New York, survey the cannon there and send on to Boston anything that would be of service. He then was to continue on to Ticonderoga, assemble as many heavy pieces of ordnance as possible and take them to Boston — a large order in view of the existing roads and the time of year. A contemporary of the former bookseller was reported to have said that he had never elsewhere seen such an ox of a man — a few years later he weighed 280 pounds — but he could move fast and could get things done. Knox quickly accomplished his mission in New York, noting in his journal that it was a most expensive place to live in, and started north, reaching Lake George in the first week of December. He found the Ticonderoga garrison so very small that he was barely able to sort out the guns and get the best of them down to the landing on Lake Champlain. There the mortars and cannon were loaded on barges and bateaux and ferried the couple of miles around to the foot of the portage. Knox had selected fourteen mortars, ranging in size from 4½ inches to 13, two 8-inch howitzers and forty-three cannon, from 3- to 24-pounders. These fifty-nine pieces had a combined weight of sixty tons, perhaps not much in our day of bulldozers and huge trucks, but a vast weight in those days of practically no roads, of oxen and manpower.

Knox somehow managed to haul these great pieces of iron and bronze up the steep portage trail to Lake George and got them on board various barges, bateaux and a petiauger. The lake was already partly frozen and they had to cut a channel about a mile long through the ice. One trip up Lake George was completed without too much trouble, but a great scow carrying three mortars and some cannon ran onto a submerged rock and could not be freed. They tried to haul it off, but the ropes broke. Heavier ones were secured from the fort and the scow at last came clear. It then sailed on to Sabbath Day Point, where a heavy wind raised waves which swamped the heavily loaded craft. This fortunately occurred in shallow water, and the scow was bailed out, the cargo shifted a little, and the journey resumed. At last all safely arrived at the head of Lake George, where they found a few more guns, sent there by Benedict Arnold in the spring of 1775.

Recourse then had to be made to heavy sleds. Knox proceeded to order these procured, along with yokes of oxen to haul them. Meanwhile he was forced to wait for a snowstorm, for, while the roads were snow-covered as far as Saratoga, beyond that village the ground was nearly bare. The cannon had reached Fort George at the head of the lake on 17 December, a month after Knox had been given his assignment. He had done well, but now the weather would largely determine his further progress. Here we can leave him impatiently waiting for a blizzard, which when it finally came was so heavy that Knox was forced during one part of his journey to struggle on foot through three feet of new-fallen snow. Weeks later, after much toil and struggle, the guns safely arrived in Boston, all except one that was lost through the ice near Half Moon on the Mohawk, endured many vicissitudes and eventually returned to Fort Ticonderoga. There it now lies in company with half of a split 13-inch mortar which also made that winter journey down the Hudson and across the rugged Berkshire hills.

A letter from Schuyler to the Continental Congress tells us that Ticonderoga was almost without troops that Christmas of 1775. What men were there most certainly were devoting almost all their time to cutting the firewood necessary to maintain life in the dilapidated stone barracks, while winter howled outside. Early in February Schuyler was trying to get out timber for repair work at the fort and at the same time he was building bateaux at the head of Lake

George. By spring a hundred had been nailed together but there was a shortage of oakum for caulking, and only thirty-five were finished.

Meanwhile, far to the north in Canada, Arnold, recuperating from the wound he had received in his unsuccessful attack of 31 December 1775, was continuing his siege of Quebec. It was a siege in name only, for at times he had fewer men than had the British defenders; and even more important, he lacked the heavy cannon essential to breaching the defenses of so strongly fortified a city. The Americans had a force of only some seventeen hundred men by the winter's end, as well as nearly eight hundred sick. By late April reinforcements had passed by Ticonderoga and moved down the St. Lawrence to bring Arnold's force up to twenty-five hundred, but he was still woefully short of cannon, powder and shot.

Britain's humane and understanding treatment of conquered Canada was a major achievement. It was the result of the thought and the work of two great soldier-administrators, James Murray, who had been one of Wolfe's brigadiers at Quebec in 1759, and his successor, Guy Carleton, later to be Lord Dorchester. Murray was removed as governor after several years of wise and considerate rule, largely through the maneuvers of a clique of British-born Canadian traders, a class the governor could neither understand nor endure. Carleton carried on the work, and it was he who a few years later largely shaped and pushed through Parliament the Quebec Act, which went far toward conciliating the population of Canada and restraining that province from joining the rebellion.

After the conquest and the Peace of 1763, a large number of Canada's so-called "noblesse" — "gentry" is a better word — returned to France, and all feudal duties formerly owed by the habitant were abolished. Peace reigned, military service was no longer required, a sound currency replaced the fiat card money of the French regime, and taxes became appreciably less. So great was the resulting prosperity and so much greater was the freedom now enjoyed by the Canadian habitant that he became a little spoiled. And so, when he was asked by both the British and the Americans to take up arms for their respective causes, he shied away and preferred to sit the struggle out. What was left of the "noblesse" and the clergy largely favored the cause of Britain, but both these classes had lost their hold on the people and so could accomplish almost nothing. Both sides succeeded in raising a few Canadian troops, but they were of small importance.

Canadian support was essential to any continued occupation of Canada. The habitant was delighted to sell supplies for hard money, but he wisely spurned the colonial paper currency. Two things were needed to secure and hold the Canadian habitant: silver or gold coin and the capture of Quebec. Unless both were forthcoming the Canadian adventure was doomed to failure. The Americans could not produce the hard money, nor could Arnold take Quebec with the facilities at his command. And so Canada was lost.

News of the invasion of Canada must have reached London at least by early October of 1775. That summer and fall the question of the revolt of the American colonies was being argued at length in Parliament, where America was not without friends. King George — and one can hardly blame him — was all for stringent action against the rebels, but he had considerable opposition to overcome, and was forced to reshuffle his Cabinet in order to make it more amenable to his will. Shortly before Christmas he was successful, and the war party was in full control. Early in January of 1776 a relief expedition was being planned for Canada, but due to the ice in the St. Lawrence it could not sail before mid-February at best.

The American army in Canada by early May of 1776 was a little over two thousand strong, with an additional twelve hundred sick, mostly suffering from smallpox. On the sixth of this month the first of the British relief troops reached the Quebec basin, and Arnold immediately raised the siege and fell back to Montreal. It was now quite obvious to all that Canada must be abandoned, the only question was how far the invading army must retreat. An attempt was made to hold Sorel, the town at the mouth of the Richelieu River, the outlet of Lake Champlain. American reinforcements continued to move northward over the border, only to contract smallpox themselves and thus add to the burden of the sick. Early in June the Americans were still trying to hold in the valley of the Richelieu. Their army amounted to 6241 in all, but only 3591 were fit for duty; smallpox and dysentery had claimed most of the rest. A contemporary report stated that some regiments "were all down with the small pox . . . not a single man fit for duty . . . sick, ragged, undisciplined, and unofficered." Three thousand men were reported sick at Chambly in early June. An added problem was that of inoculation. Vaccination for smallpox was still a generation in the future, but years before it had been found that by infecting oneself with matter from someone suffering from smallpox, preferably a mild case, one would catch the disease in a relatively innocuous form and acquire a future immunity. There was almost no risk, merely the inconvenience of being mildly sick for a couple of weeks or so, but the soldier was just as much on the sick list as if he had a real case of the pox.

The army command issued stringent orders against inoculation, but fear of smallpox was more powerful than fear of punishment, and many of the troops engaged in the practice. Whole regiments were out of action at times. And so the natural spread of the disease plus the results of self-inoculation of many of the newly arrived troops rendered the army on the borders of Canada incapable of effective action even on the defensive.

Russell Dewey came from western Massachusetts, and in March he got inoculated. His diary at this time recorded: "Nothing remarcable hapned except hungry men for we being a fixing for the small pox might not eat nor drink anything except bread and water that is we could not get anything else to eat. . . . The snow flu and winds was so high that we was affraid to go out a dore for fear we should be blowed away for our preparation brought us so low that we were almost as light as eagles."

Food was always poor and in short supply. Captain John Lacey of Wayne's Pennsylvania regiment, the son of a man who owned gristmills, wrote that the meal they were given was as coarsely ground as that milled for hogs at home and all the bran was left in it. The salt pork was miserable stuff. The soldiers would slice it up and warm it in a frying pan until all the grease was tried out. Then they threw the pork away, poured their meal into the grease and cooked it for a while. The result, Lacey wrote, was a rich and palatable cake. The only trouble was that there was never enough of it to satisfy the pangs of hunger.

By mid-June all hope of holding any part of the northern province was abandoned, and the retreat southward commenced, first to Isle aux Noix, where sickness spread rapidly in the low, humid, steaming atmosphere of the island, totally lacking in any shelter for the sick. Here, for example, in one so-called regiment of 138 men, 60 came down with smallpox in the course of only two days. In another regiment only five men remained fit for duty.

One must not think that smallpox was necessarily fatal;

on the contrary, the great majority recovered. Captain
Charles Cushing, for instance, took a company of 76 into
Canada and brought them all back again, although 74 had
smallpox while there. During two weeks in July 1497 pa-
tients entered the base hospital on Lake George, but there
were only 51 deaths during the period. The percentage, of
course, would be materially higher at a place like Isle
aux Noix where there were no facilities for caring for the
sick. Even if the fatalities were not too great, the sick were
completely out of action, and the transportation of these
unhappy people to the rear and the provision of reasonably
adequate care for them imposed a heavy burden on the
army. As fast as possible the sick were evacuated south to
Crown Point, and to the large hospital established at the
head of Lake George. The remains of the Canadian expedition reached Crown Point on the first day of July, after
tarrying a bit at Isle La Motte while on the way south. Here
all the sick still remained, and conditions were chaotic.

John Trumbull, son of the governor of Connecticut, was a
most brilliant young man, who as a child of six could read
Greek. He graduated from Harvard at seventeen, and became a painter of considerable merit, famous for his paint-
ings recording the men and the events of the Revolution.
He had, however, a most exalted opinion of his abilities and
certainly made no attempt to hide his virtues. When twenty
years and nine months old he scornfully refused to accept
from the Continental Congress a commission as full colonel
because he did not like the date of rank assigned him. Up
to this time he had given excellent service to the cause but
on account of this quibble he quit the army early in 1777
and went to England to paint. He was, however, a good and
honest reporter of what he saw, and fortunately for history
he wrote his father about the conditions existing at Crown
Point in mid-July of 1776:

At this place I found not an army but a mob, the shattered remains of twelve or fifteen very fine battalions, ruined by sickness, fatigue, and desertion, and void of every idea of discipline or subordination. . . . Last spring there were ten battalions, amounting to about six thousand four hundred men, sent from New York to join this army; there were then here two battalions of Pennsylvanians, three from New England, and one or two from Jersey, all of them strong and amounting to at least four thousand men more, which, joined with the others, make the army upwards of ten thousand strong. We now have three thousand sick, and about the same number well; this leaves near five thousand men to be accounted for. Of these, the enemy has cost us perhaps one, sickness another thousand, and the others, God alone knows in what manner they are disposed of. Among the few we have remaining, there is neither order, subordination, nor harmony; the officers as well as men of one colony, insulting and quarreling with those of another.

There was another reporter of conditions at Crown Point at this time, and a rather bitter and sarcastic one he was. Dr. Lewis Beebe had been a classmate of John Brown at Yale, and he had married Ethan Allen's sister Lucy. Naturally he detested Benedict Arnold, and as early as May of 1776 called him a traitor, probably without any justification beyond hatred. Dr. Beebe wrote that there had been "not the least preparation for fortifying the garrison, which has tumbled to ruin & decay. The generals have their hands full in riding about the camp — prancing their gay horses, the field officers set much of their time upon court martials. The captains & subs may generally be found at the grog shops, the soldiers either sleeping swiming, fishing, or cursing and swearing most generally the latter."

Even so stalwart a soldier as the engineer Lieutenant Colonel Jeduthan Baldwin was thoroughly disgusted with conditions in the army this July. In his journal he recorded that he had had enough of "this retreating, raged, starved, lousey, thievish, pockey army in this unhealthy country." He stuck it out nevertheless and continued as an engineer officer throughout the Revolution.

General Schuyler, acting essentially as a provider of supplies since illness had forced his retirement from the front, had meanwhile been busily building additional watercraft to carry the reinforcements and supplies down Champlain to Canada. He estimated that to feed the Northern Army 120 barrels of pork and flour must move out of Albany each day. This meant that nearly a dozen bateaux must start up the Hudson daily to Half Moon, the Waterford of today, there to transfer their freight to ox teams for the next leg of the long journey north to Canada. Wagoners unfortunately remembered the old trick they had learned in the last of the colonial wars of lightening their load by drilling a hole in the pork barrels, letting the brine drain out to the detriment of the pork. Unless the roads had greatly improved since the fall of Canada in 1760, these provisions would have to be shifted from boat to team and back again until each separate barrel had been manhandled five and possibly six times before it reached the waters of Lake Champlain. Then there was a straight water route to Canada until the rapids of the Richelieu below St. Jean were reached. Here the bateaux could at times pass while still fully loaded.

By the latter part of May, Schuyler, although still diligently forwarding supplies to Canada, realized that it was time to think of defensive measures, and on the last day of the month he sent thirty carpenters, who had been building bateaux on Lake George, to Skenesboro, today's Whitehall, to start work on gondolas. These were flat-bottomed, sharp-ended craft, not unlike great bateaux, but more heavily built and of relatively shallow depth. Schuyler had built two of these the year before, each sixty feet long. The defenses at Ticonderoga were still in terrible condition, as were those at Crown Point, but shortage of men prevented any attempt at repairs until as late as mid-June, although by then it was quite obvious that the Canadian attempt had failed, and that it was now a matter of resisting an invading British army.

Both Crown Point and Ticonderoga had originally been selected by the French as defenses against attackers advancing from the south. Now conditions were reversed, and the Americans must hold these points against an advance from the opposite direction. Crown Point lies on the tip of a peninusla which extends to the north at a place where Lake Champlain narrows into what almost appears to be a river — in fact the French called it one. Nothing could pass along the lake by the fort without grave risk. The bay on the western side of the peninsula, however, is quite wide and vessels could pass by the fort practically beyond range of its cannon and sail on south to the end of the bay. Troops and guns could be landed in rear of the defenses, thus cutting Crown Point off from communications with its southern base.

Schuyler quickly grasped this most important point, and decided to abandon the more northern fort and make his stand at Ticonderoga. An additional reason for his decision was the terrible condition of the fort. "The ramparts are tumbled down, the casemates are fallen in, the barracks burnt, and the whole a perfect ruin, that it would take five times the men of our army, for several summers, to put it in defensible repair." So General Gates reported once he had visited the place. Although his generals endorsed the position Schuyler had taken, the field officers of the regiments made voluble protest and signed a round robin letter opposing the withdrawal, claiming that it would leave New England open to attack from the Champlain Valley. News of the protest reached Washington, and he wrote Schuyler a rather sharp letter, criticizing his decision to abandon Crown Point. Schuyler had already given proof of his devotion to the cause,

of his selfless attention to his duty, of his freedom from
jealousy and of his ability in the field of logistics, and his
reply to Washington reveals him as a sound military thinker.
He wrote of the inherent weakness of the northern fort
against a British advance, and then went on to say that he
only wished that an invading army would leave Champlain
and try to cut through the Green Mountains into the frontiers of New England. Just let them get a score or so of miles
into the mountains, he wrote, and then turn light infantry
loose after them. From his logistical experience and from his
service in the last French war he well knew the practical
impossibility of moving men and supplies through the mountains, particularly when harassed and chivied by fast-moving
irregular troops.

Schuyler showed his foresight in another way, and time
was to prove him right. He realized that eventually it might
be necessary to abandon Fort Ticonderoga and to fall back
on to some position farther to the south, such as Fort Edward. Then, he wrote, the British advance would be greatly
hampered by the difficulty in moving their supplies over the
Skenesboro-Fort Edward portage. He included a calculation
of just how many two-wheeled carts, the largest he believed
that could be brought down from Canada, would be needed
to carry the barrels of rations and how long they would take
to make the trip between the Champlain and the Hudson
waterways.

General Thomas, commander of the invading army, had
died from smallpox at Chambly during the retreat from
Canada, and the Congress appointed General Horatio Gates
to succeed to the command of the Northern Army. Gates's
service during the latter part of the Revolution could hardly
be called distinguished, but this was more the result of existing conditions than of incapacity on his part. His suspected
but unproved involvement in the Conway cabal, which at-

tempted to oust Washington, put another black mark against his name, and the result was that historians have been loath to appreciate his many good qualities. An ex-officer of the British army who had seen considerable colonial service — he had been badly wounded at Braddock's defeat — he was a capable administrator, and as such was what the defeated, disheartened and debilitated soldiers of the Northern Army needed in this summer of 1776.

On the first day of July Gates took over his new command at Crown Point, and he did not like what he saw. Later he wrote Governor Trumbull of Connecticut: "Upon my first joining the troops (or rather the hospital) at Crown Point, all was in the utmost disorder — the pestilence raging, not a cannon mounted, the vessels lumbered with stores, the men dispirited with defeat and fatigue, and, in short, the whole a scene variegated with every distress and disappointment that could conspire to ruin an army." Gates at once got to work, sent all the sick off to the base hospital, and all the vessels then on the lake went back for a refit. Meanwhile the rest of the army moved to Ticonderoga in accordance with Schuyler's orders. The greatest of care was taken to prevent any reintroduction of smallpox.

Despite repeated orders, many of the reinforcements headed for the lake stopped on the way for an inoculation, and in at least one case the senior officers of a regiment stopped off at Williamstown for such treatment, sending the regiment on ahead under the captains. Whenever cases of inoculation were discovered or suspected the men were held in quarantine before they were allowed to join the healthy troops. A large party of desperately needed ship's carpenters stopped on the way north for inoculation. Such men were very hard to come by, and many were needed at Skenesboro to push on the completion of the fleet. Nevertheless, as soon as headquarters learned of this, the carpenters' pay was stopped, and they were ordered to return home at their own expense. By such stringent measures smallpox was at last gotten under control, and one of the greatest threats to the Northern Army practically eliminated.

Another cause of trouble was the question of command. Schuyler in Albany commanded the northern region, while Thomas had been the head of the army in Canada. Gates, as the successor of Thomas, now believed that he was in command of all the Northern Army, while Schuyler, feeling that Gates's command existed only while the army was in Canada, was certain that he was. Although they disagreed, both men were big enough to prevent any damage to the cause, and they worked in relative harmony until the Congress upheld Schuyler, and Gates became his subordinate. Schuyler, however, continued as a commander in the rear; he was, moreover, responsible for the western frontier along the Mohawk, where trouble was brewing. Gates meanwhile was in active command of the troops, where his undoubted administrative ability soon began to produce results. Conditions greatly improved, due, said one who was there, to rest, fresh meat and rum. In mid-July, for instance, Colonel Mathew Ogden's regiment had only eighty men fit for duty, while ten days later convalescents had raised the figure to three times as many.

Despite improved conditions, the camp at Ticonderoga could not have been too pleasant a place, according to reports that have survived. Colonel Anthony Wayne commanded the 4th Pennsylvania that summer and he wrote a friend: "[Ticonderoga] appears to be the last part of the world that God made & I have some ground to believe it was finished in the dark. . . . I believe it to be the ancient Golgotha or place of skulls — they are so plenty here that our people for want of other vessels drink out of them whilst the soldiers make tent pins of the shin and thigh bones of Abercrombies men. . . ."

Ticonderoga and its old French fort could not be considered safe against a determined attack from the north, for, just as was the case at Crown Point, an aggressive enemy could bypass the fort and cut off its rearward communication which was, practically speaking, only by water either to Skenesboro or up Lake George. On the east side of Lake Champlain at Ticonderoga there was, however, a rugged promontory of about the same height as the headland upon which stood the old stone fortress. This point of land, soon to be called Mount Independence, offered many advantages as a strong point to halt a British advance. It commanded the passage through the lake as well or even better than did the old fort, and had a considerable plateau on its top suitable for a campsite. It was surrounded to the west and north by deep water, and to the east by a creek and a swamp of considerable extent. Only at its rear or southern end did a neck of land tie it to the eastern shore and a safe land route to Skenesboro and the villages of the Hampshire Grants. Here then was a place which could be strongly held, but one from which a safe withdrawal could be made if the position had to be abandoned. The decision was made to fortify Mount Independence and to make a stand against the expected British advance on both sides of the lake. Work was commenced on the eastern headland on 11 July 1776.

It was at about this time that Colonel Joseph Wait reported that the Northern Army had "generals without men, and a small artillery without supplies, and commissaries without provisions, pay masters without money, and quartermasters without stores, and physicians without medicines." Gates's competent hands were busily at work remedying these conditions, and even when this was written they had taken a turn for the better. Every morning at beat of drum all stood at their alarm posts until it was daylight; then they were drilled at the manual of arms until breakfast, after which came fatigue, mostly work on the fortifications. A considerable advance guard garrison was still kept at Crown Point, and there were small outposts at Jericho and Colchester Point in the Hampshire Grants, with another at the White House at Pointe au Fer which Schuyler had failed to utilize the previous year. Now it was entrenched and supplied with cannon, and, since a swamp made the place practically an island, it furnished a strong outpost against an enemy advance. Despite all these endeavors on land, it was clearly realized that the British could approach Ticonderoga only by water, and that it was of the utmost importance to continue to hold command of the waters of Lake Champlain.

ELEVEN

Britain Wins the Lake, Too Late

THE GREAT QUESTION to be solved in this summer of 1776 was who was to control the waters of Lake Champlain. A British army was poised on the northern border, but it would not dare advance southward through the wilderness unless its only highway, the waters of the lake, could be made safe for its passage. Far to the south at Skenesboro the Americans were striving to build a fleet, adding to the nucleus on which the farsighted Schuyler had started work in the spring, when he was among the first to realize that the Canadian adventure had failed. The British, on their part, equally well appreciated that they must control the lake if they were to achieve any advance during this campaign. And so the shipbuilding race got under way at opposite ends of Lake Champlain.

The American shipyard was at Skenesboro where Wood Creek enters the southern end of Champlain. Two sawmills in the vicinity were a decided asset, and there was ample wood at hand, even if it must be sawed and spiked in place while still green. Schuyler had sent thirty carpenters there at the end of May, and within some three weeks they had completed one gondola and had a second nearly planked. These craft were flat-bottomed and had relatively low sides, carrying one cannon fixed at the bow. The boat itself was shifted to aim this bow gun, a 12-pounder carrying a ball four and a half inches in diameter. The other two somewhat lighter guns, one on each side, were mounted on the usual naval carriages. A single mast carried a square mainsail and a topsail. These vessels were only expected to sail before the wind, certainly not to beat up against it, and otherwise were rowed by long sweeps. Gondolas were easily and quickly built and carried considerable firepower for their size, with small swivel guns in their bulwarks supplementing the fire of their cannon.

Scouts and spies brought news of British actions at frequent intervals. Early in July it was reported that they were building three sloops and a schooner with a dozen guns. Next came word that Carleton was hauling warships from the St. Lawrence overland by the Chambly rapids. Fortunately this undertaking failed. The British made the attempt with rollers under the vessels, but the soft ground and the round bottoms of the hulls conspired to defeat the operation except in the case of the 30-ton flat-bottomed gondola *Loyal Convert,* captured recently from the Americans at the relief of Quebec. And so it was found necessary to take the three largest vessels, a ship-rigged sloop and two schooners, to pieces, carry the components to St. Jean and then reassemble them there, a time-consuming operation when speed was the essence of the campaign.

Skenesboro became a hive of activity. Ship's carpenters and woodcutters poured into the unhealthy settlement, battled the humid heat and mosquitoes, shouted constantly for more rum, and fell sick with fevers and dysentery. But they built the little warships. By the end of the third week in July four gondolas had been finished and sent away to Ticonderoga for rigging and equipping. The news from the north, however, showed that there was need for more than gondolas if the British ship and the schooners were to be contained. Row galleys, so called, had been built for the defense of Philadelphia, and requisition was made for someone from that region who was familiar with their construction to come to the lake. Such a man, however, was not forthcoming and there apparently was no connection between the Delaware River galleys and those built at Skenesboro. The latter were sizable round-bottomed craft, some seventy feet long, with an ample hold, a gun deck and quarterdeck, armed with eight or ten fairly heavy guns and several swivels, and carrying a crew of eighty men. Their twin masts each carried a triangular lateen sail, a type of sail not usually associated with our waters. This rig had, however, been in some use along our coasts for years, and the French had lateen-sailed chebecs on both Lake Champlain and Lake Ontario during the Seven Years War. The galleys, as their name implies, could also be rowed when necessary, but their hulls had good lines, as can be seen from drawings preserved in the British Admiralty, and they must have been able ships when under sail. The first of them was started by mid-July, and two others rapidly followed. They took considerably longer to build than did the gondolas but were well worth it. They were the battleships of Arnold's fleet. In addition to this new construction the Americans had various sloops and schooners, three of them captured the previous year and one built at Ticonderoga, probably from a keel and ribs abandoned at St. Jean by the British.

The southern end of Lake Champlain was not a pleasant place that summer. High hills shut out any cooling breezes, and the low swampy land harbored untold hosts of hungry mosquitoes. These pests were famous. George Washington, who visited Skenesboro after the Revolution, once told an acquaintance that he had never been so much annoyed by mosquitoes in any part of America as he was in this dismal hamlet. It was, however, a strategic location for the ship-yard, on deep water at the northern end of the portage from the Hudson, and it had an iron forge in addition to one of the two sawmills of the neighborhood. These mills had all been built a few years before by Philip Skene, the proprietor of the regional land patent. The other sawmill was about a mile northwest of Fort Anne at a place called Cheshire's. After the American retreat from Ticonderoga in 1777 Lieutenant Anburey of the 29th Regiment made a delightful sketch of the mill and the blockhouse that had been built to guard it. Shortly thereafter American scouts sneaked back and burned both structures. (Various mills followed John Cheshire's sawmill until in modern times a hydroelectric plant was built there. Now even this last undertaking has been scrapped and the waters of that branch of Wood Creek fall free as they cascade over a forty-foot rock precipice, exactly as they did when Anburey made his sketch of the falls 185 years ago.)

The Skenesboro shipyard was fortunate in having the sawmills to rip out the planks for the sides of the vessels and the forge to turn out the necessary ironwork, but there were other serious shortages. Skilled shipwrights were scarce, and most of them were more interested in getting high pay for building privateers along the seacoast. They had little desire for the hardships of the frontier where they must work in the wilderness under primitive conditions for uncertain pay, and that in the depreciated "continentals." Most probably insisted on being paid in hard money. Many of the men that could be persuaded to go to Skenesboro soon went on the sick list. Supplies of all sorts, from food to the blocks and cordage needed for rigging, were short at all times. There was, however, one thing which was readily available and for which there was a constant cry from the workers. That was rum, and anyone sweating out his daily stint in that stinking, humid, mosquito-infested swamp certainly deserved his daily dram. General David Waterbury, the excellent officer in charge at Skenesboro that summer, saw that they got it.

As fast as the vessels were launched they were rowed, riding high and clumsy without their ballast and guns, to Ticonderoga, where the empty hulls were rigged, equipped and armed. Then they were dispatched down the lake to be added to the fleet that was assembling in the vicinity of Crown Point. The New England regiments could produce a considerable number of sailors to form a nucleus for their crews, and soldiers were drafted to complete them.

Meanwhile the British were not idle on the Richelieu. Spies brought back conflicting reports to Ticonderoga, but all agreed that there was great activity at the shipyard at St. Jean. Ten small gunboats had been brought from England in knocked-down form, and they were quickly assembled, while countless bateaux to carry the soldiers and supplies were being built or brought up from the St. Lawrence and hauled by the Chambly rapids on wagons. The ship-rigged *Inflexible*, carrying eighteen 12-pound guns, was the backbone of the British fleet, combining as she did both firepower and maneuverability. She was far from being a large vessel, only 180 tons in burden, some eighty-five feet long on her deck. There was also the ponderous radeau with even more and heavier guns, some of them great 24-pounders. This strange craft was built like a gigantic scow, ninety-two feet long overall and thirty-three feet wide. She was nearly seven feet deep, keel to deck, and carried massive bulwarks pierced by ports for her guns. There was a small quarterdeck and a cabin. Manned by a crew of nearly three hundred, she was huge, unwieldy and clumsy. Two masts carried her great sails, but in calm weather or when the breeze was light she was kedged along, an anchor being taken a cable's length ahead in a longboat and dropped. Then the radeau was hauled up to the anchor by her windlass, and the process repeated. If there was a good wind in the right direction the craft could make amazing speed under sail (she was once reported to have covered ninety miles in nine hours, but this is somewhat hard to believe). Once this great floating fortress could be brought within close range of an enemy ship, it could wreak tremendous damage with its heavy guns served by its immense crew. The problem was to get it where it was wanted.

Another decided advantage enjoyed by the British was their warships in the St. Lawrence. Supplies, equipment and veteran sailors had only to be brought up the Richelieu as they were needed to equip and man the growing fleet. The *Inflexible* was the last to be completed, but her reassembly was done in record time: twenty-eight days from the laying of her keel she was ready to set sail. In addition to the *Inflexible*, the schooners *Carleton* and *Maria* and the radeau *Thunderer*, the fleet included a score or more of gunboats, each with one good-sized cannon firing over its bow, and with a crew of a dozen gunners, ten sailors, and an artillery officer in command. Early in October all was ready and waiting on a favorable wind from the north.

Meanwhile at Ticonderoga the garrison had been doing its best to repair and to extend the fortifications of the place. But its best was not very good, and the work progressed all too slowly, particularly on Mount Independence. Toward the end of August General Gates had an army of sixty-four hundred men fit for duty with almost two thousand more on sick report. Work had been started on the Vermont shore by mid-July. A battery of about two dozen guns was placed behind an earthen parapet just above the level of the lake on the extreme tip of the peninsula, and a second horseshoe-shaped battery was constructed farther up the hill. Advanced posts were maintained to prevent surprise, one at the White House at Pointe au Fer, another in the vicinity of present-day Burlington, Vermont. Colonel Thomas Hartley's regiment was posted at Crown Point, where the colonel went vigorously to work fortifying the place and planning to make real resistance to any enemy advance. Such action was entirely opposed to the wishes of General Gates, who reiterated instructions to Hartley that he must withdraw when the enemy should appear in force. A company of Stockbridge Indians arrived at Ticonderoga in mid-September, presumably intended for use as scouts. They all wore red and blue caps to distinguish them from the Indians of the British.

Ensign Bayze Wells of Farmington in Connecticut served on board the gondola *Providence* and kept a journal of his activities, a journal more interesting than most, although replete with outlandish spelling and weird grammar. He tells of an accident of a kind all too common in the days of muzzle-loaders. While stationed near Ticonderoga early in August, the gondola was ordered to try out its cannon. One was fired. "[Then] they spunged the bow gun and put in the cartritch one Solomon Dyer who served spung went to ram down the cartritch there being fire in the gun [a spark still smoldering in the bore] it went off while he was standing before the mouth of the cannon which blew both his hands & one nee almost of and likewise the spung rod part or all of it went through the left part of his body at the root of his arm blew him overboard we could not find him until 7th [Aug.] he rose and floted we took him up and buried him decently."

A few days later the fleet's commander, Colonel Jacob Wynkoop, looking north down the lake saw the white sails of a British flotilla approaching. He at once summoned all captains to a council of war, whereupon one of them, enjoying better eyesight than Wynkoop, borrowed a telescope and discovered the sails to be a flock of white seagulls!

The American fleet had been gradually assembling at Crown Point, as each newly built gondola was equipped and sent north from Ticonderoga. Colonel Wynkoop remained in command until mid-August when Benedict Arnold arrived to replace him. Without bothering to notify Wynkoop of the change in command, Arnold at once ordered two of the schooners to sail down the lake to reconnoiter and to furnish protection to a party of men making oars. When the vessels set their sails, Wynkoop at once fired on them and brought them to. Arnold of course was furious and the final result was that poor Wynkoop was put under arrest and sent back to Albany, quite unfair treatment to my way of thinking. He was, however, considered to be incompetent, and was apparently eased back into civil life without a court-martial.

By late August Arnold had eleven warships at his disposal, and he set sail northward, followed a couple of days later by two more vessels. He had a sloop, three schooners and one galley, with a total of forty-six guns, mostly 4-pounders or smaller; the rest of the fleet were gondolas. Four more galleys were under construction, or soon would be, at Skenesboro, but they would not be ready for battle for many weeks to come.

For a month Arnold held his fleet in the northern waters of Lake Champlain, changing station from time to time, waiting for the arrival of the galleys, and constantly writing back for more supplies, food, clothing, ammunition. At one time the fleet was near Willsboro and some of the men seem to have raised havoc at Squire Gilliland's settlement there, destroying crops, smashing windows and stealing everything movable. That at least is what Gilliland reported, but later Arnold denied the charge. In this case my guess is that Gilliland is to be believed rather than Arnold.

Occasionally the fleet engaged in target practice, but powder and ball were precious and usually each cannon was allowed but a single shot. The crews went on shore from time to time, to hunt food or firewood, and sometimes for relaxation. Late in August Arnold invited all the ships' officers on shore for a picnic. They shot at a target for a bit and then ate roast pig (one of Squire Gilliland's?) washed down with wine punch and hard cider. Later there was a similar outing at Valcour Island.

By the second week in September there was report of a twenty-gun ship being put together by the British at St. John, and Arnold talked of building a thirty-six-gun frigate, a delightful but quite impossible dream under the conditions existing on the lake that summer. Arnold was always brimming over with ideas and energy and now was seized with the idea of firing explosive shell from howitzers on the galleys. He did not succeed in this, but it is one of the earliest suggestions of the use of explosive projectiles at sea, a practice that did not become common much before our Civil War. (Such an experiment was successfully carried out at Ticonderoga that summer, when a shell was fired from a howitzer on one of the gondolas.) The British at the other end of the lake had an even more advanced idea, that of firing explosive shells from a cannon. The journal of a British officer recorded that such an experiment was to be made, but there is no further mention of the matter.

Around the middle of September the fleet was holding station a bit south of Pointe au Fer, with two small schooners constantly cruising to the northward by day and guard boats posted every night some two miles toward the enemy. Arnold was not going to be caught napping if precautions could prevent it. Soon spies brought tales of the great radeau, whose armament of heavy guns could quickly pound to pieces anything the Americans had on the lake.

Arnold decided that his best chance for success — or perhaps one had better say survival — lay in taking up a defensive position and forcing the British to attack him while at anchor. After considerable reconnoitering he decided that Valcour Island offered the location best suited to his plan. Accordingly he sailed there in the third week of September and took up position between the island and the New York shore, believing that when the British came up the lake they would pass by before discovering the American fleet. They would then have to beat their way back upwind in order to attack. By this time the three galleys had been launched at Skenesboro, rigged, supplied and armed at Ticonderoga, and early in October they sailed north — a material and most welcome addition.

The weather was getting chilly as September gave way to October, and clothing was scant in the fleet, while the supply of food was never quite enough to satisfy the hungry crews. On 6 October the galleys *Washington* and *Congress* arrived, and were greeted with a salute of five rounds for each. Morale must have enjoyed a real boost when it was learned that the galleys brought a barrel of rum for each vessel of the fleet. The *Trumbull* had reached Valcour a few days earlier.

The British meanwhile were waiting with their army at Isle aux Noix, St. Jean, and Lacolle until the *Inflexible* was ready for action, and then there was further delay pending a favorable wind. So it was not until the morning of 11 October, with snow white on the Adirondacks, that the British fleet cleared Cumberland Head, scudding along before a brisk wind from the north. Arnold had correctly predicted what would happen, and the British, their fleet well stretched out because of the different speeds of the various vessels, overran Valcour Island before they discovered the American vessels concealed in its lee. Commodore Pringle's reconnaissance was certainly much at fault.

The *Inflexible*, technically a sloop-of-war though rigged as a ship, led the armada, along with the two schooners, *Carle-*

ton, and *Maria*, while the gondola *Loyal Convert* and the great radeau wallowed on behind. A floating platform for heavy guns, rather than a real vessel, the radeau served as a supply depot for provisions and ammunition. So slow was its advance that it did not reach the scene until dusk when the battle was over. Well behind the fleet some four hundred bateaux carried the army. They put ashore at Pointe au Fer and the soldiers set up their tents while they waited the outcome of the naval contest.

As the leading British ships cleared the southern end of Valcour and viewed the American line of battle, they turned and beat upwind. Arnold at once sent out the *Royal Savage* and three or four of his more able craft to dispute the advance of the enemy, but he soon recalled them and they scurried back to take up their places in the anchored fleet. *Royal Savage*, however, misjudged the wind, went ashore on the tip of Valcour Island and was out of the fight until, after having been abandoned by her crew, she was boarded by the British, who turned her guns on Arnold's ships. The wind and the lay of the land were such that the British ships had great difficulty in getting up into cannon range of the Americans; in fact *Carleton* was the only one of the larger ships to get to close quarters with Arnold's men. The gunboats had no difficulty in rowing up into position. *Inflexible* and *Maria* never got closer than about the extreme range of their guns, and so had relatively little effect on the battle.

By about noon the gunboats were within cannon shot of the American line and the battle really started, as they hurled solid shot and canister at the anchored vessels. Just how closely the gunboats came is impossible to determine. Captain George Pausch of the Hesse-Hanau artillery company commanded one of these boats. In his journal, one of the few relatively detailed reports we have of the battle, he wrote that about twenty-seven of these gunboats advanced against the American line and that "after getting to close quarters [the attack became] very animated." By "close quarters" one would assume that he meant perhaps one hundred and certainly not over two hundred yards, but another reporter of the battle, Lieutenant James Hadden of the British artillery, a future major general, stated that the range was about seven hundred yards, a distance at which he said that the boats were relatively safe from the American grapeshot. At such a distance the British case shot, or canister, was found to have little effect on the anchored fleet, and only the solid shot did real damage. Naval grapeshot consisted of a bundle of nine iron balls, three in each of three layers, the size of the balls such that three would nicely fit in the bore of the gun from which they were to be fired. The individual balls thus were relatively large. Case shot, on the other hand, consisted of a quantity of much smaller balls, or even musket bullets, soldered up in a tin can of the correct size to fit the cannon's bore. The can burst on discharge and its contents spread like a charge of shot from a giant shotgun, murderously effective at close quarters but doing little damage once the range exceeded some three hundred yards. Arnold in his report of the battle said that the gunboats came up within musket shot (not over a hundred yards), but I doubt this, for if any material part of the battle had been fought at this range, the losses certainly would have been much greater. The schooner *Carleton* came to the closest quarters of all, and for at least part of the battle was in advance of the gunboats. Charles Terrot, a British engineer officer, said that the gunboats lay so low in the water that most of the American cannonballs passed over them without causing damage.

Carleton, commanded by Lieutenant James Dacres, managed, some two hours after the action started, to get up within close range and fired briskly for nearly an hour. Then, seriously damaged by the American fire concentrated upon her, she was forced to drop out of the fight, assisted by two of the gunboats. On board was young Edward Pellew, later to make his name as a great admiral in the Napoleonic wars and to become a British peer, now only a midshipman, but a brave one. He exposed himself recklessly while trying to get the *Carleton*'s foresail to fill and so assist her escape. The schooner had two feet of water in her hold and was in a bad way. Dacres was seriously wounded and knocked senseless. His body was about to be thrown overboard when Pellew interposed and so saved another future admiral for the British Navy.

The gunboats continued their fire until late afternoon when they fell back to a distance of nearly half a mile, too far for effective gunnery. At one time during the action Lieutenant Longcroft of the gondola *Loyal Convert,* unable to beat his vessel upwind into the fight, rowed over with some of his crew to the stranded *Royal Savage,* abandoned by her men, and turned her guns on Arnold's fleet. American fire was concentrated on the schooner, and Longcroft was forced to withdraw. At dusk the British returned and set the *Royal Savage* on fire. Her magazine blew up in a splendid explosion, and the hull burned briskly throughout the night. By dark the action was over, and Pringle had formed a line across the westerly part of the lake to prevent an American retreat.

All in all, it had been a rather bloodless battle, and the casualties both in men and vessels were surprisingly small. The American gondola *Philadelphia* sank just before dark, "hulled in so many places," reported Arnold. In recent years this gondola, in amazingly good condition, was raised from the bottom of the lake and is now in the Smithsonian Institution, a unique relic of the Revolution. Examination shows that the hull was penetrated by only a single cannonball, and a rather small one at that, but it was sufficient to cause the craft to sink.

On the British side one gunboat was lost, its magazine exploded by a lucky shot. This particular boat had been manned by a crew of about two dozen, largely Germans, and yet despite the explosion, the casualties were only one killed, one wounded and two badly burned. The gunboat was in charge of Lieutenant Dufais, one of Pausch's officers, and the captain went to his rescue, taking her crew on board his own vessel just before the damaged craft sank. Pausch's gunboat was nearly swamped by the weight of the extra men.

The total British losses were not over forty killed and wounded, and fourteen of these were suffered by the crew of the hard-fought *Carleton*. The Americans lost about sixty in all. When one considers that the action lasted all of five hours, it is rather amazing how little damage was done. But if Hadden's statement of the range during the battle being about seven hundred yards is correct, this would easily explain the relatively ineffective fire. Accuracy at such a range was almost impossible to obtain with the smooth-bore cannon of those days. It was nearly the extreme range at which cannon would then have been fired, and a range of not over some two hundred yards was sought when accuracy was desired — and that from a stable platform on dry land against a fixed target.

The American casualties were something less than ten per cent of the force engaged. For a land battle this would have been considered high, but it would not have been for a hard-fought naval engagement when ships met in close action. John Paul Jones lost a little less than half his crew in his famous action with the *Serapis,* and in our War of 1812, fought with similar weapons, Perry had more than half his crew on the *Lawrence* out of action before he shifted his flag to another vessel. *Carleton,* alone of the British ships, came to close grips with the American battle line, and her casualties were nearly half of the crew, about what would be expected in a desperately fought close-range encounter. In addition to naval gunfire, the Americans were peppered by musket fire from Indians on both the island and the New York shore, but this did little if any harm. Arnold reported that he personally had pointed most of the guns fired from the galley *Congress* that day, and one might infer that he was not a very good shot with a cannon.

By dark three-quarters of the American ammunition was gone and many of the vessels were badly battered, Arnold later reported. A conference of captains advised a retreat during the night. One by one the vessels worked their way south, hugging close to the New York shore, with all lights extinguished save a carefully screened guiding lantern in each boat's stern. The record does not tell us whether there was sufficient wind or whether they had to row with muffled oars, but by daylight the wind had died away to nothing.

When one considers the great preponderance of the British fleet over that of the Americans, this was an inconclusive fight. One would have expected a greater British success. Inability to bring his major ships to action was one reason for Pringle's failing to gain an overwhelming victory this day. Another was Arnold's correct reasoning of what would happen and to his happy choice of position. The unweatherliness of the radeau, and to a lesser extent of the gondola *Loyal Convert* can be understood, but since *Carleton* got up into the thick of the fight, it is hard to account for the failure of the *Inflexible* and *Maria* to do the same. Months after the battle Lieutenant John Schank, commander of *Inflexible* and the inventor of the centerboard, and the captains of *Maria* and *Loyal Convert* wrote a scathing letter to Pringle, stating that he had made a most unfair report of the battle, accusing him of handling the attack very badly and even hinting at personal cowardice. They wrote that the reason the American fleet escaped the night after the battle was because Pringle so arranged his line of blockade that there was a gap of a mile between its western extremity and the New York shore. They also stated that he knew of the disposition of Arnold's fleet the night before the battle. Despite its bitterness the letter apparently did not result in any trouble for either Pringle or Schank from the Admiralty, and both men had successful careers and died admirals. It is rather remarkable that the battle of Valcour Island, so petty an engagement when measured by the standards of the British Navy, should have had four future admirals among its officers.

All that night and the next morning the battered American fleet struggled southward, stopping awhile at Schuyler's Island, some eight or more miles south of Valcour. Here two damaged gondolas were sunk, and many leaks repaired, while Arnold wrote his report of the previous day's engagement. Then they struggled on up the lake under oars and torn canvas. At first there was a fresh wind, but that died away by nightfall, and the exhausted crews toiled all night at the oars, seeking to put additional miles of safety between themselves and the pursuing British.

When dawn broke on the morning of 12 October, Carleton realized that the Americans had escaped, and he at once set off in chase, but the wind soon turned against him. Moreover, the army was still at Cumberland Head, and it was advisable to move it farther south before the fleet continued its pursuit of Arnold's fleeing vessels. Lieutenant John Enys was on board the radeau, and in his journal he told how that huge, unwieldy craft ran into trouble that morning. While trying to work her way upwind, her lee boards broke, her head fell off, and the wind, coming abeam, heeled her over so that, despite her great width, water poured in her lower gun ports. This was her only venture as a fighting ship, and her future was to be that of a transporter of supplies.

It was in vain that Arnold's battered fleet struggled south, for on the morning of 13 October the rising sun shone on the sails of the advancing fleet of the enemy. The chase continued, the *Inflexible* and the two schooners far outdistancing Carleton's other vessels. By noon these three were close enough for the action to begin, and it did not last very long, perhaps some two hours at most. The galley *Washington*, commanded by General Waterbury, who had supervised her building, somehow lagged behind the other American vessels, came under the guns of all three of the British warships, and was forced to surrender. Arnold ran the galley *Congress* and five gondolas on to the Vermont shore, and set them on fire, retreating overland to Crown Point with his crews. Only a row galley, the sloop *Enterprise,* the schooner *Revenge,* and one gondola out of Arnold's fleet of fifteen escaped south to safety at Ticonderoga. All the rest were burned, sunk, or captured. In this last battle the Americans lost perhaps another twenty men, while the British did not suffer a single casualty.

And so the American fleet was utterly routed and driven from the waters of Lake Champlain. Yet it had already achieved a most notable victory, and gained the struggling United States another year of life. For its mere existence had presented to the British a threat too great to be risked. Carleton could not hazard an advance over Lake Champlain, the only route to the south and to Albany, until he had assembled a fleet sufficient in size to neutralize, at the very least, Arnold's motley warships. Meanwhile the American naval power was not remaining static, but was steadily increasing as more ships were launched and equipped. The delay entailed by the building of these two fleets was so great that when battle was ultimately joined it would not matter who won, for the season was so far advanced that the British, even if victorious, could do nothing but retire to winter quarters in Canada.

Valcour has always been considered one of our country's

decisive battles, but incorrectly so, I believe, for this really is true only if we realize that the building of the fleet was far more important than the actual fight itself. Although the battle was lost, and our fleet was destroyed, the main objective actually had been achieved before the battle was fought. The British advance was stalled, and many months of respite had been gained for the struggling American states. And so the battle really was unnecessary, for it had in effect been already fought and won by the men who sweated and sickened at the malaria-ridden Skenesboro shipyard as they launched their crude and makeshift craft into the waters of the lake.

TWELVE

The Fort Awaits Assault

WHILE ARNOLD'S FLEET was cruising the northern waters of the lake, finally taking station at Valcour Island, preparations to receive the enemy were continued at the fort. The White House at Pointe au Fer had been burned in late June and its troops withdrawn, but an outpost, occupied by some of Warner's regiment of Green Mountain Boys, on the Onion River, near today's Burlington, Vermont, was held until the end of September, when the garrison mutinied and marched south, leaving its officers no other course but to follow. A fortnight later a court-martial cashiered the unfortunate officers.

Scouting parties were sent out from time to time to report on the actions of the enemy, while the fleet maintained its screen and made such observations of enemy movements as it could. Work continued on the defenses at Ticonderoga, largely on the western shore, where redoubts were built to reinforce the old French fort. According to one who was there, however, everything went with shameful slowness.

On 11 October the sound of violent cannonading to the north caused great excitement at Ticonderoga, but it was not until noon two days later that the result of the battle was known. The enemy was now expected at any moment and activity redoubled. Work was pushed on an abatis of sharpened treetops. Dr. Lewis Beebe recorded in his journal that the approach of the British reanimated all and put new life and vigor into the entire garrison. On the night of 16 October an unfortunate ox discovered this new vigilance when, failing to answer a challenge, it was promptly slain by the simultaneous shots of half a dozen sentries. A week later all the troops were issued a quarter-pound of buckshot apiece to supplement their regular ball cartridges. Another defensive measure was the provision of twelve-foot-long spears for use in defending the breastworks — an anachronism perhaps, but more effective than bayoneted muskets in such a situation.

Within little over a week after the Valcour fight some of Carleton's Indians were prowling around the sawmill and the portage, killing or capturing an occasional straying American. The main army was slower in its advance; although the British now had entire command of Champlain, it took time to row the soldiers' bateaux on up the lake.

And so it was not until nearly the end of October that Carleton had his troops assembled at Crown Point, awaiting reconnaissance of the defenses of Ticonderoga. On 28 October enemy vessels came within sight of the fort, after landing British and Hessian regulars some three miles north of the narrows. The ships were taken under fire by the more northern works of the defenders, but no damage was done and by nightfall the enemy had retired.

That was the limit of the British advance for this year of 1776, and soon it was learned that Carleton had started to move back toward winter quarters in Canada. He had been forced to the conclusion that the fort could be captured only through formal siege and he knew that the rapidly approaching Adirondack winter made such an undertaking quite out of the question. By 4 November, Crown Point was abandoned. There was one last alarm early in December, when a ship was sighted heading for Ticonderoga. As it came closer all were alerted for battle, cannon hurriedly loaded, muskets freshly primed and slow matches lighted. Then it was seen that the vessel was only a bateau from Onion River with sails made of three blankets and a bed tick, come to sell potatoes and corn to the garrison!

On 17 November, General Gates learned from a flag of truce, who was returning after delivering to Carleton a note (which was received with utter contempt and burned unread), that the British fleet had been laid up and that the army had gone into winter quarters. Before the end of the month the lake had frozen solidly for several miles north of the narrows, sure sign that no major thrust could be made against the fort before spring. The evacuation of the major portion of the garrison started at once. Gates selected as the winter commander of the fort Colonel Anthony Wayne of Pennsylvania — "Mad Anthony," he would later be called. The general wrote Congress that Wayne had "health and strength fit to encounter the inclemency of that cold, inhospitable region."

The troops that were left at the fort bedded themselves down for the winter, determined to make themselves as comfortable as possible in the old stone barracks and the surrounding huts. By December there were only some seventeen hundred of them, and it was reported that at least a third were without shoes. This seems a bit hard to believe, for moccasins of a sort could certainly have been extemporized from the hides of slaughtered cattle. There is no question, however, but that food and other essentials were in extremely short supply, and that living conditions were deplorable. Cutting and hauling of firewood must have engaged much of the time of the healthy members of the garrison.

Early in December Wayne wrote: "I paid a visit to the sick yesterday, in a small house, called a hospital. The first object presented my eyes, one man laying dead at the door, the inside two more laying dead, two living lying between them; the living with the dead had so laid for four and twenty hours."

This was a shocking state of affairs, but it was one for which the commanding officer, Wayne himself, was responsible, and it certainly is a reflection upon the kind of discipline maintained. On the other hand, one must remember that a healthy, well-fed garrison and a sick, discouraged and partly starved one offer quite different problems in management. At this same time Wayne reported not a single pair of shoes nor even one blanket was in store. He wrote the Pennsylvania Committee of Safety, "We have neither beds nor bedding for our sick to lay on or under, other than their own clothing; no medicine or regimen suitable for them; the dead & dying laying mingled together in our hospital, or rather house of carnage, is no uncommon sight."

It very possibly was on the same day this was written that Wayne received from Schuyler a letter sent a week or so before, a letter that must have caused the fort's commander to utter caustic and blasphemous remarks. The general said nothing about supplies on the way or of improving the defenses of the place, but he was quite specific in his injunctions as to cleanliness of both men and their quarters, and decreed that barrack chimneys must be swept out every fortnight. He did, however, remind Wayne to keep scouting parties out to the north.

Perhaps it was because of Schuyler's letter that an order was issued three days before Christmas directing that all meat must be boiled and never under any circumstances fried. It was also recommended that dumplings be prepared to thicken the soldier's stew. Tar was to be burned periodically in every tent (tents in December in northern New York!) and barrack room in order to remove and purify the "putrid" air. It is apparent from Wayne's orderly book that some women were wintering at Ticonderoga, washing clothes and perhaps caring for the sick.

Christmas Day was a lively one at the old stone fort in that

year of 1776. Old Colonel Asa Whitcomb of the Massachusetts troops had a son who was a shoemaker before the army
took him from home. The son set up his bench in his father's
quarters and patched up the worn shoes of the soldiers. This
gave offense to some of the officers of the Pennsylvania troops,
who, believing themselves of finer clay, looked down their
noses at the New Englanders. Late that day, Lieutenant
Colonel Craig of Wayne's regiment, his spirits over-elevated
by the day's libations, decided that action was in order. He
burst into Whitcomb's quarters, smashed the cobbler's bench,
and then proceeded to beat the elderly colonel, bruising him
rather badly. The noise at once attracted a crowd, and a near-
riot developed as Pennsylvanian and Yankee came to the aid
of the two principals. The former went so far as to take up
their muskets and fire some two score rounds at the unfortunate New Englanders, several of whom were badly
wounded. Despite Craig's inexcusable assault Wayne took
no action to punish anyone, and the affair ended in a farce
when the Pennsylvanians produced a fat deer and offered
Colonel Whitcomb a feast of venison. The kind old man,
never really cut out to be a soldier, forgave Craig, and that
ended the affair — except for those unlucky Yankees whose
wounds would be weeks in healing.

New England winters unquestionably are harsh but they
nevertheless are interspersed with periods when outdoor work
is both possible and pleasant. Granted that cutting of firewood
must have taken much of the time of the men at Ticonderoga
that winter, it does seem that an energetic and capable commander could have done much to improve the defenses of
the place, even if Schuyler did not order the work. Such
labor, moreover, would have kept idle troops out of mischief.
Posts for stockades could certainly have been cut and prepared, as well as logs for redoubts, while planks could have
been sawed for the little ships that might be built in the

spring. This last was a matter that Schuyler had in mind, for in mid-January of 1777 he sent Captain Frederick Chapple off to salt water to recruit a company of seamen, presumbly for the vessels he planned to build on Lake George when the snows and ice of winter had thawed into April mud.

Even when making full allowance for all the difficulties arising from inclement weather, bitter cold, lack of food and supplies, illness and expiring enlistments, I cannot help but feel that Wayne could have accomplished more. Winters at Ticonderoga really are not too much different from those, say, at Boston or Albany, and that of 1776-1777 was not a particularly cold one. The lake froze across quite early, but that was all to the good, as the weather then ceased to be damp and became a healthy and pleasant dry cold. Dr. James Thatcher, who had been a medical student at Barnstable on Cape Cod at the outbreak of the Revolution, spent that winter at the fort, and his journal reported on 30 January 1777 that it had been mild, with the snow not as deep nor the weather as cold as he had feared. Nevertheless it would not have had to be very cold to make like miserable for scantily clothed men living in tents and crude huts with hardly enough to eat.

Schuyler in Albany was devoting himself to logistical planning and administration, and he was excellent in this field of activity. His directives were carefully prepared, clear and explicit, but there were, to my mind at least, two great points of weakness. Almost all thought or action was devoted to next spring, little or nothing to the present. Boats were to be built, a vegetable garden started at Ticonderoga, this and that to be done, but it was all for the future, not for now. I also cannot but wonder if Schuyler's carefully thought-out orders for securing supplies were followed up to make sure of their execution, or even if they were capable of being met in view of the scarcity of all necessities save perhaps of rum. When one studies Schuyler's letters of this period and examines his actions, one is forced to the belief that while the general undoubtedly was a supply officer of high caliber, nature had never intended him to lead an army. For one thing he was too considerate and too patient.

Enlistments were gradually expiring, and it became increasingly hard to hold the discouraged, homesick men. Late in January of the new year seven hundred reinforcements reached the fort, and this allowed the release of some of the Pennsylvania troops. At this time such fatigue duty as could be carried on was directed to building an abatis around the fort, and to work on two new blockhouses. Despite the arrival of the welcome reinforcements the garrison continued to suffer attrition from one cause or another, and by late February there were less than one thousand effectives. At this period an advance post was being maintained at the "Red House," five miles north of Crown Point, and Schuyler directed that a pair of fast horses be kept there so that prompt warning of an enemy approach could be rushed south. Once the ice broke up they would be of little use, however, since there were no roads along either side of the lake north of Crown Point.

Discontent flared into open mutiny in mid-February, when a company of Pennsylvania riflemen decided that their time was up and that they were going home come hell or high water. Wayne quelled this outbreak with drawn pistol, and the men remained. He also handled another attempt to incite mutiny, in the same spirited way and with equal success.

Winter at last drew to a close, brightened for Wayne by news that he had been made a brigadier general. Toward the end of March, as the ice in Champlain was starting to break up, Ticonderoga was held by only twelve hundred men, both sick and well, one-third of them militia whose enlistments would expire in ten days. The following month Wayne left to join Washington's army, to share the rigors of Valley

Forge, less harsh perhaps than those he had just endured, and to achieve fame at the storming of Stony Point.

On almost the last day of November 1776, Congress had decided upon the construction of a fort on Mount Independence on the Vermont shore. Schuyler was directed to execute the work that winter, but nothing would happen until, in mid-February, Colonel Jeduthan Baldwin was sent north to get the project under way. Work was started the first day of March on a bridge across the lake. Holes were cut in the ice and log crib piers sunk and filled with rocks. There had already been an earlier footbridge across the lake, but this one was much more of an undertaking. The piers were built about fifty feet apart, and chained against them were floating sections consisting of great logs covered with a plank deck, making a roadway twelve feet wide.

General Gates had gone south in mid-November to cultivate the good will of Congress, which, because of Washington's retreat from the lower reaches of the Hudson and on through New Jersey, had quit Philadelphia for the greater safety of Baltimore. At the same time Gates apparently was attempting to undermine Schuyler's standing with that body. Fortune played into his hands, for the Albany aristocrat wrote Congress a letter which gave offense to some of the members, and resulted in a resolution which stung the New Yorker's feelings.

In late March Schuyler set out for Philadelphia, to which city Congress had recently returned, to attempt to clear up what was only a misunderstanding, blown up by his enemies in Congress — the New Englanders — into undue proportions. While on the way he learned that he had apparently been superseded by Gates, and that General St. Clair had been ordered to the command at Ticonderoga. New York at once appointed Schuyler a delegate to Congress, and Pennsylvania put him in charge of military affairs in that state. In this latter capacity, during the course of only a scant two months, he accomplished a much-needed reorganization of the commissary. His request for an inquiry into his conduct was approved by Congress in mid-April, and a committee appointed.

The hearings of this group of congressmen resulted in a complete vindication and the resolution that the Champlain and Mohawk approaches should constitute the Northern Command under Major General Schuyler. Gates, hearing the news upon Schuyler's arrival at Albany, refused to serve under him, and started south to lay his woes before Congress.

Thus Schuyler was once again in command of the northern frontier — and it was he who would be responsible for meeting the British advance in 1777. We have, however, gotten a little ahead of our story, and it would seem best to go back a few months and pick up a few threads hitherto not examined.

THIRTEEN

A New Year Opens

THE HUDSON RIVER formed not only the southern portion of that great north-south throughway that was the only practical route from Canada to the American colonies, but also acted as an effective barrier between New England, where the spirit of rebellion was rampant, and the middle colonies, where Tories were much more in evidence. This was particularly so in the New York province, where at least half of the population favored the King. Since there were no bridges over the river, armed vessels patrolling its length could easily prevent transit either along it or across it, at least of a force of any size.

In the summer of 1776, Fort Washington had been built to close the lower Hudson. It stood near the New York end of today's George Washington Bridge, and Fort Lee supported it from the Jersey shore. In mid-November the British in a spirited attack seized Fort Washington, and its companion fort was promptly evacuated.

Near Bear Mountain great cliffs border the river and form the Hudson Highlands, and here in the fall of the same year work was started on Fort Montgomery on the western shore. By early November the works were well under way and they were further strengthened by a nearby redoubt named Fort Clinton. Thus, although Fort Washington and Fort Lee had fallen to the British, by the start of the year 1777 the great

Hudson Valley was guarded by Fort Montgomery at the south and Fort Ticonderoga to the north. West Point was yet to be built, but work would soon start on Fort Constitution just across the river. For the moment General Howe had no interest in sailing up the Hudson toward Albany and testing the mettle of Fort Montgomery, and it would not be until Burgoyne was in trouble near Saratoga that such a move would be attempted.

The British plans for the campaign of 1777 were for General Burgoyne — "Gentleman Johnny," some called him, a sound and experienced but pleasure-loving officer who had replaced Governor Carleton as commander of the invading army — to advance south up the Champlain Valley and on to the Hudson. Meanwhile Lieutenant Colonel Barry St. Leger, with a mixed force of regulars, Indians and Tories, was to lead a diversion down the Mohawk Valley from the west. Burgoyne was expected to reach Albany without any particular trouble, and he was then to cooperate with General Howe, commander of the main British army in New York, as the latter should direct.

There has long been a pretty story about Lord George Germain. Lord Sackville he had been when at Minden in the Seven Years War he disobeyed orders, possibly through cowardice, but more probably through pique, and was cashiered by court-martial, condemned never again to hold the King's commission. But memories are short and the power of political families was great and now he was Secretary of State for the colonies, the cabinet officer most directly concerned with the conduct of the British armies attempting to quell the Revolution. The tale was that in this campaign Germain had planned for Howe to move up the Hudson toward a junction with Burgoyne as the latter approached Albany. Orders for Burgoyne and Carleton had been prepared, the story went, but those for Howe were not yet finished when

Germain went to his office just before starting on a long British weekend in the country. Not wishing to waste a minute of his time, the cabinet officer signed the two orders that were ready, but those for Howe were left unfinished, unsigned, and unsent. Thus Howe remained in ignorance of the fact that he was supposed to advance to Albany and join Burgoyne there. The truth is that it apparently was never intended that Howe should move up the Hudson, that Burgoyne was entirely confident of reaching and holding Albany without assistance, and that Howe was sent and duly received a copy of the instructions sent the commander of the invading army. And so it is not at all fair to say, as many have, that Germain's hurry to get out of town that day was responsible in the final analysis for the surrender at Saratoga.

Burgoyne's occupation of Albany and Britain's continued hold on New York City would divide the colonies quite effectively, as only the forts at the Highlands would then prevent free access between the two cities. The forts could be captured if and when the time came, so it was hardly necessary for British planning to advance much if any beyond the proposed seizure of Albany. Further developments could be met as they occurred. The immediate objective for the campaign of 1777 was the overcoming of the defenses of the colonials at the narrows of Lake Champlain.

The American failure to hold Burgoyne or at least delay him at Ticonderoga in 1777 has always seemed difficult to explain, since Carleton had been effectively blocked the year before. But that had been largely due to the threat of Arnold's navy, and this year the Americans had only a few survivors of the Valcour fight. No attempts were made to put an effective naval force on the lake, and the reinforcements and supplies sent to the fort were on the scanty side. Journals kept at Ticonderoga that spring seem to indicate somewhat leisurely attempts at improving the defenses, and the exertions of the previous fall were apparently lacking. The reason behind this undoubtedly was the fact that nobody believed that a real attack on the fort would be forthcoming this year, and that Burgoyne's threat from the north was merely a feint to draw American troops away from farther south, thus allowing General Howe to take more decisive and less hindered action.

On 12 March George Washington wrote Schuyler that he believed that the British would bring most or all of their troops from Canada around by water to reinforce the army in the New Jersey and New York City areas, and that their naval command of Lake Champlain gave them complete confidence in their security against any possible American attempt on Canada. Washington then went on to say that accordingly he believed that "much too large a part of our force is directed to Ticonderoga," and that "I cannot help thinking [it] is against all probability" that the British should "attempt to penetrate the country by way of the lakes" so that a large force at Ticonderoga "wou'd be an useless body of troops . . . [which] the service here [in the Jersey region] might suffer an irreparable injury for want of."

Washington had ordered all the Massachusetts Continentals to Ticonderoga, but on 13 March he wrote the legislature of that state that he believed that the British would not attack the fort and that he was at once sending a major part of these troops to the lower Hudson instead. The forts at the Highlands as yet were far from strong, and a raid by the British on Peekskill made late in March led to fear that they might be about to make a serious attempt at opening the Hudson, and consequently cutting off Ticonderoga's line of supply by ascending the river to Albany.

Ticonderoga, large as it loomed in the thoughts of its defenders, was only one of many places for which General Washington must provide the defense. Fortunately for the student of history the general's orders and letters clearly reveal his constantly varying thoughts that spring of 1777.

By the end of March British actions made Washington continue to fear an attack on the forts on the Hudson, which if successful, would force the evacuation of Ticonderoga for want of provisions and munitions.

Two weeks later in mid-April he still was worrying about the chance of the British cutting off Ticonderoga's line of supply. The rest of the month produced no alarms or change of thoughts, but early in May reports arrived that the British were on Lake Champlain. These were soon shown to be false, and Anthony Wayne had cheerfully written from Ticonderoga that all was well and that "the post could never be carried, without much loss of blood."

Washington had now come around to the belief that Howe would assault the Hudson defenses, rather than move against Philadelphia, and he sent reinforcements to Peekskill. Soon he was practically convinced of an attack northward, but by the end of May had thought better of it and was anticipating a move south to the Delaware. Before long he felt certain of it. Early in June, he learned that British forces which had been on Lake Champlain at Split Rock near today's Essex, New York, had returned toward Canada, and he felt that the alarm of a British move against Ticonderoga was groundless. On 16 June, Washington wrote Schuyler that he remained strong in his belief that the Canadian troops were being moved by water around to New York to reinforce Howe. Nevertheless he ordered that four regiments should be held at Peekskill, alerted for a prompt move to Ticonderoga, if it should prove necessary. He had by this time received Schuyler's letter giving information secured from a prisoner named Amsbury, information which later proved to be amazingly correct. St. Clair at Ticonderoga was confident that this man was a spy, sent to spread false information, and the commander-in-chief, even if he did not accept this view, felt that the plans outlined by Amsbury were entirely beyond the capabilities of the British. Moreover, he believed that the garrison then at Ticonderoga was sufficient to hold it against an attack.

Congress evidently shared Washington's beliefs, for at St. Clair's court-martial in 1778 General Poor testified that General Gates had "had the strongest assurances from Congress that the King's troops were all ordered round to New York [from Canada]." This was early in June while Gates was still in command.

By now mid-June had been reached, and by hindsight we know that unless reinforcements and supplies were sent to the north within a day or two, they would have arrived too late. Under the best of conditions it would have taken practically a week to move the first of the provisions from Albany to Ticonderoga, and then several days more for a good supply to accumulate. This, moreover, assumes an ample supply of bateaux and ox teams, a situation that almost certainly did not exist. Actually it probably did take considerably longer than a week for supplies to reach the fort. Schuyler ordered some sent on 6 June, but did not expect them to arrive at Ticonderoga for over two weeks. Soldiers could have been forwarded a little, but not much, faster. And so this critical date passed with Washington confident that there were sufficient men and supplies at the northern post to foil anything the British might do on Lake Champlain. By the first day of July he had come around to the belief that Ticonderoga would be attacked, but still felt that there was a possibility that the British "fleet and a small force of Indians and light troops . . . were amusing us." He now, instead of a move against Philadelphia, expected one against the Hudson forts, a return to his earlier thinking.

Washington's mind had been in a state of confusion that

spring of 1777 when his headquarters were in Morristown. Would Howe move south against Philadelphia? By land or by sea? Or would he move north against the forts at the Hudson Highlands? A decision as to the enemy's intentions here in the New York region was difficult enough, but what about the British forces in Canada? Until almost the fall of Ticonderoga, Washington was convinced that there would be no real attack up Champlain from Canada, and he believed that the forces at the fort could easily defeat any attempt that the British would be able to make. This belief was passed on down to his subordinates. They for their part were only too willing to accept it, developed too much of a spirit of complacency and failed to reach out for enemy intelligence, fighting to get it if necessary, since intelligence often can be obtained only in that way. Furthermore, so imbued were they with confidence in the correctness of Washington's belief that they entirely refused to believe or to give any weight whatsoever to contrary evidence. Thus Washington was, in effect, constantly reassured by his subordinates in the north that all was well on that frontier. And so, with everything confirming his own conclusions, he was able to devote himself to the more imminent problem of what Howe was going to do. Ticonderoga was left with an insufficient garrison and was still short of essential supplies. Moreover, those in command had really adopted a defeatist attitude, despite their brave words.

And so the campaign of 1777 opened with everyone confident that Ticonderoga would not suffer any serious attack, men and supplies were diverted elsewhere, and improvement of the fort's defenses continued at but a leisurely rate. More attention was devoted to building the great floating bridge than to improving and adding to the more essential redoubts and earthworks. Actually, the defenses, instead of benefiting from fatigue work during the course of the winter, had deteriorated, particularly on the Vermont shore, where the abatis had been burned for firewood, and now would have to be entirely replaced. The scanty survivors of the Valcour battlefleet had received no additions and, confined in rear of the new bridge into the narrow waters of the lake, they would be unable to maneuver, and could be utilized only as floating batteries anchored in place to await destruction from the heavy guns of the British fleet. The great bastion of the northern frontier was in desperate shape.

Colonel Baldwin's daily journal for late winter and spring of 1777 shows no sense of urgency or need for haste. He was prompt in his return trip to Ticonderoga, taking about a week for the difficult winter journey from his home in Brookfield, near Worcester, Massachusetts, although he spent several days at Albany while on the way. Soon after his arrival at the fort he tried to persuade Wayne to get some of his men at work sawing out boards and cutting timber for the great new bridge to which project the engineer officer seems to have devoted almost all his time for the next fortnight. Then he drew up plans for a new hospital, and at last in the middle of March started planning the fort on the Vermont shore that Congress, long before winter had locked Ticonderoga in ice and snow, had ordered built. Undoubtedly Baldwin was badly handicapped by lack of men, but there is nothing in his journal to show that he felt any need for haste or any worry over the slow progress achieved. He was a good man, and apparently a reasonably competent engineer officer, but he certainly lacked the drive of an Arnold, a Sheridan or a Patton. It was not until the first of April that plans for the proposed fort on the Mount at last went off to Schuyler in Albany for approval.

While our story is that of the old French fortress of Carillon at Ticonderoga, we must not lose sight of the other events of the Revolution. The Champlain Valley was only one of several places where the war was being fought. The capture of Fort Washington on the upper end of Manhattan Island in mid-November of 1776 had been followed by the retreat of the main American army into New Jersey, closely followed by the British. A small force had been left at Peekskill under General Heath as a cover for the Hudson Highlands.

Conditions became well-nigh desperate for the American cause as the year of 1776 drew to an end. Washington's army was fast wasting away through sickness, desertions and expiration of enlistments. Food and clothing were scarce and morale was approaching its lowest ebb. It is true that Carleton's invasion from the north had stalled in front of Ticonderoga and recoiled back into Canada, but the enemy held New York City and much of New Jersey, and could occupy Philadelphia at will, outnumbering Washington's unhappy army by more than two to one. Newport, then a place of much greater importance than today, was also in British hands and constituted a threat to New England. On 12 December Congress fled Philadelphia for the greater safety of Baltimore, but a day later General Howe decided to suspend operations for the year and to retire into winter quarters. It was a grave question whether there would be any American army left by spring.

Then on the night of Christmas Day in a blinding storm, half rain, half sleet, Washington crossed the Delaware and overwhelmed the German troops garrisoning Trenton. He followed up this startling victory eight days later by defeating the British force in Princeton and driving it headlong in retreat. The enemy now abandoned all of New Jersey save for Amboy and New Brunswick, while Washington fell back into the hill country at Morristown to wait the coming of spring. The long campaign of 1776, which had commenced with the British evacuation of Boston, at last was over. Washington's prestige, which had sadly declined after the Battle of Long Island and the loss of Fort Washington, rebounded to a new high through Trenton and Princeton, and Congress gave him practically a free hand as the military commander-in-chief.

When spring at last brought dry roads to New Jersey, the two armies shadow-boxed for a few weeks without material result. By the end of June, however, the British had pulled all their troops into the close vicinity of New York City, abandoning all of Jersey. It was obvious that some new move was afoot. What would it be? A move up the Hudson toward Albany? Possible but most unlikely, thought Washington. He had learned of Burgoyne's return to Canada and was practically convinced that part, at least, of the troops in Canada would sail down the St. Lawrence and on around by water to reinforce Howe in New York. Then, he feared, a descent would be made on Philadelphia.

In the first week of June Major General Arthur St. Clair had been ordered north to take over command at Ticonderoga from the newly promoted General Wayne. St. Clair was a former British regular officer who had seen much service in the last French war before resigning to seek his fortune on this side of the Atlantic. He at least partially achieved this through marriage with a niece of James Bowdoin of Massachusetts, a lady who brought him a fortune of fourteen thousand pounds, a great sum in those simpler days. He invested in western Pennsylvania lands and was a prominent citizen of those parts when the Revolution broke out, and he again took up his sword, this time against his king. St. Clair was directed to concentrate a major part of his forces on Mount Independence, and Schuyler furthermore gave him careful instructions for maintaining the health of his troops, including making certain that their food was properly cooked.

Schuyler believed that three thousand men could hold Mount Independence, while the navy on Lake George would be able to block that avenue of advance even if the old French fort on the New York side should be lost. Then, if the British invested the Mount, as it was usually called, the militia could be called out to march to its relief.

Unfortunately, there was no Lake George navy. Schuyler had planned to build row galleys on that lake, and a 14-gun schooner had actually been launched in June, but there were not guns and rigging to equip her completely. A second smaller schooner, almost certainly unarmed, was in commission and two other craft were still on the stocks. Even if these last could be hurried into the lake, there was no equipment to complete them. Thus the Lake George navy upon which Schuyler was depending to cover the western passage from Champlain to the Hudson never came into existence, save in his plans and hopes.

Baldwin's journal for the spring of 1777 contains almost as much about dining, wining and tea-drinking with the wives of some of the officers and local inhabitants as it does about more serious matters, but on 6 June he notes the arrival of Kosciuszko, the Polish engineer officer, and on the twelfth General St. Clair reached the post. The new commander must have been somewhat unhappy over the conditions that he found. Only a fortnight before, Lieutenant Colonel James Wilkinson wrote General Gates that no dispositions had been made for defense against an attack and no alarm posts assigned. Quite an indictment of Mad Anthony as a commander! But Wilkinson was a toady and an intriguer, so perhaps his accusations lacked justification. A particular protégé of Gates, he would a few months later be promoted brigadier general by Congress for bringing the most welcome news of Saratoga, although he slowed his trip considerably by stopping for two or three days while on the way in order to visit his fiancée. One sharp-tongued congressman had suggested that perhaps a pair of spurs would have been a more suitable reward than the brigadier's star. But this is a digression, and we must return to Ticonderoga, where on the same day that Wilkinson wrote his letter a gale broke both the new bridge and the great log boom just north of it, just as a scouting party returned, chased away by the enemy before they had learned anything of value.

American information about the enemy was most faulty this spring, particularly as to what was brewing north of the Canadian border. The British counter-reconnaissance screen was effective, and little information passed to the south. Their fleet closed the waters of the lake, while Indians prowled the woods. By mid-June these redskin allies hovered around Ticonderoga, making an occasional kill of a straying colonial. At this time a prisoner was brought in who reported that the enemy was ten thousand in number and would attack the fort in force, at the same time sending an expedition driving up the Mohawk Valley, and all this before the end of the month. The minds of the Americans were closed, blissfully trusting in the belief of a feint, and it was decided that the prisoner was really an enemy agent, sent to spread false information.

A few days later the report of a scout seeped back from Willsboro, some forty miles north of the fort, that a great body of men had landed there, but St. Clair refused to believe it. Only when Burgoyne's army had actually invested the fort would it be appreciated that this really was a major assault. Nevertheless there was a slight realization that the feint theory might after all possibly be wrong, and should it prove so it was planned to hold the old French fort for as long as possible and then to fall back on to Mount Independence, there to continue the fight. All this, however, was really

KEY

A   Old fort in very bad condition, wanting repair; could not be defended with less than 500 men.

B   Stone redoubt, about 200 men would defend it, overlooks the line Y, opposite the Lake, in Fort Independence.

C   Blockhouse for 100 men.

D   French redoubt upon the low ground for about 200 men, commanded by the opposite side.

E   New breastwork for 200 men.

F   New fleche for 100 men.

G   New redoubt for 150 men.

H   New redoubt for 100 men.

I   Redoubt upon the low ground for 250 men, commanded by the opposite side.

K   Jersey redoubt upon the low ground for 300 men, commanded by the opposite side.

L   Redoubt upon the low ground for 100 men.

M   Redoubt upon the low ground for 100 men.

N   French lines upon the high ground, overlooks all the works on Ticonderoga side, for 2000 men, and not less, considering the great length and importance of the place.

O P Q R   New works, in addition to the French lines.

S   High ground, occupied by the enemy, and overlooks the French lines.

T   Mount Hope, overlooks ground S, occupied by the enemy.

U   Blockhouse, burnt by the enemy.

V V   High hill, overlooks Ticonderoga and Mount Independence.

X   The bridge.

MOUNT INDEPENDENCE

Y   Line upon the low ground, commanded by the opposite side B, for 800 men.

Z   Barbet battery.

2   Line only marked upon the ground.

3   Picket fort for 600 men.

4   Blockhouse for 100 men.

5-6   Line, with three new made batteries, for 1500 men, and not less.

7   Blockhouse for 100 men.

8   Battery made by the enemy.

9   Road made by the enemy to cut off the communication from Mount Independence to Skenesboro.

Scale of a Mile
of 60 to a Mile

only in the land of dreams, and, if any detailed dispositions had been planned for a defense of the fort, no attempt was ever made to implement them. In view of what little evidence we have it seems that no plans were ever made for any real attempt at resisting a British advance.

The end of June, then, saw an American force of about twenty-five hundred men attempting to hold works on two sides of the lake which required at least four times that many. The old stone fort itself could only hold a garrison of some four hundred and could quickly be battered into submission by Burgoyne's heavy cannon. The French lines, now a series of trenches following the trace of the great log wall against which Abercromby's men had dashed in vain, offered a good defense if properly manned. But they were over six hundred yards long and to be effective would require more than the entire force available for use on both sides of the lake.

There were, moreover, on the New York side several redoubts and water batteries, as well as the outworks on Mount Hope Hill which covered the road to Lake George. The picketed fort on top of Mount Independence was intended to hold one thousand men, while the various blockhouses, batteries and trenches on that height of land required many more. Early in June St. Clair had been ordered to concentrate on Mount Independence, but it does not appear that he made any real attempt to obey these directions. It was most obvious that Ticonderoga could not hold out against a determined attack. All that could be hoped for would be to delay the enemy for as long as possible.

On 19 June General Schuyler reached the fort, and next day he held a council of war with the general officers, St. Clair, Poor, Patterson and the worthless French adventurer Roche de Fermoy. The council decided (1) that both sides of the lake could not be held with the forces available, but that it should be attempted if possible; (2) that the New York side should be the first to be abandoned, and that all cannon and stores not essentially needed should at once be transported across to the Vermont shore; (3) that the Vermont defenses were insufficient and should be improved, as should the obstructions placed in the lake; (4) that it would take at least six weeks to do all this; and finally (5) that it was prudent to provide for a retreat, and steps should be taken to do this. While it is barely conceivable that it was the intent of the council to do all possible to provide for the making of a vigorous defense on the Vermont shore at least, to my mind what their various resolutions really meant was that they had decided upon retreat, a decision clothed in ifs and whens and other such qualifying words and phrases, but an admission, none the less, that retreat was inevitable. In this they were entirely right, barring a sudden and quite impossible influx of many more troops and supplies, and they could, when facing the actual facts, have arrived at no other decision. What was lacking, however, was a determination to fight, and to delay the enemy and make him fight hard before a retreat from the Mount could be forced on the defending troops. The abject and shameful surrender of Fort Ticonderoga a fortnight later was the direct result of this weak and equivocal decision of Schuyler's council.

FOURTEEN

The Last Surrender

GENERAL JOHN BURGOYNE was a professional soldier of experience and ability, yet at the same time a member of Parliament, a courtier and a man about town. Later in life he would write plays, one or two of which were quite successful. He was one of three generals sent to Boston in 1775 to assist General Gage, and he witnessed the Battle of Bunker Hill, although he took no active part. Burgoyne returned to England early that winter and next year, 1776, he was sent to Canada as second in command to Governor Guy Carleton in the latter's attempt to drive the invading Americans from Canada and pursue them to the south.

The arrival of British reinforcements in Canada, greatly assisted by the ravages of smallpox in the American army, quickly achieved the first of these objectives, but, as we have already seen, the failure to secure naval control of Lake Champlain stalled further British advance and the army retired to winter quarters in Canada. Burgoyne then returned to England, matured his thoughts on the American campaign and presented the King with a plan for a new invasion from the north. The result was that he was put in command of the 1777 expedition. It has been said that while in England he had endeavored to supplant Carleton in the command, but this does not seem correct, nor was it necessary, for in August of 1776 orders were sent the Canadian governor —

orders he did not receive until the following spring — to restrict his active command to Canada.

Early in May, Burgoyne returned to America, and his dilatory nature was soon made evident, for it was not until a full month later that he requisitioned the carts and horses needed to haul his guns and supplies across the land carries he must pass. Moreover he did this only when his artillery officer, the competent General Phillips, reminded him of the omission. Thus a month was already lost, a month that might well have allowed the expedition to reach Albany. Whatever were his other capabilities, and they were numerous, Burgoyne lacked drive.

The plan the general had offered the War Office for an advance from Canada had called for 8000 regular troops plus artillery, 2000 Canadians and 1000 Indians, over 11,000 men in all. When the expedition at last assembled at Cumberland Head on 20 June, it numbered but 7213, mostly regulars, 3724 of these British and 3016 German troops, while the Canadians were represented by less than a tenth of the number originally required.

Although Burgoyne had failed to think of the overland haulage of his artillery until reminded of the omission, he planned to carry a great train of cannon along with his army. After the surrender at Saratoga he was severely criticized for providing so much artillery. In this, however, he was entirely right. Only through the battering down of its walls could one expect to seize a well-defended fortress in those days. Stockaded forts protected only by palisades of logs could be overcome by relatively light guns, but a masonry structure such as Ticonderoga and its earthen outworks and redoubts required much heavier weapons: 18- and 24-pounder guns and great mortars up to 13 inches in bore. The artillery train consisted of 128 cannon in all.

The uniforms the troops had worn the year before were in

bad shape, and no replacements had come from home. Now, partly in order to secure patching material, but also because it was appreciated that a short jacket would be more suitable in the woods, the tails of the uniform coats were cut off. At the same time the three-cornered felt hats were trimmed down into caps probably much like those already worn by the light infantry, and tufts of colored hair designated the various regiments and lent a jaunty touch. Some British soldiers got into difficulties with the habitants when caught cutting off the tips of the tails of Canadian cows in order to secure white hair that would take a brightly colored dye effectively. Many, eventually all, of the German troops were issued long overalls striped blue and white, probably not unlike modern bed ticking. They apparently had buttons on the legs which in effect made them both breeches and leggings in a single piece of apparel. Even the horseless dragoons were given these, and let us hope that their huge, clumsy boots were then replaced by some lighter form of footgear. Each British soldier carried a knapsack, blanket, haversack of provisions, canteen, hatchet, one fifth of the equipage for a tent, a musket and sixty rounds. The total weight was about sixty pounds.

A new frigate, the *Royal George,* this year had been added to the 1776 fleet, but most or all the other vessels, save the *Invincible,* had been disarmed and were used as transports. The five American survivors of the Valcour fight, safely ensconced behind the bridge at Ticonderoga, presented no threat to the British possession of the waters of Lake Champlain. The enemy moved south by water, but it was planned that the herd of fifteen hundred horses would go overland through the woods to Crown Point. How would the five hundred two-wheeled carts move south? Horses could be led through forest paths, but carts required construction of a road. Eventually both horses and carts reached the southern end of

Champlain, but we do not know by what means the latter got there.

Burgoyne's army reached Crown Point late in June and on the thirtieth of that month advanced elements were only four miles from Ticonderoga; British troops on the west shore of the lake, Germans on the east. Next day Indians were prowling all around the outskirts of the fort, and the two frigates had moved up almost within gunshot of the narrows.

At this time, when only Indians were in contact with the fort's defenses, and while it was still believed that no real attack was coming, St. Clair ordered the abandonment of the Lake George landing, after removal of such stores as could be gotten away, and the destruction of the defenses at that place. The signal for setting the torch would be smoke from the burning sawmills at the lower falls on the creek flowing from Lake George into Champlain. This latter destruction was decreed the next day, 2 July, and all the American defensive works, provisions and watercraft on Lake George and the creek went up in flames. The little garrison on Mount Hope fell back to the old French lines, thus abandoning to the British all access to Lake George and possible retreat by that route of escape. The enemy promptly moved in, occupied the deserted outpost on Mount Hope and brought up light artillery. They soon extended their lines down to the sawmills, where the bridge over the creek had been burned by the retreating Americans. Although cannon fire from the fort's outworks forced a British withdrawal from the mills to a somewhat less exposed position, the investment of Ticonderoga was complete. Only Mount Independence was as yet left unassailed.

On this day, the second, British skirmishers approached the French lines, now held by a considerable force of colonists. General St. Clair ordered the Americans to hold their fire and to make certain that they complied he directed them to sit down in their trenches with their backs to the enemy, and to remain so until further orders. Wilkinson, who tells the story in his memoirs, noticed a Britisher skulking behind a stump just a good musket shot away. He pointed the man out to a sergeant, whom he told to try a shot. The sergeant fired one shot, the man dropped, and every soul in the American trenches jumped to his feet and started firing at nothing as rapidly as he could pull trigger and reload. The artillery joined in, and at least three volleys of musketry and cannon fire ripped out before the men could be controlled. The British scampered away apparently unhurt. A party was sent out to bring in for burial the man the sergeant had knocked down, but as soon as it approached the redcoat jumped to his feet untouched. Wilkinson remarked that there were some five hundred British along the front, and that about a thousand Americans and eight cannon opened fire. No one was killed and only one British lieutenant wounded! Such was the discipline and marksmanship of the fort's defenders.

Up until this time St. Clair had persisted in his wishful thinking that the British were only feinting with a small force, screened by many Indians, but the prisoner taken in this ridiculous affair at last disillusioned him. This man, a sulky Irishman, at first refused to talk. He was put in a cell, and a compatriot, an American officer disguised as another prisoner, was introduced, along with a flask of rum. The man soon talked, revealing what St. Clair should have grasped much earlier, that the British were really in force.

By 3 July, Burgoyne's men had moved up more closely to surround the place, but little action occurred, although the Americans delivered a vigorous artillery fire on their abandoned post on Mount Hope and on any exposed enemy troops that they could see. The next day, the first anniversary of the birth of our country, the great radeau at last arrived and started unloading the heavy siege artillery. Engineer

Twiss, who was still only a lieutenant at thirty-two, but who would live to command the Royal Engineers and die fifty years later a full general, was sent on 5 July to look over Mount Defiance, also sometimes called Sugar Loaf. British forces had already occupied the mountain, probably around noon of the previous day. Twiss reported that cannon could be gotten up to the top and that they would be able to fire effectively on both the old French fort and the works on the Vermont shore. The range would normally have been considered excessive, some fourteen hundred yards, but the added elevation given by the mountain made fire just practical in his estimation. Burgoyne acted promptly on this report and two light 24-pounders were ordered up to the top of Defiance.

In the summer of 1776 young Colonel John Trumbull had become disturbed when he noticed how Mount Defiance overlooked the defenses of Ticonderoga. His fear was that if any enemy should get artillery onto the mountain, the fort would become untenable. He was laughed at — everyone knew the place was inaccessible, and besides the range was too great for artillery fire, almost a mile. Trumbull nevertheless persisted and pulled his rank sufficiently to have a heavy French gun on Mount Independence double-shotted and pointed at the crest. The balls were seen to strike halfway up the mountain side. Trumbull then crossed over to the western shore and, with General Gates and others looking on, had a 6-pounder on the ramparts of the fort pointed at Defiance. The three-and-a-half-inch cannonball struck near the top. Trumbull had proved his point as to range, but so what? The place was inaccessible, was it not, so cannon could never be gotten up there. The future artist, accompanied by the lame Benedict Arnold and Anthony Wayne, among others, then climbed the rocky hillside and looked down on the fort, lying apparently almost at their feet. Where men could go they certainly could drag cannon —

with the utmost difficulty perhaps and only through the hardest of labor, but still it could be done. Trumbull's discovery was nothing extraordinary, for Lieutenant Brehm back in 1759 had told Amherst that cannon could be gotten to the crest of Mount Defiance. No one else, however, until Trumbull came along, had given thought to the matter and his concern, although he had proved his point, was evidently pooh-poohed by Gates and the other senior officers. Nothing was done and Sugar Loaf was left neglected and forgotten. Trumbull wrote a memorandum advocating the abandonment of all the existing defenses at the narrows and the substitution of a small five-hundred-man fort on the top of Defiance, claiming that this at infinitely less cost of men and supplies would effectively block the lake. He was overoptimistic in this, for the range was too great for accurate fire and a waterborne expedition could easily have passed the narrows during the hours of darkness. On the other hand hindsight tells us that the mountaintop should have been covered by some sort of defense to prevent the British from occupying it. But again we must remember that not only was everyone certain that no serious attack would be made, but vastly more important was the fact that there were not even enough men to man the main defenses, let alone scatter themselves around elsewhere on mountaintops.

A large British working party started to hack out a road toward the summit on 4 July and all would have been ready for the battery to open fire on the sixth. By some mischance, however, the British activity on Mount Defiance was noticed by observant Americans. There is a story that some thoughtless person, very likely one of the Indians, lighted a fire, or it is possible that Twiss's scarlet jacket might have been noted against the background of green pine trees on the summit and inference drawn of what portended. Whatever might have been the case, St. Clair soon learned that the enemy was there, and he at once called a council of war, apparently quite early in the morning of 5 July. The council, consistent in the defeatist philosophy which permeated the place, decided upon immediate abandonment of Ticonderoga as soon as darkness fell; and the members furthermore recorded their perturbation by adding that they felt it would be great good fortune if a successful retreat could be accomplished. No one apparently had the slightest stomach for battle in that summer of 1777.

The decision to give up the fortress without any fight was privately announced to various senior officers — the quartermaster learned of it at three P.M. — but it was to be kept secret until dark as far as all others were concerned. The story has often been told that cannon fire from Mount Defiance first gave the Americans knowledge of the British feat, but this apparently is not correct, according to Burgoyne's own statement, and he certainly should have known. Moreover, there do not appear to have been any cannon in position until well after the American retreat had gotten under way. Lieutenant William Digby of the 53rd Regiment noted in his journal that at about midnight of 5 July he met a gunner captain taking the two guns up the mountain in great secrecy. The American retreat had then been going on for hours.

Shortly after sunset on 5 July the great floating bridge to the Vermont shore started to become a bedlam as men poured across the lake, and frantic but largely unsuccessful attempts were made to move cannon and supplies to the comparative safety of the eastern shore. Utter confusion reigned everywhere, and discipline, dubious and tenuous under the best of conditions, collapsed, while men and supplies struggled up the rough road over Mount Independence which led to the boat landings and the escape road to Castleton. The sick and some supplies were put on board the five survivors of the Valcour fleet, two galleys, two schooners and a sloop, and into the great number of bateaux lined up along the shore. The retreat, despite its confusion, was apparently not disclosed to British eyes until the French adventurer Roche de Fermoy, contrary to specific orders, set fire to his hut high up on the Mount. It burned brightly and like a great torch illuminated all the surroundings. The retreat was now most evident, yet Burgoyne, sleeping soundly on one of the frigates, did not learn of it until daylight, when Brigadier Fraser had already taken it upon himself to start a pursuit. Light infantry poured over the bridge, left usable although somewhat damaged by the fleeing garrison. It was covered by the fire of several cannon on the Vermont abutment, tended by a crew of four gunners — but all were dead drunk from a keg of Madeira they had somewhere filched. Redcoats got up on to the Mount just as the last of the Americans scurried away toward the hamlets of the Hampshire Grants. Fraser sent his light infantry on to bark at their heels, meanwhile preparing his brigade for a vigorous pursuit.

The fleet and the nearly two hundred bateaux had been loaded with sick, but also, it is feared, with many able-bodied men who should have taken the Castleton road. Thus most of the provisions and essential supplies had to be abandoned. St. Clair afterward claimed to have carried much of these safely away, but Burgoyne reported their capture, save for three hundred barrels of powder, soon to be seized or blown up when Skenesboro fell. A high wind was blowing, making the embarkation difficult, but by daylight all were safely away and headed up the narrow lake toward the security of the defenses at Skenesboro.

Once the vessels were a few miles to the south of the narrows all sense of haste vanished and progress became leisurely. The great bridge and the boom with its huge logs bound together with chains whose links had been forged from inch-and-a-half-square iron bars would surely hold the British fleet up for many hours if not for days. Why hurry? By early afternoon they had at last reached Skenesboro. Hardly had they started to land when they were thunderstruck to learn that the British also were almost there, and that this place must also be abandoned, and in the greatest of haste. Bateaux were started south up Wood Creek, loaded with women and the sick, while the torch was put to the stockade, buildings, baggage and all remaining supplies. It was a mighty bonfire.

The British had moved at daylight and they had moved fast. The great bridge had been set on fire by the Americans, but the damage was speedily repaired. Troops rushed across it, while the navy prepared to break it and secure passage up the lake. Only a scant half-hour and a few well-directed cannon shot were needed to break this obstruction which had caused the colonials so much work, work which could have been utilized more effectively elsewhere. By eight in the morning the two frigates and some gunboats had pushed through the gap in the boom and bridge, and by midafternoon they were within a couple of miles of Skenesboro. Infantry was rushed ashore to struggle up over the intervening mountain chain in an attempt to cut off the American retreat up Wood Creek. Meanwhile the warships continued up the east branch of Champlain, met the five American vessels in a sharp skirmish, and destroyed them. Two struck their colors, while the remaining three went up in smoke and flames. The Americans fled, abandoning the raging furnace of Skenesboro to the victors. Their hold on the Champlain waterway, first grasped by Ethan Allen over two years before, was gone, and Champlain had become a British lake.

From almost every point of view the defense of Ticonderoga in 1777 was shameful. The high command was certain that no serious attack would be made; intelligence of the enemy was almost entirely lacking during the critical weeks; the decision to make the defense on the Vermont shore was not implemented; no attempt at a delaying action was undertaken; and finally the craven abandonment and retreat were decided on hurriedly and without any intelligent plans made for their execution. It was indeed fortunate for the American cause this summer of 1777 that time, space and the wilderness were to combine to slow the further progress of the British. There was little that the Americans did in the Champlain Valley this year that would have prevented an aggressive commander from occupying Albany. How he would have maintained his army once there is, however, another question. Perhaps he could have, or, more likely, the British New York force could have broken through the forts on the Hudson and opened water communication for the supply line.

It is always easy to be wise after the event, particularly in war; still, I cannot but feel that the attempt to hold Ticonderoga was wrong. With the forces and supplies then available it was hopeless, since it was well appreciated that a garrison of about ten thousand was needed to man all the works. But even if there was a full complement, an energetic enemy could still have bypassed the defenses and secured access to Lake George. Then, unless the Americans came out of their lines into the open field, the British could have contained them while forces moving up Lake George crossed the mountains, as had Rogers almost a generation before, and cut off Lake Champlain in their rear. A defense only on the Vermont shore was more logical, but it could have held only up to the time that troops had crossed East Creek and reached the eastern shore of Champlain in rear of the Mount.

The most logical point to hold would have been Fort Edward on the Hudson. True, considerable land would have thus been abandoned to the enemy, but it was mostly wilderness, and the few inhabitants were largely Quakers or Loyalists. The American supply problem would have been far more simple, that of the invaders more difficult. Here at

Fort Edward the two routes from Ticonderoga met, that by the upper end of Champlain and the alternate route across Lake George. A single strong fort at this point would block all access from the north, while at the same time possessing excellent communication to sources of supply in its rear. It is, of course, easy to say this today, but anyone who then had dared suggest giving up so famous a fortress without a fight would have sounded his own political death knell. Nevertheless, that was just what did happen in effect — a craven and frantic abandonment of the place before the British had even commenced their attack.

FIFTEEN

Surrender at Saratoga

THE MAIN American army, demoralized and disheartened as it was by the sudden loss of Fort Ticonderoga, nevertheless covered its retreat by effective rearguard action and got safely away. St. Clair led it to Castleton, Vermont, a march of some thirty miles, that first day. He planned to move westward to Skenesboro, not then realizing that the British had anticipated him. Despite St. Clair's orders Colonel Seth Warner, a former Green Mountain Boy in command of the rear elements, decided to stop for the night at Hubbardton rather than continue on to Castleton, a few miles farther. He had about a thousand men in all, but he did not take the trouble to establish any outposts. During the night some of Burgoyne's Indians, for once at least performing their intended function, scouted the American position. At daybreak Fraser struck the bivouac while the men were preparing breakfast. Many of Warner's men ran, but others, falling back into the woods, put up a brave defense. Eventually the British outflanked them and drove them from the field. It was a hard-fought skirmish that produced considerable casualties. St. Clair learned of the action at about the same time that a messenger arrived with the news from Skenesboro, and the American army fell back eastward to Rutland that night. Two days later it was at Manchester. St. Clair then continued south and west, joining Schuyler at Fort Miller on the Hudson on the twelfth, nearly a week after the fall of Ticonderoga. Here had also been collected those of the army who had escaped by way of Skenesboro. On this same day Fraser's troops, after their victory at Hubbardton, rejoined Burgoyne's main force at Skenesboro. The two opposing armies, one thoroughly disorganized and demoralized, the other exhausted by the vigorous action of the preceding week and outrunning its supplies, sat down to catch their breath. They were a little over a score of miles apart, some six thousand British and German regulars and over one thousand Canadians and Indians on one side, about twenty-eight hundred continentals and sixteen hundred militia on the other.

On 8 July a small British force advancing south from Skenesboro along Wood Creek had run into a considerable party of Americans at Fort Anne, and a brisk little battle took place. The British advance was checked, but the Americans fell back and abandoned the field to the invaders. A party of Indians, sent forward to aid the British, balked at the last minute and refused to enter the battle, an action quite in keeping with Indian behavior throughout the colonial wars. The Indian wanted to loot, to kill and scalp the helpless, not to do battle with those who could defend themselves. It seems probable that it was at this affair that the Stars and Stripes was first flown in battle, for Lieutenant Hadden of the 53rd Regiment describes a captured American flag as having thirteen red and white stripes with a "constellation."

Ticonderoga was lightly garrisoned by the victors and the war moved southward into a temporary stalemate as Burgoyne tarried at Skenesboro. The British general had procrastinated in getting the expedition started from Canada that spring and had wasted a good month in commencing his advance. On the other hand, his investment of Ticonderoga, once he had arrived there, was prompt and effective. He believed the American garrison to be twice what it actually was, yet he proceeded with dash and even perhaps a touch of rashness. Had the Americans been much greater in number than the twenty-five hundred they actually were, there was little they could have done against Burgoyne's double envelopment which, avoiding a direct attack, threatened their rearward communications on both flanks. Only a determined sortie by the defenders could have forestalled Burgoyne's well-planned actions. The American abandonment of the Mount Hope position made easier the British seizure of the Lake George landing and the disruption of that avenue of supply and of possible retreat, but such a small detached post could easily have been bypassed had the Americans made a serious attempt to hold it. Meanwhile, the German troops advancing on the east bank of Champlain would soon have cut the rearward communications of Mount Independence. All in all, Burgoyne's assault on Fort Ticonderoga was a well-planned and well-executed affair. Moreover, the pursuit of the retreating Americans to Skenesboro and Hubbardton could hardly have been bettered. Yet Burgoyne reached Skenesboro on 6 July and it was not until over three weeks later that he reached the Hudson, only some twenty-three miles away.

It is customary to explain this apparently extraordinary delay by saying that men sent north by Schuyler from Fort Edward had so damaged the road by destroying bridges and felling great pine trees that it took the British a month to open it again. Actually, the road was made usable from Skenesboro to Fort Anne in only six or seven days, and the road onward to Fort Edward through "the pitch pine plains" had only a few felled trees and was cleared in a matter of hours. Others hint or state outright that Burgoyne was paying more attention to his bottle and his mistress, the wife of an unnamed commissary officer, than to carrying on the war. Neither explanation is correct. What delayed the British advance was the logistics of colonial warfare. Men must be fed and cannon and ammunition carried forward. By hindsight it became easy to say that Burgoyne took too much artillery onward after the fall of Ticonderoga, and this probably was true. At the time, however, the British general had no way of knowing it. He had to be prepared for all contingencies, and heavy artillery was the ace in the game of colonial frontier warfare.

As far as Skenesboro the invading army possessed perfect water transport all the way south from St. Jean on the Richelieu, but the moment it advanced farther, either from Skenesboro or from the foot of Lake George, it faced the problem of overland transport. Burgoyne of course had appreciated this, but not to a sufficient extent. He had requisitioned five hundred small Canadian carts, each capable of carrying eight hundred pounds, or one day's rations for 267 men. Fifteen hundred horses had been called for to be driven south through the woods along the shores of Lake Champlain, certainly a difficult operation. Lieutenant Hadden in his journal wrote that the horses were shipped up the lake in flatboats, a simpler procedure, one would think, than attempting to herd them through an empty and roadless wilderness. Probably both methods were used. A few ox teams were picked up from the settlers south of Skenesboro, but there never was enough wheeled transport.

Burgoyne has been subjected to criticism for not drawing his troops back to Ticonderoga and ferrying them across Lake George, but the cold facts of logistics clearly show that this would not have solved the problem. He wisely realized that if he were to advance to Albany he must build up a reserve of provisions as well as move his artillery forward. Moreover, his army now numbered a bit over seven thousand and every day ate up ten tons of food, which must be moved forward every twenty-four hours before anything could be added to the reserve. If Burgoyne moved his troops over Lake

George, he could not also move his supplies, for there were not enough boats. Accordingly he determined to move the troops, the light artillery and some provisions overland from Skenesboro, while the heavy artillery and most of the supplies went by Lake George, thus utilizing both avenues at the same time. Three or four hundred bateaux would have been needed to carry the army, and it would have taken nearly two weeks to get these boats from Champlain up into Lake George. Hadden recorded that the portage road was not too bad, and that two hundred American prisoners kept it in repair. He wrote that it took eleven days to move up enough boats into Lake George to carry the heavy artillery and the supplies. All this would have to be repeated at the much longer carry from Lake George to the Hudson, where, it was later found, the bateaux were so racked in transit that they required much recaulking.

The British commander had an unusual, and by the standards of his day an almost unthinkable plan in mind. Nearly a century later Ulysses Grant achieved fame and victory at Vicksburg by abandoning his lines of communication and plunging into enemy territory without any way of replenishing his supplies save off the country. Burgoyne in 1777 dared the same plan, but he realized that he could not live off a most sparsely inhabited country and would have to accumulate a reserve of provisions before he could risk cutting his ties with Canada. Much of the apparent delay in the advance to the defeat at Saratoga was an intentional action requisite to the accumulation of a month's provisions for his army, at least twenty-five hundred barrels of pork, beef, peas and hard bread.

The plan for an advance by two routes was sound and correct. Whatever action he took, the army would have to kill time at some location until the supplies had been advanced. They could do this quite as well along the Skenesboro–Fort

Anne road as they could by waiting at Ticonderoga or at the head of Lake George. Moreover, their presence on the more easterly route continued to offer a threat of an advance against New England that the Lake George route did not present. The mistake that Burgoyne made was the failure to push a light force farther south at the earliest possible moment. He certainly could have occupied and held Fort Anne without waiting to clear the road, and this could have been done within a day or two after the skirmish of 8 July, instead of waiting until 23 July, the day after the road was finally cleared of the felled trees, all of which had been cut down after the 8 July affair.

Burgoyne had assembled the component parts of his army at Skenesboro by 12 July, but it was not until two weeks later that he moved on to Fort Anne, occupied two or three days before by Fraser's advance troops. Two days later Fraser was within a mile or two of Fort Edward, where on 27 July there occurred an incident which was to have great effect on the American cause. That was the death of Jane McCrea, an event too well known to describe in detail. Jane was visiting in the near vicinity of Fort Edward a Widow McNeil who, oddly enough, was a cousin of Brigadier Fraser. The house was raided by some of Burgoyne's Indians and Jane was carried off on horseback. The current story, one of great propaganda value to the American cause, was that she was killed by the Indians, either wantonly or in the course of an argument between two of her captors, each of whom claimed her as his prize. Later research has made it appear that she probably was accidentally shot by American pickets firing at the Indians. It is certain anyway that she was killed and scalped, and her scalp was taken into the British camp, where it was recognized by her fiancé, a Tory officer. Jane at once became the occasion for widespread propaganda throughout the northern colonies, and her death was the cause of a great increase in the turnout of militia against the British invasion. Burgoyne was shocked by the incident and tried further to curb the excesses of his Indians, with the result that almost all of them quit the expedition in disgust and went home. Soon only about fifty of his original five hundred Indians remained. Actually, they were a small loss, having on the whole done more harm than good, particularly when they slaughtered the horses they found, horses so necessary to the army. Burgoyne had intended that his Indians should "spread terror without barbarity," and he had so directed them in a rather fatuous speech made in the early days of the expedition. On the whole his endeavor was to a considerable extent successful; certainly the actions of his Indians were more restrained than they had been in previous wars.

While at Fort Edward, Burgoyne expressed much concern over what he considered the excess baggage carried by his officers. He issued orders begging that this baggage be reduced to a minimum, saying that an officer could, if he wished, carry all that he needed in a knapsack. The general himself seems to have been the major offender in this direction, if the story is true that some thirty of the Canadian carts were loaded with his wine, his equipment and the baggage of his light of love. Although tradition puts the number at thirty, I have as yet been unable to find an authoritative contemporary source for this report and it may be unfair to the general, whom the more I study, the more I like. Even if he did fill up thirty carts and take a lady along with him on his expedition, he only acted in conformity with the spirit of his times, when much more than now rank had its privileges and took advantage of them.

After almost two weeks spent at Fort Edward the army moved forward a few miles to Fort Miller, a place name but no longer a fort, and here Burgoyne made probably the greatest of his mistakes, the dispatch of a force of Germans to

Bennington. From the very beginning he had wished to penetrate eastward to the Connecticut River and thus threaten
New England, but this operation had been forbidden him.
His orders were clear and specific — "Get to Albany." Burgoyne maintained faith in his plan and endeavored to continue to feint a threat toward New England so far as was
possible within the bounds of his mission. A great store of
wagons, provisions and horses was said to have been formed
by the Americans at Bennington, and the general determined
to seize the place, securing both provisions and horses for his
hitherto foot-slogging cavalry detachment, until now forced to
act as infantry. The extent of this store was probably much
exaggerated in the reports received at headquarters, since the
region was still sparsely settled and of no great productivity,
but there evidently was some sort of a cache of supplies held
in this hamlet. There was a guard of some four hundred
men, soon to be greatly augmented for a day or two by New
Hampshire militia marching westward under General Stark.

Instead of sending British light infantry, Burgoyne picked,
for reasons not entirely clear to us, the slow-marching Germans and the dismounted cavalrymen. He gave them the
broad mission of penetrating eastward as far as the Connecticut River, gathering all the horses they could, learning the
feelings of the inhabitants (Baum, the commanding officer,
could speak no English!) and then returning to the main
army by the way of Brattleboro. It was a most foolish move.
Burgoyne changed his written orders to verbal ones at the
last minute and directed Baum to march directly to Bennington, but we do not know whether he made any change in the
Connecticut River mission. Baum led his men eastward and,
nearly at Bennington, met the American militia, spread his
force of about eight hundred out into overly dispersed units,
and suffered utter defeat and death. The battle of Bennington, contrary to popular belief, was actually fought on New

York soil by a force largely of New Hampshiremen. Baum had soon realized the difficulties in which he was becoming involved and had sent a plea for help. An additional body of Germans plodded to his aid, delayed by heavy rain and atrocious roads, but it arrived near the scene of battle too late, and itself was badly mauled during its retreat to the Hudson. This unsuccessful foray to the eastward cost Burgoyne over eight hundred men.

On 3 August, over a week before Baum's expedition left Fort Miller, Burgoyne heard from General Howe in New York that the latter was moving against Philadelphia and planned no action up the Hudson unless Washington moved in that direction. Sir Henry Clinton would be left to hold New York with a force too small to take offensive action up the river. Reinforcements, however, were expected from England. This may have given Burgoyne something to worry about, but at this period he seems still to have been confident of reaching Albany through his own exertions alone. For a month, 14 August until 13 September, the army waited at Fort Miller while supplies were being pushed forward. Meanwhile, the tale of Jane McCrea, soon followed by the wondrous news of how Stark's militia had attacked and annihilated the German regulars at Bennington, was a marvelous incitement to new enlistments and the turnout of militia forces. The roads became thick with men moving north and west "agin Burgine," and soon Gates, who had replaced Schuyler early in August, had a sizable army at his disposal. On 22 July the American army had fallen back from Fort Edward for a few miles, and a week later it continued on south to Stillwater, where it entrenched and soon began to grow daily in strength.

The month-long wait at Fort Miller would be fatal to the British invasion, yet there was nothing else that Burgoyne could do until he had advanced the supplies necessary to further forward movement. The campaign, basically sound in its essentials, failed because the high command did not sufficiently appreciate the logistical problems of colonial warfare, and grossly inadequate provision was made for moving the supplies, once the waters of Champlain had been left behind. Burgoyne had wasted a month before he thought of ordering horses, and then through one cause or another he never received more than a third of the fifteen hundred for which he had contracted. Had the difficulties of wilderness transport been properly appreciated and sufficient provision made to overcome them, Burgoyne might have been in Albany by late July or early August, well before any effective American army could have assembled to oppose him. Later, when he had returned to England, Burgoyne wrote: "In such an undertaking as mine . . . for one hour he [the commander] can find to contemplate how he shall fight his army, he must allot twenty to contrive how to feed it."

There were many women with the expedition, just how many it is hard to say, but orders allowed three to march south with each company to act as nurses and laundresses in accordance with the custom of the times. This would produce a total of probably between three and four hundred. In addition there were a very few wives of officers, and of course Burgoyne's lady love, the wife of the complaisant but nameless commissary. On 14 August the army received a most notable addition, Baroness von Riedesel, wife of the general commanding the German troops, and her three little girls. She was a lively and cheerful person who at once was in everyone's good graces, but, and more important to us, she wrote home many letters that give us further insight into the life of the expedition. She had come to Canada early in the year while the army was still north of Lake Champlain, but had been sent back to safety at Trois Rivières. She recorded many observations and happenings in her letters, such as

what she said was the common scandal of many of the
Canadian priests having pretty young housekeepers. She
visited with the nuns of the Trois Rivières convent who,
made merry with wine, disguised themselves and did a Cos-
sack dance for her benefit. Then they dressed the baroness
up as a nun, which badly scared the little daughters, who
feared their mother was really entering the convent. Wherever she went and whomever she was with, she enjoyed
life and made others happy to the best of her ability. One description of her says that she was small and rather too plump,
another that she was Amazonian in figure.

By midsummer von Riedesel relented and allowed the
baroness to join him at Fort Edward. From her we learn
that Burgoyne, although he spoke highly of Riedesel, snubbed
him, a major general, by excluding him from the councils of
war, which various British officers, much junior in rank to
the baron, attended as a matter of course. Despite this obvious unfairness the Briton and the German got on together
pleasantly, and Burgoyne had only favorable reports to make
of Riedesel, who spoke fluent English. The baron had seen
the fallacy of the Bennington expedition, but his earnest pro-
tests fell on deaf ears, recorded Baroness von Riedesel.

Bennington must have been a shock to Burgoyne's complacency, although his letters written at the time show no
sign of it. Despite his early belief of his ability to reach Albany unaided he must have begun to have doubts. Regardless of any such possible qualms he intended to carry out his
orders. He attempted to be cheerful in a letter to Germain,
written from Fort Miller on 20 August, but it is obvious that
he had started to worry, as he wrote: "Wherever the King's
forces point, militia, to the amount of three or four thousand,
assemble in twenty four hours; they bring with them their
subsistence, &, the alarm over, they return to their farms. The
Hampshire Grants in particular . . . now abounds in the

most active and the most rebellious race of the continent, and hangs like a gathering storm upon my left." There is little of Burgoyne's former confidence remaining. On 3 September he learned of St. Leger's retreat from the siege of Fort Stanwix, and at last realized that no immediate help was forthcoming. By this time, however, he had nearly accumulated the reserve of provisions he had determined upon, and on 13 September in conformity with his instructions, he bravely crossed the Hudson, knowing that he was thus voluntarily abandoning his communications with Canada. He believed that the American forces between him and Albany numbered at least fourteen thousand, but in obedience to his orders he advanced to attempt to execute his mission.

A scant ten miles below Saratoga, today's Schuylerville, a height of land looms above the Hudson. The place is very close to halfway between Fort Edward and Albany. Here Gates took his stand and dug his defenses. By mid-September he had between six and seven thousand men, perhaps a thousand more than had Burgoyne. Woods masked the American position so that effective reconnaissance was almost impossible. Burgoyne knew that Gates was in force and that, in order to reach Albany, he must drive him from his chosen position.

There is little need here to tell of the ensuing battle in detail; it has been amply covered by many writers. On 19 September the British army advanced, spread out over a wide front. Gates at once moved forward from his defenses against the British right, which was perhaps a mile and a half inland from the Hudson, and the two forces joined in furious battle over a wooded area, interspersed with a few open fields. The fight was intensely sustained on both sides for three or four hours. The Americans, attacking from woods against troops lined up in open fields, perhaps enjoyed a slight advantage, but this was balanced by the artillery of the British.

Finally Burgoyne became hard pressed, with heavy losses and little ammunition remaining. Riedesel, who had been moving the Germans along the river road, heard the noise of battle and marched part of his forces to the sound of the guns, arriving just in time to save the day. Soon it was dusk and Gates withdrew his men, leaving the field to the sadly battered British.

Technically, perhaps, the victory went to Burgoyne, but his losses were nearly six hundred, while the Americans suffered only about half as many casualties. The battle did much to raise the spirits and strengthen the morale of Gates's army. They had attacked and for half a day held their own against British and German regulars. As the news spread through the colonies more volunteers rushed toward Stillwater to swell Gates's forces, which meanwhile were strengthening their defenses, replenishing their ammunition, and preparing for another battle.

Burgoyne now fully realized the difficulty of his situation. On 21 September, two days after the battle, a message was at last received from New York. In it Clinton said that he would attack Fort Montgomery in the Hudson Highlands on about 22 September. Burgoyne replied that he badly needed a diversion to the south, and that he would remain where he was until about the end of the second week in October. He feared that any retreat on his part would free Gates to march against Howe, and he believed that he would best do his duty by continuing to threaten Gates, even if he could not longer hope to advance without aid from Clinton or Howe. And so he settled his command down in close vicinity to the scene of the recent battle, and dug his defenses, determined to play a waiting game. There he remained for seventeen days, consuming his sadly reduced supply of provisions, and hoping that a diversion on the lower Hudson would cause Gates to fall back to the south.

No help came. The two armies were in close contact and

outpost and scouting actions were constant, actions in which the British usually suffered more than did their enemies. Burgoyne's provisions were running low despite a reduction in the daily ration. Clinton did move up the Hudson and seize Fort Montgomery, but this did not loosen Gates's hold. At last the British realized that lack of action was fatal, and that something must be done or the army would succumb to starvation. Accordingly on the morning of 7 October Burgoyne in a desperate attempt sent out about a third of his force to feel out the enemy defenses. Such procedure was called making a reconnaissance in force, and its purpose was to brush aside pickets and outposts so that the true strength of a position might be determined. Burgoyne promptly learned the answer as the American army poured out from its defenses like a swarm of angry bees and drove the British back to their starting point. Then, urged on by Benedict Arnold, who, now without a command, had ridden madly to the sound of musketry, they broke the British and drove them into their defenses. A further advance, again led by the indomitable Arnold, seized the western redoubt held by Breymann's Germans and burst the British defenses wide open. Night came at last. Both forces were exhausted and disorganized, but the battle was over and the fate of the campaign of 1777 decided. Burgoyne realized that he could advance no farther, and that he must choose between starvation and retreat. Two days after this second battle the British army turned its face northward and sadly plodded through heavy rain over roads deep in mud toward its ultimate surrender at Saratoga.

Help was on the way but it was too little and it came just too late. Clinton, as he had promised, moved up the Hudson against the Highland forts, but not until 3 October. He had received reinforcements from England a week or so before, and thus felt able to make a diversion to aid Burgoyne. Clinton, an able general, took three thousand men up the Hudson in frigates and transports. Soon he received another message from Burgoyne telling of the latter's troubles, but still giving no hint of approaching disaster. Meanwhile preparations for attack on Fort Montgomery proceeded, and shortly through clever maneuver and a determined attack with the bayonet the British overcame the fort's defenders. But sad to say, the spirited defense of the Americans and the blood lust of battle caused the victorious British to massacre many of the captured garrison. The supporting Fort Clinton soon gave up. That night the Americans burned their river defense vessels, and, save for a boom across the Hudson, the river was open to a further British advance.

Clinton wrote a brief note to Burgoyne telling of his success, and it was concealed inside a hollow silver bullet; Sergeant Daniel Taylor put this in the pocket of his civilian clothes and rode off northward. Unfortunately, the sergeant fell into American hands, and he swallowed the bullet, but his action was observed. An emetic produced the bullet, which today, still enclosing its original message, is in the museum at Fort Ticonderoga. Needless to say, the unlucky sergeant was promptly hanged.

A British force under General Vaughn was now dispatched on up the river. It reached Esopus, today's Kingston, New York, by about 15 October, and promptly burned the town. Vaughn was now only about forty miles from Albany, and that city was practically defenseless since all available troops had marched against Burgoyne. For some unknown reason Vaughn failed to advance any farther, although he could well have reached Albany in a day. It was no matter, for it was now too late. On 16 October Burgoyne had surrendered his army.

SIXTEEN

The Fort Holds Fast

WHEN BURGOYNE MOVED on across the Hudson toward surrender at Saratoga he left as a garrison at Ticonderoga the Prince Frederick Regiment of German troops and the 53rd British, supported by the frigates *Maria* and *Carleton* and a few gunboats. Brigadier Powell held the command, his headquarters in the Vermont defenses, and his troops were deployed on both sides of the lake. At the Lake George landing there was a detachment of a dozen seamen and their two officers, and a few hundred yards away a camp of about a company of the 53rd. Between the two stood a large barn used at night to hold American prisoners, who by day loaded stores and provisions at the landing for transport up Lake George. A small armed sloop was moored by the wharf. Near the bridge over the creek at the lower end of the portage and in the vicinity of the sawmill there was a block-house, while another British detachment, probably about a company in size, camped along the road to the old French fort, near another barn which held additional American prisoners. The fort itself was occupied by some one hundred men, about three companies, and finally on top of Mount Defiance a blockhouse was under construction. Here were seventy-two artificers, a sergeant's guard, and a 12-pounder brass gun with ample ammunition. Except for those in the fort itself, all the troops on the western shore of the lake were highly vulnerable to a surprise attack.

On the eastern bank of the lake the rugged southern end of Mount Independence rises high above the neck of land, between Champlain and East Creek, which connects the Mount with the mainland and the road to the Vermont settlements and Skenesboro. The German troops and about a half of the British held the Mount, the southern crest of which was rimmed by an abatis, a defensive line with three batteries and as many blockhouses, none of them as yet finished. The entire garrison was perhaps five hundred in all, far from enough to defend the whole Mount against a real attack, but ample to cover the rugged southern extremity against an attack not of major proportions, particularly one that brought no artillery. Additional security was furnished by the two frigates, anchored bow and stern so that their broadsides could sweep the flat approach to the Mount, and some gunboats covered the same avenue from East Creek on the other side of the low-lying neck. Thus by mid-September the narrows at Ticonderoga were strongly held on the Vermont shore, while across the lake in New York, except for the men in the old stone fortress, the troops were widely dispersed and in no condition to meet even a minor raid.

General Benjamin Lincoln was one of Washington's tried and trusty generals, one of the few on whom he could rely. On 2 August Lincoln arrived at Manchester in the Hampshire Grants as commander of the troops assembled in that region. His mission was "to divide and distract the enemy" and of course to offer such protection as he could against any British threat against New England. He moved from time to time in the area between Bennington, Manchester, and Pawlet, keeping constant reconnaissance on the two roads to the north, one to Rutland and the other toward Skenesboro and Fairhaven. Meanwhile he sought opportunity "to amuse the

enemy," as he expressed it. A raid on Ticonderoga seemed to
fit the need, particularly since it was reported to be lightly
held at the moment. There were known to be American prisoners there who might be released and stores which could be
destroyed. Any threat to his rear would certainly give Burgoyne cause for thought.

On 13 September, Lincoln ordered the dispatch of three
expeditions, each of about five hundred men. One, sent
against Skenesboro, found the place abandoned by the British, while the other two groups marched to attack the
British at Ticonderoga. Colonel John Brown, whom we first
met in 1775 when the Green Mountain Boys kept Vermont
in ferment, led the force which was to attack the old stone
fort, while a Colonel Johnson was to test the defenses of
Mount Independence with the other five hundred militiamen. Brown approached the head of the portage along the
western slope of the mountains which separate Lake George
from Lake Champlain, and reached the vicinity undiscov-
ered on 17 September. He concealed his men in the woods on
the western side of Mount Defiance and proceeded to spy
out the British dispositions.

Brown's basic mission was to release the American prisoners, to destroy the provisions at the Lake George landing
and to make as much general trouble as he could. Should
he find it feasible he was to attack the fort itself, but this
was not at all the main objective of his mission. Hitherto
it has been believed that this expedition constituted a serious
attack on Ticonderoga, but a recently discovered letter of
General Lincoln to General Gates has brought out the interesting fact that a real attack on the fort itself was planned
only "if an opportunity should offer without risking too much."

The action which followed was a relatively minor one, and
one actually of little importance, for Burgoyne's fate was already sealed; but it is of interest on two counts. During it

there occurred the only attack in its history on the old stone
fort itself, for Allen's sudden seizure never developed into
what could be called a real attack, and the whole action of
some four days is well documented by reports by members
of both of the opposing forces. Too often we have only the
story of one of the opponents. Lieutenant John Starke commanded the frigate *Maria* and he left a fine map and a story
of the affair, while Brown's reports to Lincoln give excellent coverage from the American side. Brigadier Powell sent
several reports to Carleton, and the chief of the artificers
on Mount Defiance wrote a long letter telling of the engagement. And so for once in a Revolutionary affray we know
quite well the thoughts and actions of both parties.

At daybreak on 18 September Brown assaulted the camp
near the Lake George landing, capturing all the British and
releasing the rejoicing American prisoners from their barn.
Meanwhile forty Vermont Rangers under Captain Ebenezer
Allen (apparently no near kin of Ethan), after working their
silent way up the western face of Mount Defiance in the
dark, pounced on the partly finished blockhouse. All the artificers, and perhaps even the sergeant's men, were soundly
asleep, and all but nine were killed or captured. Brown's
men moved on to the landing, where without difficulty they
seized the sailors and the sloop. Then they went, a wild and
exultant mob, down the portage road to the bridge over the
creek and its nearby blockhouse. The noise of the waterfall
over the ledges at the sawmill had drowned out all sounds of
the actions which had already taken place farther to the
west. The British again were completely surprised and the
blockhouse was soon surrendered.

The detachment guarding the prisoners at the second barn
on the road to the old fort was also overcome without difficulty. It certainly would appear that all the people on the

New York shore were sound asleep that September morning and no sentries out at all. Brown then moved on and without opposition occupied the French lines, thus gaining possession of all the British posts on the western shore save for the old stone fortress itself. His total losses were three or four killed and five wounded, while those of the British were even less. In all he secured 293 prisoners and released 118 Americans. Altogether a most satisfactory action up to this point. The British in the fort had been alerted by the last skirmish, and Brown's men made no further advance, but brought up to the lines two 6-pounder guns they had found near the bridge, guns intended for the top of Mount Defiance. These took the fort under fire, while Captain Allen's men on Defiance started action with the 12-pounder they had found there.

The Vermont defenses appear to have first realized that an attack was being made at about six o'clock, an hour after the action had started, and it was the gunfire from Mount Defiance that gave notice. Johnson's attack against the southern end of Mount Independence, supposed to start at daybreak, had been delayed. Just as it was about to start, the frigates, roused by the cannon fire of Allen's men, started to pound the edge of the woods with grapeshot. Johnson's men held themselves within the woods, shouting Indian war cries and discharging their muskets, but never showing themselves. The attack failed to take place then or later. Thus by early morning there was a stalemate, the Americans fired their captured guns from the French lines and from Mount Defiance, while Johnson's men on the Vermont side did nothing.

At this point it is of interest to note that here was nearly duplicated, in a small way to be sure, the situation which St. Clair had so feared: the old fortress assailed by a force five times its number, and with cannon firing at it from Mount

Defiance. Yet the attackers accomplished nothing, fearing the losses which would result from a final assault, and the fort was held. All of which goes to show in what a panic St. Clair must have been two months before, and how unnecessary was the mad haste in which he evacuated Ticonderoga.

Cannon fire continued the next day, the nineteenth, "without doing much damage," Powell reported. The British brigadier may have been almost criminally careless in his lack of security on the New York shore, but he proved stubborn in his defense and could not be bluffed into surrender. General Warner apparently took over command from Johnson on this day, but Brown was left free to act as he thought best. Gunfire and stalemate continued on for another day, but the twenty-first was enlivened by two events. A welcome reinforcement of one hundred Germans arrived to give cheer to Powell. They almost certainly were brought by St. Leger, who, after his march down the Mohawk Valley had stalled in front of Fort Schuyler, at today's Rome, New York, and had returned by way of Oswego to Montreal, where he received orders to join Burgoyne. He got as far as Ticonderoga, but there were no carts and animals to get him over either portage to the Hudson, and he never gained Burgoyne's unfortunate army. By nightfall of the twenty-first a heavy fog set in. Again a cow, this time temporarily more fortunate than the ox that had wandered into the lines in the fall of 1776, strayed into the German lines. Here were highly trained, regular troops, yet they evidently acted like the rawest militia. A general alarm rang out and "a most thunderous cannonade" from all over the Mount and from all the warships burst forth to wake the echoes. This continued until almost daylight, although the offending cow was soon captured and taken into the lines, where she was probably converted into beefsteaks.

Lieutenant Starke had some interesting remarks to make about the action on the Vermont shore:

The defence of Mount Independence is mentioned in the same letter [Powell to Burgoyne] as a gallant and spirited service! It certainly was so if men are to judge from the quantity of ammunition fired; but it is an undenyable truth that the Mount was never attacked by the rebels otherwise than by paper [i.e., letter demanding surrender]. The only living creature (except paper messengers) who approached it after September 18th, was a poor stayed [strayed?] cow. . . . A most thundering cannonade from all quarters of the Mount and from the vessels ensued. . . . Indeed it must be confessed the cannon were fired every night, from the several batteries, and also from the vessels, as a preventative, and to scour the woods if the rebels should chance to be there, and so great was the ardor of the garrison that when the fire of the vessels seemed to slack at any time, they were hailed and told it was the brigadier's orders to renew it. It must have been a pure and noble flame for military glory which burnt so much powder, and not the effect of f——r, as some have insinuated; for every person of truth and candor must allow that nothing had been done in the repair of the fences [defenses?] of the Mount or of Ticonderoga, from the time the Rebels had destroyed and abandoned them July 7th, till they come back to attack them Sept. 18th. The guns on the French lines at Ticonderoga, and the round and grape shot, everywhere very numerous, were nearly in the same state they were left. And so secure were the garrison in their own prowess, that no scouts were ever sent out to gain intelligence, but all strangers were allowed to come and go where they thought proper.

Brigadier Powell expected the enemy to storm either the fort or the Mount, perhaps even both at once, the next morning before the low-lying fog had cleared away, but nothing happened. The appearance of the southern end of Mount Independence, the steep bluff crowned with its batteries and blockhouses, was enough to chill the stoutest heart, even without the crossed fire of the naval cannon which covered the low approaches over which the troops would have to advance. Nor did anything take place on the other shore, where the stone walls of the French fort scowled across the barren landscape that stretched to the old French lines. The sporadic fire of the two 6-pounders produced little result, and the 12-pounder on Mount Defiance was but a threat which accomplished little or nothing. It perhaps was this day that a flag of truce approaching the fort was fired on by the defenders, and three of its party of five killed. Such treatment of a white flag by British troops seems most unlikely, yet the story was reported by one of that nation who was there, and he wrote that it was Powell himself who ordered the fire. Brown realized that his artillery was useless against the walls of Ticonderoga. He felt confident that he could take the fort by assault, but believed that the resulting losses would be high and would not at all justify the capture, particularly since there seemed no chance that Mount Independence would fall to the Americans during the current engagement.

Brown accordingly destroyed the hundred and fifty bateaux he had seized in Lake Champlain below the sawmill falls, as well as all but a score of the fifty he had found on Lake George. His force, reported now to be about 420 — the remainder were probably conducting the prisoners south by land — climbed aboard the three-gun sloop, two British gunboats and the bateaux. They set forth up Lake George to see what could be done to annoy the British at the southern end. Burgoyne had marched his men and his two-wheeled carts over the Skenesboro–Fort Edward road, but his artillery and heavy supplies had moved by water over Lake George, his main line of communication since Skenesboro had been abandoned. Old Fort George at the southern end of the lake was the unloading point, but the fort was of little use, small and commanded by neighboring heights. This latter objection had just been shown by Brown's attack to be a dubious one, but in colonial days it was a military fetish that a fort commanded by higher ground in the vicinity would be untenable.

And so Diamond Island, a few miles to the north, was made the bastion of the lake head; at the moment it was garrisoned by Captain Aubrey and two companies of the 47th.

The expedition got under way late in the afternoon of 22 September, expecting to surprise the British on Diamond Island the next morning at dawn; but a heavy storm churned up the waters of Lake George, forcing the boats ashore by midnight while only halfway to their objective. A former American sutler, now apparently serving the British, had been picked up that day while coming north down the lake from Diamond Island. Brown put him on parole, but he made his escape that stormy night and managed to reach Captain Aubrey with warning of the coming attack.

It was not until nine in the morning of 24 September that the attack was made on an alerted garrison, who had several cannon emplaced behind ample earthworks. Brown advanced his armed ships directly against the front of the island, while the men in the bateaux, divided into two parties, were to attempt a landing on the two flanks. The island defenses were taken under fire for nearly two hours, but without material result. The British cannonading, however, disabled the sloop and one of the gunboats, while the landing parties were able to accomplish nothing. Brown had lost four men and several others were wounded before he was forced to realize that his attempt must fail. Reluctantly he abandoned the assault, withdrew his boats, then ran them ashore and burned them, along with everything that he could not carry away. Then his men, well loaded down with plunder, most of it clothing, took to the woods and marched east to Fort Anne. Among the spoils was a Continental standard abandoned at the hurried evacuation of Ticonderoga the previous July. Brown forwarded it to its former owners with the sarcastic request: "Please present my compliments to those gentlemen who in their hurry slipt off and forgot them [the colors],

— hope never to have the like occasion to present them . . . with our own colours."

All in all, Brown did well in this raid on Ticonderoga and the British communications northward. He was energetic, did considerable damage to the enemy, and yet showed discretion in avoiding a pointless assault on strongly held defenses, although urged on by overzealous subordinates. He had served his country well as a delegate to the first Continental Congress; he had traveled to Canada early in 1775 to determine the feelings of the habitants and the British merchants to the cause of revolution. Yet there evidently was a side to his character that does not ring so true. He hated Benedict Arnold with a fervent hate, and showed it in every way. That is quite understandable and no reflection on Brown, though some of his accusations and vituperations today sound a little too shrill. Largely on account of his feud with Arnold, Brown had resigned his commission in a Connecticut regiment early in 1777, and he led this attack on Powell's men as a militia colonel. Upon its completion he returned to civil life in Pittsfield. In the summer of 1780, when Brant and Sir John Johnson were raiding the Mohawk Valley, he again turned out with the militia levies, and was killed at Stone Arabia, a little west of Johnstown, New York.

SEVENTEEN

Two Centuries of Peace

IN 1888 a boy of eight was playing with his brother on the grass-covered mounds that hid the old walls of Fort Ticonderoga. A stone in a partly exposed bit of masonry was dislodged and a little bronze tinder box dropped into sight. Stephen Pell first saw and seized the treasure, only to fall into immediate argument and perhaps a scuffle for its possession, for Howland Pell claimed that since his was the foot that had loosened the stone, the tinder box should be his. Stephen, however, held fast to his find, and today it forms the prize exhibit in the case in the Fort Ticonderoga museum devoted to the memory of the late Stephen Pell.

We are, however, getting far ahead of our story of the fort, and we must retrace our steps over a century and again pick up the thread of history. General Powell had burned and abandoned Ticonderoga when he learned of Burgoyne's surrender at Saratoga. The fort was never again occupied by a garrison, although from time to time raiding parties of British made it their headquarters for a day or a week. Many cannon still remained in the various defensive works, too heavy to be removed except by water. The British had no present need for these guns, while the Americans most certainly did. Britain, thanks to her ships, commanded Lake Champlain, and periodically they were sent cruising up the lake to Ticonderoga to keep an eye on the fort and make certain that the Americans did not get any cannon loaded on bateau or barge. One or two of the raiding parties who harried the upper Hudson and the Mohawk camped for a bit at the fort, and emissaries of Haldimand and Ethan Allen met there to discuss the possible reunion of Vermont with Britain, secret schemings of which even today we do not know the whole story. Beyond such happenings, minor in view of what had gone before, the stone fortress remained empty and abandoned. Nothing was left but the walls and these soon started to collapse.

The Revolution ended and settlers surged into the valley of Lake Champlain. Naturally they needed stone for their cellars, or, in the case of the more ambitious, for the walls of their new homes. Why go to the trouble of quarrying when all the stonework of the fort lay free for the taking? And so they took it away, rolling it down to the lakeside or carrying it away in ox-drawn wagons. No one tried to stop them, for no one cared. The fort was no longer of any military value and its new owners made no objection. The fort lands had been either Crown property or a part of a land grant to some now exiled loyalist who no longer was there to attempt to reclaim them. The state of New York assumed ownership, and in 1790 its regents donated the land to Columbia and Union Colleges as grants to aid them in their activities. Such action in aid of education was quite customary at that period.

William Ferris Pell (1779-1840) was a New York merchant dealing largely in the import of marble and rare woods. He often had occasion to make the trip between New York and Montreal, using the only route then, the Hudson-Champlain waterway. Steam had come to Champlain in 1808; in fact, the second successful steamboat in the world, the *Vermont,* had followed closely on Fulton's *Clermont* and was puffing her way back and forth over the waters of Lake Champlain well before the War of 1812 broke forth and slowed the advance of steam propulsion on the lake. One of MacDonough's fleet that was victorious at the Plattsburgh naval fight had been started as a steamer before military necessity had changed her construction to that of sail. Once the war was over, steamers (or to be more correct, perhaps, small steam-driven vessels) ran regularly on schedule on Lake Champlain.

For several years Mr. Pell moved up and down the lake admiring the scenery of the Champlain Basin. The ruins of the fort on the Ticonderoga headland caught his eye and soon he arranged to lease the fort lands from their scholarly owners. Then in 1820 he bought them and built a summer dwelling. Within a very few years this burned to the ground, and in 1826 he built the Pavilion to replace it, a summer residence that has lasted down to our day. The Pavilion is almost unique in America, the summer dwelling-place of a family which has maintained possession for 138 years.

In 1839 Archibald Pell, who customarily preceded his father north from New York each year, was killed when his usual salute to the arriving family blew up the cannon. William Ferris Pell at once lost his interest in Ticonderoga. By this time steamboating on Lake George and Lake Champlain had become one of the most favored ways of passing a summer vacation. Steamers ran up the Hudson from New York, and others the length of beautiful Lake George. At the northern end of the latter lake one took a stage coach for the short ride down to the Pavilion, now operated as a hotel for the fashionable trade, where, after a pleasant lunch, one could tarry a bit and climb over the ruins before taking the steamer for Burlington and the north. And so for many years, as long as the northern tour remained fashionable, the Pavilion continued as a hotel. Members of the Pell family, who still retained ownership, often visited the place in summer, and so it was that Stephen Pell found his tinder box and before many years had passed made his promise to himself to restore the old French fort.

By 1908 the fort lands were divided in ownership among seventeen descendents of the original owner and there were a number of squatters who had never been evicted. The hotel had ceased operation, and was now a farmhouse with a horse stabled in one of the bedrooms. Stephen Pell had grown up to serve on board the *Yankee* in the Spanish-American War, and in 1901 he married Sarah, daughter of Colonel Robert M. Thompson, a man who had done much to develop the International Nickel Company. Sarah Pell shared in Stephen's dream of restoring the fort, and at last in 1908 a start became possible through the financial aid of Colonel Thompson. A young English architect was engaged to supervise the work. (Years later he returned home and entered Parliament. Today he is Lord Bossom of Maidstone in Kent.)

Fifty and more years ago little was known about colonial and military archaeology. The study of the early days of Egypt, Persia, the American Indian, all these were being carried on, but our colonial and Revolutionary periods had received almost no attention. There were no real experts to turn to for help in restoring the fort, and so Stephen Pell and Alfred Bossom had to rely almost entirely upon their own knowledge and common sense. Despite continued depredations over many years, as well as gradual natural erosion of the ruins, a considerable part of the fort remained. One of the three original barracks within the fort still stood, badly damaged indeed, but with more than enough of its walls remaining to show clearly the height, window spacing and many details of construction. Of the other two stone buildings surrounding the courtyard little remained but their foundations.

The walls of the fort were grass-covered mounds over which wandered grazing cows, but when workmen dug into their sides they at once encountered the original walls of the fort. These walls had not really been built of stone — they were of earth, covered by a rather thin stone facing, too thin for the frigid winters of the region where frost can wreak havoc in only a single winter. Time and frost loosened many of the stones composing the walls during the years after the Revolution when there was no garrison to make repairs. The post-Revolutionary settlers quickly took away the stone facing from the upper half or two-thirds of the walls. The earth, hitherto held in place by the facing, collapsed and covered the base of the walls that remained, giving almost complete protection over the years.

The first year's work was devoted to restoring the West Barracks, and Fort Ticonderoga was officially opened to the public, with President Taft in attendance, in the summer of 1909. The ambassadors of Great Britain and France, as well as the governors of New York and Vermont, were also present at the opening ceremonies.

The work of restoration continued over the years, progressing as rapidly as funds became available, for it is a costly business rebuilding an old fort, particularly when all the money is raised among one's family and friends, with no assistance whatever received from state or federal government. Digging out around the old walls produced many relics of all sorts, far too many and too varied to itemize. The best of them are now displayed in the museum in the fort, a military museum which also contains a great many other exhibits procured from varied sources both here and abroad. Stephen Pell was foresighted in acquiring land to protect the fort from unfortunate real estate developments, and today some thousand acres are owned on the New York shore. John Pell, Stephen's son, some years ago gave the fort a great many more acres on the Vermont side, land which includes most of the Revolutionary defenses on Mount Independence, as well as an ample shore frontage that guarantees that the view to the east from the old stone fortress shall not be defaced.

In 1931 Stephen and Sarah Pell, sole owners of the fort since acquiring the rights of the other Pell heirs, established the Fort Ticonderoga Association, a nonprofit educational corporation, and gave to it the fort, the museum and all the lands. Stephen Pell lived until 1950 to see the reconstruction of the fort complete save only for the East Barracks, and he was succeeded as president of the association by John Pell, his son. And so the old colonial and Revolutionary fort, once scene of actions of such vast importance in the history of our country, today during the summer season is host to a throng of visitors from all over our country, who learn the story of the old stone fortress and enjoy the glorious view of Lake Champlain and the Vermont shore, with the Green Mountains forming the backdrop. They go away again a little richer in their knowledge of those men who some two centuries ago served their countries so well.

Bibliography

ALLEN, ETHAN. *Narrative of Colonel Ethan Allen's Captivity*, Walpole, N. H., 1807.

AMHERST, JEFFREY. *The Journal of Jeffrey Amherst*, ed. J. C. Webster, Toronto, 1931.

AMHERST, WILLIAM. *Journal*, ed. J. C. Webster, London, 1927.

ANDERSON, T. S. *The Command of Howe Brothers*, New York, 1936.

ANON. Journal of Campaign in Canada . . . in 1776 . . . & 1777, MS. at U. S. Military Academy, West Point, N.Y.

BALDWIN, COL. JEDUTHAN. *Revolutionary Journal*, Bangor, 1906.

BALLANTINE, JOHN. MS. Diary, American Antiquarian Society.

BAXTER, JAMES P. *The Journal of Lieut. William Digby*, Albany, 1887.

BEEBE, DR. LEWIS. "Journal," *Penn. Magazine History*, Vol. 59.

BLOOMFIELD, MAJ. JOSEPH. MS. Journal, Morristown Nat. Park Library.

BOUGAINVILLE, L. A. "Journal," *Quebec Archives*, 1923-1924.

BREHM, LT. DIETRICH. MS. Report in Gage Papers, Univ. of Michigan Clements Library.

BRODHEAD, J. R. *Documents . . . Colonial History of New York*, Albany, 1856——.

BROWN, COL. JOHN. "Letters," *N. E. Hist. Gen. Reg.*, Vol. 74.

BURGOYNE, LT. GEN. JOHN. *Orderly Book*, Albany, 1860.

——. *A State of the Expedition from Canada*, London, 1780.

CARROLL, CHARLES. *Journal*, Maryland Hist. Society, Baltimore, 1876.

CARVER, JONATHAN. *Travels*, London, 1778.

CASGRAIN, ABBÉ HENRI. *Levis Papers*, Quebec, 1889-1895.

——. *Montcalm and Levis*, Tours, 1899.

CHAGNY, ANDRÉ. *François Piquet,* Montreal, 1913.

CHAMPLAIN, SAMUEL DE. *Voyages of Champlain,* New York, 1907.

CHITTENDEN, L. E. *The Capture of Ticonderoga,* Vermont Hist. Society, Rutland, 1872.

CLARKE, T. WOODE. *Bloody Mohawk,* New York, 1940.

DE KERALLAIN, RENÉ. *La Jeunesse de Bougainville,* Paris, 1896.

DE LERY, CHASSEGROS. "Journal," *Fort Ticonderoga Bulletin,* July, 1942.

DU CREUX, FATHER FRANÇOIS. *History of Canada,* Champlain Society, Toronto, 1951.

ENYS, LT. JOHN. MS. Journal, Dominion Archives, Canada.

EPPING, CHARLOTTE S. J. *Journal of du Roi the Elder,* Univ. of Penn., 1911.

FLICK, ALEX. C. "Gen. Henry Knox's Ticonderoga Expedition," New York State Historical Assoc., XXVI, p. 119.

FORBES, ELI. *A Family Book,* Salem, 1801.

FORCE, PETER. *American Archives,* 4th and 5th Series, Washington, 1837-1853.

FREEMAN, DOUGLAS. *George Washington,* New York, 1948, II & III.

FRENCH, ALLEN. *The Taking of Ticonderoga,* Cambridge, 1928.

GAGE Papers, Clements Library, Univ. of Michigan.

GIPSON, L. H. *Lewis Evans,* Philadelphia, 1939.

———. *Great War for British Empire,* Vols. I-IX, Caldwell, 1936, New York, 1939-1956.

GORDON, WILLIAM. *History of Rise of . . . United States,* London, 1788.

HADDEN, L. JAMES. *A Journal . . . Burgoyne's Campaign,* Albany, 1884.

HALL, HILAND. *The Capture of Ticonderoga,* Vermont Hist. Society, 1869.

HAMILTON, EDWARD P. *The French and Indian Wars,* New York, 1962.

HARDY, CONSTANTINE. "Diary," *N.E. Hist. Gen. Register,* Vol. 60, 1906.

HAWKS, MAJ. JOHN. *Journal,* N.Y. Soc. of Colonial Wars, New York, 1911.

HITCHCOCK, DR. ENOS. "Diary," *R.I. Hist. Soc. Pub.,* 1899.

HOLBROOK, STEWART. *Ethan Allen,* New York, 1940.

HURLBURT, JOHN. "Diary," *Magazine of Am. Hist.,* 1893, p. 395.

JESUIT RELATIONS. *Lettres Edifiantes et Curieuses,* Toulouse, 1810.

KNOLLENBERG, BERNHARD. *Washington and the Revolution,* New York, 1940.

KNOX, CAPT. JOHN. *An Historical Journal of the Campaigns in North America,* London, 1769.

KNOX, GEN. HENRY. Papers, Mass. Hist. Society.

LACEY, JOHN. "Memoirs," *Penn. Mag. Hist.,* Vol. 25.

LINCOLN, GEN. BENJAMIN. Papers, Mass. Hist. Society.

LOCKWOOD, JOHN H. *Westfield and Its History,* Springfield, 1922.

London Gazette, 1777.

LOSSING, B. J. *Life and Times of Philip Schuyler,* New York, 1860.

MAHAN, A. T. *The Major Operations of the Navies in the War of American Independence,* Boston, 1913.

MERRIMAN, SAMUEL. "Diary," in George Sheldon, *History of Deerfield,* Deerfield, 1895, I, 661.

MONYPENNY, CAPT. ALEXANDER. MS. Orderly Book, Fort Ticonderoga Library.

NEW YORK STATE ARCHIVES. *The American Revolution,* Albany, 1926.

NICKERSON, HOFFMAN. *The Turning Point of the Revolution,* Boston, 1928.

O'CALLAGHAN, E. B. *Documentary History of the State of New York,* Albany, 1849-1851.

PARGELLIS, STANLEY. *Military Affairs in North America,* New York, 1936.

PARKMAN, FRANCIS. *The Jesuits in North America,* Boston, 1867.

——————. Papers, Mass. Hist. Society.

PELL, JOHN H. G. *Ethan Allen,* Boston, 1929.

PORTER, COL. ELISHA. MS. Journal, Fort Ticonderoga Library.

POWELL, BRIG. H. W. "Letter to Sir Guy Carleton," *Fort Ticonderoga Bulletin,* July, 1945.

RIEDESEL, BARONESS FREDERIKA VON. *Letters and Memoirs,* New York, 1827.

ROGERS, MAJ. ROBERT. *Journal,* Dublin, 1769.

ST. CLAIR, MAJ. GEN. ARTHUR. "Trial of," *New-York Hist. Soc. Collections,* 1880.

SALTONSTALL Papers, Mass. Hist. Society.

SCHANCK, LT. JOHN. "Letter to Captain Pringle," *Fort Ticonderoga Bulletin,* July, 1928.

SCHUYLER, GEN. PHILIP. "Court Martial of," *New-York Hist. Soc. Collections,* 1879.

SEWALL, HENRY. Diary and Letters, Mass. Hist. Society.

SMITH, J. E. A. *History of Pittsfield*, Boston, 1869.

SMITH, JUSTIN H. *Our Struggle for the Fourteenth Colony*, New York, 1907.

SMITH, WILLIAM HENRY. *The St. Clair Papers*, Cincinnati, 1882.

STARKE, LT. JOHN. MS. map and description of Brown's 1777 attack, Fort Ticonderoga Library.

STILLE, CHARLES J. *Major General Anthony Wayne*, Philadelphia, 1893.

STONE, WILLIAM S. *The Campaign of . . . Burgoyne and . . . St. Leger*, Albany, 1877.

————. *Journal of Captain Pausch*, Albany, 1886.

————. *Memoirs . . . of Baron Riedesel*, Albany, 1868.

THATCHER, DR. JAMES. *A Military Journal*, Boston, 1823.

TILGHMAN, LT. COL. TENCH. *Memoir*, Albany, 1876.

TRUMBULL, JOHN. *Autobiography*, New York, 1841.

WALLACE, WILLARD M. *Traitorous Hero*, New York, 1954.

Index

ABERCROMBY, GENERAL JAMES, 72;
size of his expedition, 73;
marches against Ticonderoga,
77-82; his defeat, 84-85
Albany: founded, 24; in 1643, 30
Allen, Colonel Ethan: characterized,
106; captures Ticonderoga, 110-
112; in command, 115; captures
Fort George, 116; attempts to
hold St. Jean, 117-118; goes to
Philadelphia, 120; captured at
Montreal, 120
Amherst, Major General Jeffrey:
commands in America, 87;
moves against Ticonderoga, 91-
93; invests Ticonderoga, 94-96;
advances to Crown Point, 99
Appalachian Mountains, 8
Arnold, Major General Benedict:
tells of cannon at Ticonderoga,
104; commissioned to seize Ticonderoga, 105; reaches Castleton and demands command,
109; at capture of Ticonderoga,
111-112; seizes St. Jean, 116-
117; in command of lake frontier, 118; demoted, 121; hint of
future treachery, 121; Kennebec march, 128; lays siege to
Quebec, 132, 134; commands
Champlain fleet, 152; at Valcour battle, 153-157, 161; campaign of 1777, 213

BALDWIN, COLONEL JEDUTHAN: engineer at Ticonderoga, 137; returns, 170; 1777 Journal, 179,
182

Bateaux, 13-15
Battles: Champlain with Indians,
21-22; siege of Fort William
Henry, 56-63; Carillon, 75-84;
Valcour, 155-157; capture of
Fort Ticonderoga, 1759, 91-96;
1775, 110-112; 1777, 195-197;
Hubbardton, 200; Fort Anne,
201; Bennington, 207-208;
Freeman's Farm, 211-212;
Bemis Heights, 213
Beebe, Dr. Lewis, 137, 163
Bemis Heights, battle of, 213
Bennington, expedition to, 207-208
Bigot, François, 43
Black Watch, heavy casualties of,
84
Bleury, supplier to Fort Ticonderoga,
52-53
Boats. See Watercraft
Bossom, Alfred Charles, Lord, 228
Boston, besieged, 103
Bougainville, Colonel Louis Antoine
de, 50; describes 1756 condi-
tions, 51-52; describes Indians,
56, 64; describes Fort William
Henry massacre, 68
Bourlamaque, Brigadier, defends Ti-
conderoga, 92, 94-95, 97
Braddock, General Edward: defeat,
16; expedition against the
French, 37
Brehm, Lieutenant Dietrich, recon-
noiters Ticonderoga, 88-89
Brown, Colonel John: sent to Canada, 105, 125; assails Ticonderoga defenses, 218-220; retreats by Lake George, 222-223;
death, 224

Burgoyne, Lieutenant General John: 188-189; size of his army, 189; assails Ticonderoga, 192; his delay, 202-203; his plan, 204; complacency vanishes, 210-211; crosses Hudson, 211; surrenders, 214

CAMPAIGNS: Champlain Valley, 1756, 42; British plans for 1757, 55; for 1759, 87; for 1777, 173-174; progress of 1777, 180-181
Campbell, Major Duncan, 83
Canada: falls to Britain, 100; feelings of population, 133; retreat from, in 1776, 134
Candles, lack of at Ticonderoga, 52
Cannibalism, 57
Cannon: Washington's need of, 103; Knox carries to Boston, 130-131
Canteen at Ticonderoga, 46
Carignan-Salières Regiment, 33
Carleton, Sir Guy: escapes from Montreal, 128; a wise governor, 132; commands 1776 advance, 146; retreats to Canada, 164
Carroll, Charles, 14
Champlain, Samuel de: his 1609 expedition, 19; battle with Iroquois, 21-22; location of battle, 23
Chebecs, 147
Church, Dr. Benjamin, commissions Arnold, 105
Clinton, Major General Sir Henry, moves up Hudson, 213-214
Council of War, 19 June 1777, 186-187
Crown Point, 20; fort built at, 34; Johnson to attack, 37; southern bastion of Canada, 38; Warner takes, 115; Schuyler abandons, 139; Carleton occupies in 1776, 164
Currency, Canadian, 46

DACRES, LIEUTENANT JAMES, 156-157
Delaplace, Captain William, 102; warned, 108; surrenders, 112
Dieskau, Baron von: reaches America, 37; moves against Lake George, 38; his defeat, 39
Discipline, lack of, 192, 220

EVANS, LEWIS, 14, 16

FELTHAM, LIEUTENANT JOCELYN, 103; asks Allen's authority, 112; his report, 113
Foldboats, 92
Forks of the Ohio, 36
Fort Anne, battle of, 201
Fort Carillon. See Fort Ticonderoga
Fort Chambly, 128
Fort Edward, 17, 38; possible defense at, 198-199; road, Fort Anne to, 202; British reach, 205-206
Fort Frontenac, 16
Fort George, 116
Fort Le Boeuf, 35-36
Fort Lydius. See Fort Edward
Fort Miller, 206
Fort Necessity, 36
Fort Niagara, captured, 100
Fort Orange (Albany), 25; in 1643, 30
Fort Ticonderoga (Fort Carillon): location, 18; commenced, 40; progress, 41, 43; called Carillon, 42; lack of progress in 1756, 48; state, 1756-1757, 49; capacity, 50, 186; outposts, 50; fuel requirements, 53; 1758 preparations against, 73; 1758 French defenses, 75-77; British attack, 1758, 82-84; 1759, 91-96; partly destroyed, 98; scandal at, 101; conditions, 1759-1775, 102; captured by Allen, 110-112; reinforced, 121, 124; conditions, July 1775, 124; winter, 1776-1777, 165-169; abandoned, 195-197; British ad-

vance from, 202, 205; British defenses, 1777, 215-216; abandoned by British, 225-226; quarry for settlers, 226; reconstruction, 228

Fort Vaudreuil. *See* Fort Ticonderoga

Fort Washington, 172, 180

Fort William Henry, 42; description, 54; Rigaud's raid, 54-55; Montcalm attacks, 56-63; the massacre, 64-69

Freeman's Farm battle, 211-212

French Canadians: their attitude, 125; their support essential, 1776, 133

GALLEYS, 147

Gates, Major General Horatio: commands Northern Army, 140; maligned by history, 141; disputes command with Schuyler, 142; replaces Schuyler, 170; controversy with Schuyler, 170-171; removed, 171; returns to command, 208; defeats Burgoyne, 211, 213

Germain, Lord George, 173-174

Gondolas, description, 138, 145-146

Grapeshot, 156

Green Mountain Boys, 106-107; plan Ticonderoga attack, 109

HOWE, LORD GEORGE AUGUSTUS, 73; death, 77

Howe, Major General Sir William: his plans for 1777, 176; plans no aid for Burgoyne, 208

Hubbardton, battle of, 200

Hudson, Henry, 23-24

Hudson River defenses, 172-173

INDIANS, DESCRIPTION, 56-57

Intelligence: from St. Jean in 1776, 146, 149, 153; from Champlain frontier in 1777, 176; faulty American, in 1777, 183

Intendant, Canadian, 43

Inverawe, legend of, 83-84

Iroquois: obtained muskets by 1640,

25; Huron and Algonkin wars, 25; raid St. Lawrence settlements, 25; capture Father Jogues, 26; location of Mohawk towns, 28; with Montcalm in 1757, 58; at 1758 battle, 81

Isle aux Noix, 127; smallpox at, 135

JOGUES, FATHER ISAAC, 26; tortured by Indians, 27-28; his arduous trip to the Mohawk, 27-28; aided by Dutch, 29; escapes and reaches France, 30-31; sent as emissary to Mohawks, 31-32; returns to found mission, 32; martyrdom, 32

Johnson, Sir William, 38; at 1758 battle, 81; captures Niagara, 100

KALM, PETER, 13

King George's War, in Champlain Valley, 35

Knox, Colonel Henry, 130, 131

LA CHINE MASSACRE, 34

La Marine Regiment, 37

Lac St. Sacrement (Lake George), 31

Lincoln, General Benjamin, 216-217

Logistics: Amherst's campaign, 89-90; American, in 1776, 138; Burgoyne's campaign, 203-205, 206, 209

Lotbinière, Michel de: directed to build fort at Ticonderoga, 39; financial operations, 46-48; his horses, 47; owns canteen concession, 51; his actions legal, 52

Loudoun, Lord: depletes forces in Champlain Valley, 55; relieved, 72

Lydius post (Fort Edward), 17

McCREA, JANE, 205, 208

Montcalm, Marquis de, 37; reaches Canada, 42; captures Oswego, 42; at Ticonderoga, 48; cap-

Montcalm, Marquis de (*continued*)
    tures Fort William Henry, 58-
    63; attempts to stop massacre,
    65; responsibility for massacre,
    69-70; organizes defenses of Ti-
    conderoga, 75-76; defeats Aber-
    cromby, 82-84
Montgomery, General Richard, 127;
    killed, 128
Montreal surrendered, 1775, 128
Montresor, Captain John, report on
    Fort Ticonderoga, 108
Monypenny, Captain Alexander, 74
Mott, Captain Edward, 109; com-
    missions Allen, 113; his letter,
    121
Mount Defiance: occupied by Brit-
    ish, 193; seized by Brown, 218
Mount Independence, 143; work at,
    150; Congress orders fort, 170;
    1777 American attack, 219
Muster roll, Indian, 58

Navies: American, building at
    Skenesboro, 145-147; British at
    St. Jean, 146, 149
New Amsterdam (New York), in
    1643, 30-31

Ohio Company, 35
Oswego: founded, 10; fall of, 16;
    captured by Montcalm, 42

Pack horse, capacity of, 8
Parsons, Colonel Samuel: learns of
    cannon from Arnold, 104; plans
    seizure of Ticonderoga, 108-109
Pay, soldiers', 40
Peculation, 43-44, 45, 46, 47
Pell, John: gives land to Fort Ticon-
    deroga, 229; succeeds Stephen
    Pell as president of Fort Ticon-
    deroga Association, 230
Pell, Stephen, 225; restoration of
    Ticonderoga, 228-230
Pell, William Ferris: buys Fort Ti-
    conderoga lands, 226-227
Pellew, Midshipman Edward, 157

Pointe au Fer, 127; outpost at, 144;
    abandoned, 163
Poor, Thomas, reconnoiters Ticon-
    deroga, 41
Portages, 8; Fort Edward, 8; Ni-
    agara, 8-9; Fort Stanwix, 9; Os-
    wego, 9
Powell, Brigadier, 215, 220-222;
    burns Fort Ticonderoga, 225
Prideaux, Brigadier John, killed at
    Niagara, 100
Pringle, Commodore: at Valcour
    battle, 154; accused by subordi-
    nates, 159

Quebec Act, 132

Radeaus, 91, 149
Raids: Iroquois, on Hurons and
    French, 25; French, 1666, on
    Mohawk Valley, 33; Schuyler's
    of 1691, 34; Rigaud's on Fort
    William Henry, 54
Rations: French, 45-46; British,
    1758, 74; transport require-
    ments, 89; 1776, 135, 138
Riedesel, Frederika, Baroness von,
    209-210
Riedesel, Baron Friedrich von, op-
    posed Bennington expedition,
    210
Rifle, use in 1758, 74
Roads, colonial: Boston to Albany,
    5-6; New York to Albany, 6;
    Pennsylvania, 6-7
Rogers, Captain Robert, 17; recon-
    noiters Ticonderoga, 40
Roubaud, Father: describes Indians,
    56-57; at William Henry mas-
    sacre, 66

St. Clair, Major General
    Arthur: commands at Ticon-
    deroga, 181; abandons outposts,
    191; decides to abandon Ticon-
    deroga, 195
St. Jean: British activity at, 126; be-
    sieged, 128; British build fleet
    at, 146, 149

Saratoga: settled, 35; battles of, 211-213; surrender at, 213
Saunders, Admiral Charles, 99
Schenectady, raided, 34
Schuyler, Peter, 34
Schuyler, Major General Philip: ordered to northern command, 122-123; builds boats, 138; abandons Crown Point, 139; his foresight, 140; his plans and orders, 168; friction with Gates, 171; restored to command, 171; visits Ticonderoga and holds council, 186
Shell, explosive, 153
Shot, case, 156
Skene, Major Philip, 109; his mills, 148
Skenesboro (Whitehall), 145; conditions at, 146, 147-148; abandoned, 197
Smallpox, 136, 142; inoculation against, 134-135, 141
Spears, 164
Spruce beer, 52
Starke, Lieutenant John, describes Brown's attack, 218, 221

Taylor, Sergeant Daniel, swallows bullet containing message, 214
Thompson, Colonel Robert M., 228
Trumbull, Colonel John: describes conditions at Ticonderoga in 1776, 136-137; proves his point, 193
Twiss, Lieutenant William, explores Mount Defiance, 193

Uniforms, British and German, 190

Valcour, battle of, 155-157; losses, 158; retreat from, 160-161

Vaudreuil, Pierre François de Rigaud, Marquis de, 38; orders fort built at Ticonderoga, 39; clashes with Montcalm, 42; not involved in peculations, 44

Warner, Seth: takes Crown Point, 115; at Hubbardton, 200
Washington, General George: first engagement of Seven Years War, 36; his thoughts on Ticonderoga, 175-178; expects no attack, 178; crosses Delaware, 180
Waterbury, Brigadier General David, builds fleet at Skenesboro, 148
Watercraft: log dugout, 11; birch canoe, 12; elm-bark canoe, 12; bateau, 13-15; gondola, 15, 138, 145-146; barges, 16; sailing vessels, 16; whaleboat, 17; foldboat, 92; chebec, 147; radeau, 149
Waterways: Connecticut, 7; Hudson, 7, 11, 17-18; Chesapeake, 7; Potomac, 7; James, 7; Mohawk, 9-10; St. Lawrence, 11
Wayne, Brigadier General Anthony: describes Ticonderoga, 142-143; commands at Ticonderoga, 1776-1777, 165; quells mutiny, 169; promoted, 169
Webb, General Daniel: commands Champlain frontier, 55; his letter, 61; fails to reinforce Fort William Henry, 62
Whaleboats, 17, 74
Whitcomb, Colonel Asa, 167
Wilkinson, Colonel James, 182-183
Wolfe, General James, 99
Wynkoop, Colonel Jacob: commands fleet, 151; fires on own ships, 152; relieved, 152